ALL IN THE FAMILY

ALL IN THE FAMILY

ON COMMUNITY AND INCOMMENSURABILITY

Kennan Ferguson

Duke University Press   Durham and London   2012

© 2012 Duke University Press

All rights reserved.

Printed in the United States of America on acid-free paper ∞

Designed by Heather Hensley

Typeset in Arno Pro by Copperline Book Services, Inc.

Library of Congress Cataloging-in-Publication Data appear
on the last printed page of this book.

CONTENTS

ACKNOWLEDGMENTS

We feel both enlarged and implicated by our families. A child's sartorial choices, a parent's embarrassing outburst, a partner's professional reputation: we instinctually feel that each reflects on ourselves as members of their families while being in many ways outside of our individual control. A book's authorship has the same complexity of commitments and responsibilities, since we each exist in composite networks of influence, usufruct, conversation, contestation, and glad handing. The customary apologia about those acknowledged, that "their contributions are substantial while the mistakes are my own," is such an overt lie that it invites the more psychologically minded to inquire into the roots of such denial.

So my acknowledgments here are as much an indictment as a recognition of gratitude. The following people are responsible for this book in much the same way as family members are responsible for one another: thus the admixture of pride, embarrassment, resentment, requital, and possibly rage they will no doubt feel at being included in such a motley and extensive community. And, as with any extended family, others remain excluded, probably (though not entirely) due to being inadvertently forgotten: my apologies to you.

Valuable comments and brutal critiques of the first three chapters of the book came from Cheryl Hall, Steven Johnston, Carolyn DiPalma, Michael Gibbons, Pat Boling, Libby Anker, J. Donald Moon, Mika LaVaque-Manty, Sandy Schramm, Lilly Goren, Dustin Howes, Elizabeth Markovits, Christina Beltrán, P. J. Brendese, Robyn Marasco, Char Miller, Mary Hawkesworth, Laura Grattan, John Tambornino, Simon Stow, Timothy Kaufman-Osborne, and Kam Shapiro.

Chapter 4 emerged from discussions with Melissa Orlie, Kathy Ferguson, Carolyn DiPalma, William Connolly, Verity Smith, Matthew Moore, Raia Prokhovnik, Cheryl Glenn, and Crista Ratcliff, whose commentaries (and occasional silences) helped form this chapter. (My thanks also to Pendle Hill and Swarthmore College, whose collections of Quaker literature proved invaluable.) My gratitude to Verity Smith, Jane Bennett, Caroline Winterer, and Stephen White for providing their animal spirits for chapter 5. Margaret Price both inspired chapter 6 and proved its most trenchant critic. And the final chapter benefited from the wisdom of Marla Brettschneider, Michael Shapiro, Mort Schoolman, and Kathy Ferguson. Finally, I engaged in early discussions of the ideas underpinning the book with Tom Dumm, Neal Milner, Sankaran Krishna, Nevzat Soguk, Erin Manning, and Larry George.

I am also indebted to two anonymous reviewers of this book (anonymous to me, though not to the reader, since their encomia likely appear on the back cover) whose serious and measured judgments on the original manuscript led to extensive revisions. And, of course, to the careful shepherding of the book by the staff at Duke University Press, especially my editor Courtney Berger, whose suggestions were no less essential and helpful, and by Christine Choi, Robert Demke, and Fred Kameny. Shannon Kolpin, supported by the Department of Political Science at the University of Wisconsin, Milwaukee, and Nancy McCann also provided valuable editorial assistance.

Earlier portions of chapter 4 and 5 appeared as "Silence: A Politics" in *Contemporary Political Theory* 2, no. 1 (2003), 49–65, and "I ♥ My Dog" in

Political Theory 32, no. 3 (2004), 373–95. My thanks to Palgrave Macmillan and Sage Publications, respectively, for publishing these earlier versions.

Finally, my own family has proven central to my thought in this book. Dick and Jean Ferguson, Rona Ferguson, and Danny Collins; Susan Eichner, Tom Considine, and Tess Eichner Considine; and Elizabeth Kennan, Michael Burns, and Alex Kennan have all taught me more about family than has any book of political philosophy. Others who have welcomed me to the practices and passions of their families have included Mary and Richard Price; Elizabeth Garland and Judith Frank; Steven Johnston and Judy Gallant; Kamuela, Jan, Mason, Puna, and Pila Young; Cheryl Hall and Denise Roemer; Fred Mogul; Valerie Morignant; Ivy Ratafia and Scott McLeod; Jim Snyder and Scott Plummer; Tamara Zwick and Matt Leish; Kristie Hall; Jasmine Alinder and Aims McGuinness; Tom Mertes and Lissa Wadewitz; Mary Zerkel and Ian Morris; Nancy Lou Bochan; Robert Lawrence and Anda Iamnitchi; Cristina Kerner; Steven Tauber and Megan Hogan; Dean Chadwin and Alleen Barber; and Justin, Edie, and Mose Wolfe. Finally, this book has been shaped by the memory of family members no longer alive, especially Corrine Bochan Eichner and Norman Eichner, Gladys Ferguson, and Violet Kennan. And my deepest and most heartfelt gratitude goes to Carolyn J. Eichner, whose guidance, editorship, and inspiration make her a co-conspirator of the ideas herein.

FAMILIAL INTENSITIES

WHY FAMILY?

The pull of the family strongly affects its members, both in its contemporary Western idealized nuclearity and in its less atomized historical antecedents or culturally multivarious conceptualizations. People often feel their families to be the locus of their true identities, where the falseness of their social selves can fall away. Others, less sanguine, find their families oppressive but somehow inescapable, often attempting to build their own, better familial structures. Nor can this importance be escaped by leaving a family behind. Doctors as well as psychiatrists, states as well as strangers, demand answers about individuals' families in the hope of better understanding those individuals.

Structurally, politically, and personally, families function as the most important determinant for most people.[1] And yet contemporary political theorists spend relatively little time on the roles that families play.[2] As befits a culture based on the ideology of liberal individualism, family life usually seems better left to anthropologists, sociologists, and public policy experts. The ideological use of a deliberately normativizing discourse of "family values" forms one major exception, of course, but even this approach tends to be used unproblematically: deployed by politicians or attacked and discounted by its opponents. Few inquire into the power and status that such uses attempt to draw upon. The particularities of familial experiences, and the relative importance such engagements have for people in their quotidian existence, get left behind.

The critique of the family as a patriarchal institution has been done elsewhere.[3] Some of what follows dovetails with those familiar feminist criticisms, in large part because the history of the family as the exemplary touchstone of political life remains closely tied up with the genealogy of sex and gender. The authority of the patriarch and the patriarchy of the state mutually constitute one another, as many of these feminist theorists have pointed out. But this book is less concerned with these particular models of the family (though it is difficult to disentangle the contemporary Western imaginary from the nuclear heterosexual child-rearing model) than with the generality and commonality of imbricated communal oft-trans-generational relationships.

WHOSE FAMILIES?

"Imbricated communal oft-trans-generational relationships"? In the common nomenclature, these locales are "families." Children get raised, by someone, and develop bonds with and make demands on them. Adults choose people to fall in and out of love with, live with, travel with, invest and get old and play with. Love, envy, gratitude, anger, jealousy, helpfulness, violence, caretaking, and sharing play their own important roles in these connections. Each of us is imbricated in networks of these ties, from our childhoods to our individual lives to our chosen relationships to our institutional dependences.

Each of these families, of course, has its particular form. One might consist of a man, woman, son, daughter, dog, and station wagon; another could be a twelve-year-old boy, his aunt, and her lover; still another could be a gay man, his ex-wife, and his current boyfriend. A grown woman who has cut all ties with her controlling mother but remains close to her step-grandfather and his daughter-in-law's daughter from a previous marriage has her own peculiar and specific relationship. It is not the form of each family that is significant, for the purposes of this book, but the concrete and pragmatic reality of familial life, of the intimacy and attention and feeling and interest that we feel for those close to us. Families matter because they matter to those within them (and often to those excluded from them), and those matterings have infinite variety and organization.

In an academic work about the family, one might expect a careful and precise definition of which affective communities count as such: how, in other words, will "the family" be defined here? Such a definition would likely include a dynamic of biological reproduction, a locus of a cultural socialization, an existential historicism, a sense of emotional and communicative immediacy, and a sphere of physical intimacy. For reasons that will become apparent through this work, including the provable insufficiency of any of these characterizations, no such definition appears here. Rather than regulating an ideal form, I prefer to accept families as they are, in a kind of democratic determination. Presume that all families are made up of different and constantly negotiated affective ties that exceed their formalization in law, biology, parenthood, or even our own minds. (Many people are surprised to find themselves still connected to a parent or sibling they thought they left behind and who was no longer of concern for them, for example.) Those who hold that some kinds of families somehow *count* less than state-sanctioned ones may be correct in some ways (e.g., such families may lack legal claims on one another), but the intensities and continuities of those relationships exceed the definitions of such moralizing. Using the self-identifications of "family" serves better, in that the reasons why people claim (or reject) familial ties where they do underlie the concerns of community and incommensurability are explored herein.

To whom can such a project be addressed? Unlike a moralist, I do not aim to reinforce, defend, or shore up the family from the dangerous forces of the modern world. Unlike a normative theorist, I develop no attempt to determine the underlying superstructure of all families. Unlike a policy activist, I lack interest in showing how a marginalized sense of family turns out to be more like the imagined conventional family than expected.

Instead, this book examines what political and social thinkers can *learn from* familial dynamics. That emotional connections develop their own attendant complexities, that force always coexists with equality, that authority can be diffuse and heartfelt at the same time: these are lessons learned and passed down in families. That they are true at the individual level makes them at least important for macropolitics.

INCOMMENSURABILITY

Perhaps the most overt, and most consequent, of these lessons is the ever-present knowledge of incommensurability, a knowledge that many sociologists, political scientists, and philosophers constantly forget. For them, families often serve as a model of a functioning society, a locale where sameness prevails, where language and values and goals are held communally, where the pull of individualism is most firmly held in check by the bonds of common purpose. In common political idioms and in the presumptions of public policy, families stand in rhetorically for stability, unity, and continuity.

It actually takes very little critical thought to recognize the superficiality and inaccuracy of such a picture. Families appear to function smoothly only to those on the outside; in reality they are dens of hurt feelings as much as skinned knees, of arguments and negotiations and silent resentments as much as love and support and fellow feeling. In their everyday functioning, in their continuous building, and in their abrupt disconnections, families take up our energy and our attention. And the fact, generally true, that we know the members of our families better than we know anyone else does not make the negotiations internal to those families any more seamless or easy.

How well do you know your parents, your children, your lover(s)? All too often, the answer is: not as well as you thought. Each one still has the potential (and often the inclination) to make an unforeseen claim, to ask for something unexpected, to abruptly change direction—in short, to surprise you. Each partner, parent, child, and other family member is distanced from every other by temporality, space, inclination, personality, interests, and interrelationships with people outside and inside the family.

One philosophical term acutely describes this reality: incommensurability. The fact of human differences, of the reality that two people never fully understand one another, is closely tied up with the differences in their motivations, valuations, and histories.

On the one hand, such disparity and distance make up the rich bricolage of human life. The infinite depth of others, as Emmanuel Levinas noted, provides the very complexity of experience (as well as the demands upon us) to make us ethical, responsive beings.[4] That we can never completely comprehend those to whom we are closest makes life endlessly interesting, intriguing, and insoluble. It its most dramatic form, such incommensurability leads to a familial life of delight, learning, and wonder.

On the other hand, however, it leads to a familiar catalogue of complaints about those with whom we share our most important emotions, thoughts, and ambitions. Other people are unpredictable, which leads to disappointment; they are unreliable, which leads to anger; they are unclear, which leads to miscommunication. They want different things for us than we want for ourselves; they want different things for themselves than we want for them. In its most dramatic form, such incommensurability leads to a familial life of disillusionment, anguish, and violence.

The concept of incommensurability in contemporary philosophy was largely introduced by Thomas Kuhn. In locating incommensurability at the heart of scientific change, Kuhn both popularized the concept and tied its definition to a problematic invocation of insolubility.[5] By describing change in scientific knowledge as involving a group at a particular theoretical location whose members are fundamentally unable to "recognize, understand, or accept entities revealed through observations made from an alternative theoretical perspective," Kuhn properly recognized the problems and dynamics inherent in the shift from one perspective to another, but he also reified so-called competing perspectives into totalized, overarching categories.[6]

Yet, of course, families do operate. Even if there are multiple insoluble incommensurabilities between us, we live in and with families. Decisions get made, arguments resolved or forgotten. In the practical actualities of our lives, the fact of incommensurability does not result in insoluble problems or in irredeemable breaks, at least usually. We need not turn to ancient Greece or to esoteric knowledge in order to see the fallacy of assuming that such incommensurabilities lead inexorably to unending conflict or moral stasis (though, of course, such investigations may help explain why and how they can).[7]

In political theory, the "incommensurability question" links most closely to debates internal to liberal theory. Those theoretical positions which developed from Isaiah Berlin's recognition that different people's sense of what is good may never be reconciled or even reconcilable (what is generally termed "value pluralism") take incommensurability as a tragic condition of humankind and philosophy.[8] But in many ways the value pluralism debate misses the realities of incommensurability. Making moral claims about incommensurability (that it is a tragic condition of human life, for example) also causes its constant and constituent nature to disappear.[9] This book aims in part to displace this question: to show how incommensurability is neither an insoluble problem nor an unfortunate situation to be overcome, but rather the continuing condition of engaged human (and even transhuman) existence, the condition in which we have already happily or unhappily led our lives even within our own families.

Though my criticisms here focus primarily on this liberal tradition, they are not meant as salvos in the ideology battles recurrently raging within political theory. Much of liberalism cannot (or does not) account for the inter- and transpersonal dynamics that underpin these conclusions about incommensurability and community, but most approaches presented as alternatives to liberalism (e.g., communitarianism or republicanism or a host of others) share many of the presumptions that lead liberal theory astray: a belief in plurality as a problem, a sense that incommensurability subverts political action, a trust in the locus of logical analysis to lead to normative solutions to which rational persons will comply. My aim is neither a search for an authorizing discourse for political identities nor an attempt to build connections to overcome incommensurability. Instead, grounded in taking people's lived lives seriously, it is to identify and learn from the particular and quotidian practices and functionings of meaningful living with others, what Michel de Certeau calls the "practice of everyday life" and Thomas Dumm refers to as "politics of the ordinary."[10] And an ideal locus from which to examine these lives is one with which we are all not only conversant but implicated, although in infinitely diverse and pluralized ways: families.

POLITICAL FAMILIARITY

The specific importances of families in our lives have two interrelated political operations: their conceptual anchoring of our interpersonal connections and their emotional locus of our affective intensities. In the next chapter, I attend to how these have determined the *concept* of the family in the traditions of political philosophy. Why, I ask, have the rhetorics of family been metaphorically synchronous with state power? To answer this question, I note first how the forms of families within liberal societies function to naturalize and depoliticize power, both through their size and through their practices. But second, and more important to their functioning, families are the location where most of our political and ethical negotiations take place, where we learn to make sense of our simultaneous connections to, and distances from, other human beings. Family is, in other words, the site of community most intensely practiced by most people. It has thus served theories of politics of the modern age, especially those interested in justifying state authority, as an almost ubiquitous touchstone, a location of affective, authoritative, and reproductive ties which can be used for (and contrasted with) contractual or formalized national power.

The third chapter explains how those theories justify certain presumptions about unity in the world of contemporary political thought; it is, in short, an attack on the presumption that community requires the elimination of incommensurability. The targets range from political conservatives to progressives, reactionaries to liberals and libertarians, all of whom propose an end to substantive political engagement through a matrix of community. In their imagined communities, they dream of mechanisms and economies of exchange that mitigate true opposition, that allow for the final unity of community to shine forth. To explain why this can never be achieved, the chapter turns to Immanuel Kant and gay marriage: the latter as an exemplary form of a recently emergent political divide in countries around the world, and the former as the philosopher who best explains (but does not solve) this divide.

But how, overall, do these dynamics work in families themselves? The next few chapters attempt to answer these questions by turning away from theoretical abstraction and instead to the particular, ontic, phenomenological character of families themselves, using family behaviors, identities, and practices to show how incommensurability and families already coexist. In these chapters, I focus on how we *negotiate* incommensurabilities, that is, how our everyday attempts to both reinforce and overcome the distances between us play out in our familial life. The presumptions internal to political commentary and political science which presuppose sameness as the basis for community are undermined by the ways that people live their lives.

Chapter 4 examines one modality through which families can negotiate commonality and incommensurability: through *not talking* about issues which cause conflict. This use of silence goes against the negative implications generally given to silence. We generally presume that silence operates as oppression: when people, movements, groups are silenced, it is seen as a form of subjugation. Certain theorists have recently turned to reconceiving silence in a new way: as resistance to oppression, seeing how students, or prisoners, or women use silence as a mechanism with which to protect their autonomy. However, neither of these interpretations entirely satisfies, because, as the chapter shows, silence can also be used to develop community. It is used, for example, not only by families but also by religious traditions and musical composition in order to open new spaces for the development of collectivity and interaction. Silence ultimately has no definitive politics precisely because it can operate in such plural, multiplicitous, and overlapping ways.

The fifth chapter turns to a creature often understood to be a member of the family, but one often ignored in most philosophical and political discussions. What do dogs teach us about the nature and inclusiveness of families? Most notably, they undermine the conditions generally set for political actors: they do not aspire to equality, they do not want to vote, they do not even make claims to humanity. And yet the time and energy and love (especially love) that we expend on them make clear that our formal commitments to political abstractions (by and large) hold considerably less significance than our emotional and familial connections. The profound incommensurability between dogs and humans neither precludes love nor excludes them from family; instead it interrupts our conceptions of the proper sphere of politics.

Such an interruption does not depend on nonhumans: other humans in our families can have even greater impact. In the sixth chapter, I examine how the imaginative experience of familial relationships in one familiar range of events—the onset of what is commonly termed "disability"—can demand a reimagination of what initially seems obvious. The experiences of love and care for another, this chapter argues, have the potential to change our conceptions of space: we can begin to see it as pluralized, dichotomous, or multiplicitous. Whereas most people presume space to be normatively empty, formal, and universal, the experiences of caregiving can allow space to be more properly apprehended as profoundly different for different people. Here too, familial relationships undermine the presumption that community demands or requires a collective, unified experience; in fact, the requisites of caring for another pull the caregiver away from universalism into the particularities of divergent space.

The book concludes by returning to the linguistic field in which commonality and incommensurability always already coexist. If one is truly interested in the quotidian and everyday practices of human experience, looking at the philosophy of language—especially some of its historically significant debates—proves an excellent summary of where a similar debate has already taken place. People use the same words, meaning similar (though not identical) things by them, leading to profoundly different conclusions. The idea that language should be policed so as to be universally agreed upon and unambiguous has tempted many, but has proven to be unworkable and indefensible. Language works precisely because of its slippages and reformulations: these give language its power and those who use it (or are used by it) their home in it. Language, in other words, recapitulates familialism.

Yet this conclusion begs the causal question, in that it presumes community's basis in that which it attempts to prove. If we are formed by our families, our languages, our connections to others, and if we simultaneously form our own families, sentences, and connections, what kind of causal relationship is this? Who, ultimately, is in charge of or responsible for our connected subjectivities? This question turns out to be unanswerable. Few linguists would argue that people cannot create original paragraphs, conversations, and narratives within the limits and structures of a given language; few family theorists would argue that people do not become who they are alongside and within a network of people both given to them and chosen by them. Instead of attempting to answer this causal question, the discussion in this book examines the mechanisms of these dueling formulations of pregiven structures and personal creativity, which are here called "negotiations." Negotiation happens every time an individual reconceives what raising a child means, every time a couple weds, every time an event affects the presumed normality of life (as well as every time an author uses grammatical rules to structure a sentence). Negotiation is how we live our lives as both communal creatures and individual actors, feeling and creating our way through roles, expectations, obligations, and potentialities. We learn these skills and their limitations in our jobs, in our writing, in our plans for the future, in our casual interactions with others, and—probably most importantly—in our families.

Thus the goal of this book, and of the arguments herein, cannot be to formulate the "proper" set of policies to encourage "healthy families," or to shore up one mode of family against another, or to decide what sorts of political and ethical commitments make family life stronger. In a prescriptive mode, it is not about families at all. Families do not operate under prescriptive models, but negotiative ones: we operate within our families along complex lineages of obligation, love, anger, sadness, and protectiveness. We respond to other family members along lines which are both predetermined and original. We rehearse and repeat arguments, grow apart and together, care for and hurt one another. The purpose here is to learn from those realities, to recognize that the prescriptive models used for politics and sociology and policy and philosophy usually fail when stacked up against the experiential natures of families. It is to learn from how people live their lives rather than telling them precisely how and why to live them. It is to take families seriously, for a change.

Chapter 2 | **THE FUNCTIONING FAMILY**

Why do political philosophers turn repeatedly to the family to explain power? From Plato to Foucault, the family has served as both an exemplary location of politics and a source for resistance to larger forms of power. Whether a model for the *polis* or a micropolitical site of subject formation, theorists posit the family as the central model for political order and disorder.

Yet this modeling takes a bewildering variety of forms. For various writers, family has one or more of the following functions. It justifies authority, underpins conceptions of power, explains states, serves power emblematically, organizes community, centralizes power, naturalizes monarchy, stages patriarchy, motivates attachment, differentiates political power, formulates normative sexuality, and provides the emotional intensity of political life. It is not particularly interesting to determine which of these interprets the relations between family and politics most accurately, since all seem somewhat correct yet limited. Instead, the question arises: why so many functions, in so many places and times? Whatever the justification desired, the family seems an irresistible and aeonian spring from which political authority can draw refreshment.

The family's important role in politics generally takes a traditional, grounding role. Of course, in contemporary political culture, issues and debates are often framed in terms of what is best for "working families" or "the nation's families" or even "family morality." But those debates concern the proper treatment of families by political institutions and actions, where families serve as a particularly powerful interest group. That is, they assume that families are secondary where law, policy, and institutions are primary, that the success or failure of families depends on the particularities of politics.

This may well be true. The form of the family, as many historians have pointed out, has changed profoundly over time and through space and culture.[1] Kinship networks and familial concern surely exist within certain periods and social formations; to presume that any particular makeup is natural and universal shows a profound ignorance of human experience. But the assumption that families are formed by politics ignores an equally important reversal: *politics depends on families.*

Conceptions of legitimacy, authority, and political identity did not form in a historical vacuum. Western political philosophy, in its long history of developing justifications and organizing state power, has fundamentally relied on the family as a source of political organization. For many theorists, paternal authority forms the basis of authority; as the most natural and fundamental kind of power, the patriarch provides the proper model for the legitimacy of all forms of organizational and political power. The mysticism of "God the Father" and "the father" both underlie claims to the proper and authentic uses of earthly authority.

This may seem a counterintuitive claim. The dominant narrative of the emergence of modernity presents European thought as the simultaneous overthrow of theology in the name of reason, and of kinship networks in the name of formal, disinterested legal order. The first of these stories has proven a fertile field for debunking, and contemporary scholarship in intellectual history has widely investigated the claim that the magical thinking of the church was dissolved by rational order. But the concomitant assumption, that with the birth of modernity rights-bearing individuals (not families or kin groups) now have relationships to states, has been far less critiqued.

This familiar story ignores at least one important aspect of the intellectual development of civil individualism. If God no longer forms the basis for political legitimacy, as in the divine right of kings, then other legitimizations must take his place. In each of these histories and theoretical traditions, theorists search for conceptual or metaphorical models from which political authority arises. In each of these various models, one pattern appears repeatedly: families are the site of natural, prepolitical authority, and the proper state is that which develops from and properly expands that source of power. The following section outlines a very few of the many nodes providing those connections, examining how family has long underpinned conceptions of political power, both as representational of authority and as a symbolically differentiated source of power.

A BRIEF HISTORY OF POLITICAL FAMILIES

Both Diocletian and Constantine issued extensive family laws, which made up a large share of their jurisprudence.[2] Constantine, especially, foregrounded the rule of the paterfamilias, minimizing the power of wives to act independently. By formalizing an authority that creates the legitimacy of family life, to an extent that at times intruded on decisions previously made privately (such as denying cohabitation rights between free women and slaves), he connected legal and familial authority closely together.[3] Children and wives were expected to obey the orders of the paterfamilias, including those concerning marriage and divorce. In turn, the paterfamilias had certain responsibilities to his family: marrying daughters properly, not beating sons unduly, listening to family member's opinions before ruling on issues.[4] Ideally, this led to *concordia*: the ideal of a perfect and continuing harmony of the various parts of a family.[5]

Augustine, too, combined the authority of society with that of marriage, encouraging the future centrality of the family in Christendom. In Augustine's theopolitics, the first natural relationship "of human society" is the "bond of husband and wife."[6] From this it follows that, short of one's relationship with God, the family is the social bond from which all others follow: it serves as a model of authority and obeisance.

And of course God himself has shaped that familial relationship. Augustine's admiring account of his mother Monica's role in her own family serves correspondently for the proper relationship with God. Monica never blames her husband, she forgives his infidelities, she always reasons with him when his temper has subsided. Wives, she says, "should remember their condition and not proudly withstand their masters."[7] Some contemporary interpreters see Monica's central place in the *Confessions* as merely replicating Roman patriarchy in the religious sphere, and Augustine does clearly mean to perpetuate patriarchal familial dynamics.[8] But his exaltation of Monica does something further: it shows the reader how the proper attitudes of submission, forgiveness, and continence make one not only happier but more successful. By recognizing her appropriate place in the family, Monica provides an example of how to properly respect authority and to make both oneself and the larger group happily functional.

The Christian world never relinquishes the centrality of the family in its ethics and organization. As Albrecht Koschorke has shown, the imagery of the "holy family" not only forms conceptions of families in the Middle Ages but continues to underpin the contemporary mythological structures.[9] Indeed, a form of authoritarian paternalism intrinsically prevails in monotheism: God as Father provides the most familiar trope, but the church develops considerable Mary idolatry into its structure as well. The dynamic between mother and child so beloved of Christian art over the centuries clearly links the holy and the human, attitudes of care to those of obedience, and the centrality of parenthood to sanctity.

It is in part against this structure that Thomas Hobbes famously restructures political theory. Hobbes's state of nature has no families, no extended networks of kinship. Indeed, part of Hobbes's project literally defamiliarizes: he presumes that the prepolitical world is a state of unencumbered individuals, lacking family, clan, or social networks. It is the very equality of isolated individualism that makes life insupportable without the overarching power of the sovereign.

Yet the demand for a solution to this radical individualism continually hearkens back to the ways which families solve the same sorts of problems. As Richard Allen Chapman notes, Hobbes fills *Leviathan* with families, with fathers exerting power, even with an overt parallelism between familial and state governance.[10] Even as he undermines kinship, Hobbes conceives power and authority along familial lines, explaining the domination necessary for sovereignty. In Chapman's words, Hobbes "uses the family constantly as an analogy for the state, as justification, as historical example, as a heuristic device to explain political structures and functions, and as exhortation."[11]

John Locke, in disentangling the modern conception of the state from the theological forms of authority, justifies and limits government in his *Second Treatise of Government*. He famously transforms Hobbes's threatening state of nature into a far more comfortable conception.[12] In Locke's rendition, society comes about slowly, only once property must be preserved and abstracted from immediate needs. The narrative of the *Second Treatise*, however, does not proceed quite that cleanly. As Locke explains this movement from the state of nature to that of government, he suddenly breaks off his narrative to explore the question of "paternal power." It transpires that the power of the father predates all other forms of power, but that it is a form both limited and mutual.

This strangely positioned chapter attacks the parallelism of paternal and monarchical power proposed by Sir Robert Filmer (as did Locke's *First Treatise of Government*). While the details of their debate need not be rehearsed here, the traces are clear: Locke builds his theory of the legitimacy of the commonwealth in ways which depend intimately on the position and responsibility of parents (mostly fathers, though Locke at times recognizes the natural rights of mothers to be superior).[13] Parents naturally have power over their children, Locke argues, but this power ends once the minors reach the age of reason, and the parents also have responsibilities to their children (such as education).[14]

Though Locke sees no necessary connection between paternal and political power, he does reluctantly admit that, historically, one developed from the other. Locke argues that "the natural fathers of families by an insensible change became the political monarchs of them too."[15] This transfer makes sense only if the proper use of kingly power is the development and expansion of the property rights of individuals, just as a patriarch trains his children from infancy to maturity. The father's government teaches his sons to become "accustomed . . . to the rule of one man, and taught them that when it was exercised with care and skill . . . it was sufficient to procure and preserve to men all the political happiness they sought for in society."[16] Just as we can criticize bad fathers, so can we criticize bad kings; this is simply a matter of the quality of authority. Thus the transformation is in forms of power rather than in power itself. Not in question is the right of parents (or kings) to rule in their respective spheres; indeed the force of Locke's argument for relative obeisance depends on the parallel.

Though usually positioned as Locke's opposite, Jean-Jacques Rousseau places the family at the origin of politics even more dramatically. "The most ancient of all societies," he writes at the beginning of *On the Social Contract*, "and the only natural one, is that of the family."[17] Calling the family "the prototype of political societies," he explains how other forms of governance are dependent on the exchange of similar favors.[18] The father's love for the children's security is the original compact. From that, all else remains merely a question of scale and distance. Indeed, he points out, marriage itself must be battled over by church and state, as it is simultaneously a civil contract, a religious compact, and the basis of society.[19]

Family plays a central role in Rousseau's second and third discourses as well.[20] In the state of nature, the only state where humans have been totally self-sufficient and thus free, no families could exist. "Males and females," Rousseau hypothesizes, "came together fortuitously as a result of chance encounters [and] left one another with the same nonchalance. The mother at first nursed her children for her own need; then, with habit having endeared them to her, she later nourished them for their own need. Once they had the strength to look for their food, they did not hesitate to leave the mother herself."[21] Humans do not need parents; for Rousseau, it is only as they come to need one another that kinship relations become important. Families come about as the first stage toward the social. Though he follows Locke in ultimately identifying property as the necessary spur for the emergence of political society, he clearly places the creation of familial emotional bonds as the beginning point of property. Rousseau refers to the "first revolution": the uniting of "husbands and wives, fathers and children in one common habitation. The habit of living together gave rise to the sweetest sentiments known to man: conjugal love and paternal love."[22] This attraction led inevitably, he continues, to gender differences, to pride and envy, and thus to the need for property. (Marx and Engels follow Rousseau closely in this genealogy.)[23] Because of families, people become softer and interdependent, and what we see as progress from this state is, in reality, the "decay of the species."[24]

John Stuart Mill, in his turn, uses the family as a fulcrum for citizenship. Sometimes this is as a set of recommendations: in *On Liberty*, for example, he argues that families must reproduce at the proper rate for a society, and that states have an obligation to make sure that the proper forms of education are being followed in the home. But far more importantly, Mill argues, the form of the family and the functioning of oppression are interconnected. His protofeminist book *The Subjection of Women* repeatedly returns to the family, using marriage as an example of profound social injustice that unnecessarily subjects women to men.[25]

Mill's form of political individualism is closely tied to his image of the family as made up of equivalent, if not legally equal, partners. The directional causality of his egalitarianism has been much debated: whether individualism should be first bred within the family to later transpire in the political realm at large, or whether Mill's commitment to formal equality enables him to critique the inequalities within the family.[26] But it is clear that Millian individualism should extend to women both in public life and in the home; whatever limitations women are thought to have are direct results of their social and legal subjugation. When he addresses the question of women's value and creativity, for example, he argues that the stultifying effects of their oppression in their everyday lives has limited their abilities.[27] Mill inherits this concern from Mary Wollstonecraft, who argues for the liberal values of friendship and equality to replace the oppressive state of marriage.[28]

As many feminist critics of Mill point out, he argues that women are more naturally suited to the care and raising of families, and that even if given free rein, most women would continue to be interested in "domestic management."[29] This early version of difference feminism leads Mill on the one hand to celebrate the realm of the private family sphere, arguing that it has its own kind of worth, and on the other to privilege those few "exceptional" women who can use the moral values that emerge from these interests to the benefit of public life. In addition, Mill argues, once women were no longer legally forced into oppressive situations, feminine "weakness" would disappear. Legal equality, in his vision, "would abate the exaggerated self-abnegation which is the present artificial ideal of feminine character . . . but on the other hand, men would be much more unselfish and self-sacrificing than at present, because they would no longer be taught to worship their own will."[30]

Strong echoes of Mill's sort of celebration of family life as emblematic of a better, more caring and well-ordered *polis* appeared in the feminist aspects of the Progressive movement and in the fight for suffrage. Women, it was commonly argued, would bring a domestic tranquility to public life through their kinder and more nurturing instincts.[31] In turn, the feminine virtues would percolate through the rough-and-tumble of political life, lessening corruption, infighting, and war. Women, heretofore untainted by politics, could bring the lessons of raising a family and organizing a household to the largest household of all: government.

Even the political philosopher most enamored of the state as the totalized ideal of human experience, G. W. F. Hegel, positions the family within a similar matrix. All moral life, he argues in his *Philosophy of Right*, arises from three interrelated and developmentally hierarchic organizations of individuals: the family, civil society, and the state. The family founds the basis of ethical life, where the completion of such concepts of engagement and responsibility reach their naturally fulfilling ends. Marriage, for example, seems initially a limitation of freedom, but because it leads to a greater, more encompassing "substantive self-consciousness," it is in fact a liberation from the empty liberty of singular subjectivity.[32] Indeed, such connection comprises one of the most basic and fundamental goals of ethical life: the subsumption of two personalities into a greater whole.

But the advent of the social destroys family: "civil society tears the individual from his family ties, estranges the members of the family from one another, and recognizes them as self-subsistent persons."[33] Only the state, he argues, can holistically complete the authority and order of the family with the freedom and self-realization of civil society. This of course entails the wholesale subsumption of women into a purely domestic familial sphere, as some commentators point out, but—equally important—it uses the family as the locus where all people aspire to being subsumed.[34] The human existence within families, where one is freed by one's obligations to others, serves for Hegel as a minor and preliminary version of the liberation of the nation-state.

Other analogies of communal association have served to justify political power, of course, but the longevity of the family has been dramatic. Even those correlative constructs which emphasize distance from the family end up rooted in familial forms. Michel Foucault, for example, famously argues that patriarchal power differs from the more modern "pastoral" form of power, in which the government is dedicated and self-sacrificing.[35] "What enables [the concept of] population to unblock the art of government," according to Foucault, "is that it eliminates the model of the family."[36] In this conception, the limitations of patriarchal power (its immediacy, its focus on individuals, its particularity) proves incompatible with the needs of a large, instrumental, and territorial sovereignty. The family becomes only a segment or site of power, a "privileged instrument for the government of the population."[37]

But this distinction is not only too clean, it is also strangely simplistic. For, as the examples of Mill and Wollstonecraft (as well as modern political discourse) show, the model of the paterfamilias never entirely disappears. Foucault minimizes the extent to which familial tropes continued to inform the work of political philosophers, and the ways in which issues of family continue to form democratic political practices. In Europe, for example, the continuation of patriarchy and monarchism determined much conservative political activism, while liberal calls for political society to serve and protect the family can be clearly seen in both the later Dickens novels and Émile Zola's *Les Rougon-Macquart* novels. In the United States, too, the model of the government as family not only informed the early-twentieth-century Progressive movement (such as in the banning of alcohol to protect families) but also proved central to the conservative revolution of the 1980s. The pastoral form of power did not supplant the familial form but instead commingled with it, resulting in a conflation of patriarchal and pastoral modes of care and control.

FAMILY VALUES

Why does the family hold such importance for all these various periods and all these influential thinkers? What makes this model (or this trope) such an appealing source of intellectual sustenance? One might think that its power is merely an unacknowledged inheritance from previous thinkers, or that once political philosophy makes such connections they are difficult to renounce. But other narrative inheritances are happily jettisoned: the very newness of new political theories arises from their changes in focus or intellectual dependence. Yet the family reappears, imbricated through theories as disparate as those mentioned above.

The family does not only underpin conceptual justifications of authority; it also has centralized power for the contemporary nation. Political readings of the historical emergence of the state have emphasized the necessity of a celebration of the nuclear family in the creation of state power. Robin Fox, for example, has argued that as the Westphalian state system emerged, its major adversary was the clan.[38] If the state has absolute or near-absolute authority, other loyalties, especially those arising from extended kinship groups, have to be sundered. Rather than directly attacking such affiliations, Fox argues, liberal state authority rewarded and reproduced individualism, both for people and for families. Insofar as people are citizens, their primary relationship is with the state, instead of with alternate organizations, religious affiliations, or, most importantly, distant cousins and other relatives.[39]

The nuclear family fits neatly with an individualized citizenry. Within the idealized family, one's loyalties are limited to one's intimates. Reinforcing separate, self-contained family units encourages the dissolution of larger affiliations. Fox argues, "in promoting the self-sufficiency of the nuclear family unit, the state is in effect attacking the essence of kinship, which lies in the extension of consanguineal (or pseudo-consanguineal) ties beyond the family into strong and effective kinship groups."[40] Families allow for reproduction and childcare, she notes, while depoliticizing the nongovernmental possibilities inherent in relations. What we think of as nuclear families, in other words, *defamiliarize*: they make more difficult the otherwise likely affiliations that arise from kinship.

For those who live within such liberal societies, these family forms seem both vital and normal. Their constant appearance in liberal political theory serves the important function of naturalizing power dynamics. Power differentials always exist in families, ideally in an ordered and ordinary way. Therefore, according to this philosophical subtext, power differentials always exist everywhere. The closer we can come to the natural direction and subjugation of families, such a narrative assumes, the more properly our society is ordered. In other words, such philosophies smuggle the importance of families in our lives into the importance of politics in our lives. Distant and concentrated authority is parasitically justified by intimate and negotiated power. And this is only possible insofar as families already have great importance and centrality in our lives.

Families function so ceaselessly in political thought precisely because they function so ceaselessly in life—they are locales where the impossibility of overcoming human distance clashes most fiercely with the human incapacity to be alone. The family acts as a nidus, in which human concerns, conflicts, and cares rest. Thus the appeal of the family in political philosophy. Once a small-scale ideal commonality can be built (or at least bought into), the only obstacle to a perfectly functioning larger community is the question of scale.

These family dynamics, even those displaced and reformed by political normativities, continue to play a central role in political discourse. Their location in our lives, the fact that they function so well and so often, makes them a ceaseless spring from which to draw new meanings, new histories, new laws, new methods. If authority is to be created and recreated, it must always reference known and lived authority, and those emotional locations of natality serve the nation equally well.[41] Thus do families reappear at moments when authority must be rooted in experience or emotion, whether by contemporary politicians or long-gone philosophers.

Yet these families have a constant unreality about them. Even in Locke's time, it is as difficult to believe in the prevalence of forbearing, powerful, kind, and stern patriarchs whose families fully obey and respect him as it is to believe in the reality of a state of nature, a land without law or society. Locke may have thought the former as real as the latter (like Hobbes pointing to the Americas as a true state of nature), but his readers understand him to be engaging in an imaginative exercise. The families that justify half of Locke's political philosophy are as fictional as the state of nature that justifies the other half.

Wittgenstein famously noted how bizarre it was to read books on ethics which failed to even mention "a genuine ethical or moral problem."[42] Similarly, is it not strange to read so many renditions of families which fail to mention any actual conflicts or issues which arise within families? If the family is important precisely because it is the locus of negotiations of unity and difference, the lack of (philosophical) discussion of such negotiations seems more a sleight-of-hand than an actual willingness to engage in these questions. Of course families function easily, ceaselessly, and naturally, the political philosopher implies; any failure to do so is a problem of that particular family, not an issue endemic to families themselves. Isn't that, after all, Tolstoy's point about the happiness of families?

THE FAMILY DYNAMIC

The very situatedness of ethics causes grave problems for the formalization toward which philosophers aim: the need for universality in moral judgments conflicts most with historical particularity and locality. The claims of moral philosophy tend to the overwhelming absolute; philosophical self-consciousness of its "own origins and potentialities," to use Bernard Williams's terminology and idea, makes the possibilities of ethics as a "satisfactorily functioning whole" impossible.[43] Even when confronted with absolute ethical positions we entirely agree with, we often make decisions and act in ways which entirely undercut those positions.[44]

Attention to the details of ethical practices provides more insight regarding morality than do logically coherent superstructures. But it is the latter which grabs the intellectual imagination. Linda Zerilli describes the constant return to "the political pretensions of epistemology that have a way of creeping back into our thinking."[45] Drawing on Hannah Arendt and Wittgenstein, Zerilli suggests contesting this creep by attending to "political actions," those behaviors and practices by which we not only come to build our own worlds but help create the worlds in which others live as well.[46] It is in our actions, our everyday decisions, she points out, that our commitments emerge; one can never ultimately predict or predetermine them.

And our families play a central role in these decisions, both as a source of action and as a locale wherein those actions have their effects. Familial conflicts, familial obligations, and familial love shape who we are and motivate these actions, even in their most dramatic forms. The still-fascinating tales of Antigone's sacrifices and Medea's vengeance echo in contemporary newspaper stories and television programs about parental dedication or domestic violence. In each, the conflicts between family dynamics and legal and moral rectitude are put in the starkest of terms, implicitly asking viewers of these dramas to judge the propriety of actions taken.

These conflicts need not even be so dramatic to matter. For most of us, even the most politically committed or religiously observant, questions of how to make a living or how to promote a just society fade into the background in comparison to our relationships to our loved ones, our attempts to negotiate closeness to and distance from our lovers, our parents, our children. The clichés of the businessman who engages in illegal action for money he can never spend or the mother who endangers her children by staying in an abusive relationship are merely the most overt versions of these intensities. All of us betray ideals, usually without realizing we are doing so, on behalf of not only our own selfish interests but for those we love and are surrounded by. Indeed, if the intensity of emotion involved marks the most important aspects of our ethical lives, these personal engagements overwhelm the abstractions. How much energy is expended by people trying to change aspects of their lovers, parents, and children, compared to how much is expended to change the world at large or make their neighborhood an abstractly better place to live? To take a violent, but sadly familiar, example, compare the number of "domestic" murders (where, for example, George cannot allow Martha to leave him and would prefer to kill both her and himself) with the number of attempted assassinations of political leaders. We care far more about those close to us than we do about those who can change the world at large.[47]

Which is more likely to have been said, in your own life, in the past week: "You said you would take out the garbage!" or "Gay people have the right (or, conversely, no right) to marry!"? More importantly, which phrase has, as it were, a higher resonance? Which sentence registers a moral claim that most immediately affects the claimant? The first, obviously, has little perceived "real" import, at least as far as the macropolitical level is considered "real." But that is not to say it fails to charge a defect of justice or that it is unimportant to the speaker. In fact, one of these sentences could well come before or within a domestic argument that each interlocutor tries very hard to "win," whatever that could mean in such a context.

Such a demand (namely, the one made when reminding of a responsibility to take out the garbage) should properly be understood as profoundly moral. It bespeaks a presumed ethical responsibility, stipulated by one person of another, absent an authoritative ground of legal reinforcement. In fact, this absence of external reinforcement (the lack of garbage police) reduces the claim to a truly moral one; the "you said" becomes the merit upon which the argument turns. Possible responses, such as "I meant to but forgot," "Why do I always have to do it?" "I'll do it later; I have to finish my homework," themselves evoke moral reasoning to justify the lapse.

The moral and ethical components of these exchanges are of course well known: philosophical arguments often use such everyday details as examples of how moral arguments work. One often sees them in philosophy textbooks or essays exploring the necessity of rule-following, for instance. What these examples almost always misconstrue, however, is that the importance of their use in people's everyday lives far exceeds the importance of the larger use of the general rules they are meant to explain. That is, the authors of philosophy textbooks incorrectly assume the examples merely show how moral argumentation works, so that it can be better applied to the important realms of law, public ethics, or business. They fail to realize that, for themselves as much as for their audience, such uses are not nearly as important as the actual usage of the claims. What they miss: the moral claims internal to families are to most of us more compelling, more important, than the macroethical principles they resemble.

HIGH STAKES

Two major points have been made so far: that the family conceptually underpins liberal conceptions of politics and power, and that the family usually serves as the location where people, in their quotidian lives, most readily and vociferously engage in power struggles. But the connection between these two contentions cannot be reduced to a simple causality. It would be as false to argue simply that liberalism has looked to the family simply to justify itself as it would be to hold that families are important only in so far as they have produced a contemporary *polis*.

The claim made here is a larger one. Families hold such primacy, however they are structured or defined, precisely because they embody the central political problematic of community and incommensurability. *The family is where people have the highest level of identification with one another, but also where their differences and distances seem most important.* Those to whom we are closest are also those we feel need to be both most like us and whose differences provoke the most dissatisfaction or intrigue. These constant negotiations of similarity and difference, of likeness and remoteness, make up the emotional push and pull of the family, and their complexities never end (as any family counselor can attest).

This means, in turn, that predictions of identification can never be as simple as they may seem to someone outside of a family. What theoretical unity can properly represent the admixture of embarrassment, love, disdain, and respect an adolescent feels for her father? Or the combination of affection and exasperation at the center of a fifteen-year marriage? Or the negotiations of information, influence, and power which emerge when a new mother asks her own mother for parenting advice? None are simple connections, let alone absolute identifications in the way family has traditionally been thought about. Instead, they are complex, plural relationships, reinforcing lines of connection, defensiveness, and mutuality.

Their consequences can surprise. Gay rights, for example, emerge very differently when concretized. A young woman comes out to her parents. How they respond is in part determined by their religious beliefs, in part by their culture, but often just as importantly by their relationship to their daughter. Their apparent political progressivism may be threatened and disappear, or their religious objections may be overcome by their concerns for their daughter's happiness. What is bearable at a distance becomes unbearable in such close intimacy, or vice versa.

Family life concerns home, money, and intimacy; love, desire, anger, and hate are the possible consequences. It is precisely this volatile and vitalizing concoction that makes the role of family so important, in both personal and political venues. Second-wave feminism politicized the personal; no longer can political theorists unproblematically conflate the private with the unimportant with the female with the unpolitical. But paying attention to the family can do more than that—it can personalize the political. Human passions should no longer be excluded from the realm of the legitimate, where philosophy has so long attempted to move them.[48]

It is already well recognized that families play a large role in electoral politics. Politicians often make (or at least justify) decisions according to how they will affect "working families." These claims function precisely because they take advantage of the intensities of the emotional landscapes we already operate within. At their most basic level, they may help perpetuate what Gill Valentine has named "geographies of fear": the excitement of life around the unfamiliar and threatening, which depends on the possibilities of dramatic disruption of that life.[49] Thus the idea that abductions by strangers are more threatening to children than swimming pools, or the common assumption that terrorist attacks are likely to involve a family member: these erroneous assumptions arise from the intensification of fears already extant within familial life.[50]

Even most investigations of the politics of the family have not understood this dynamic. When close attention has been paid to the family, it has still been primarily to suggest changes and improvements to familial life. Susan Moller Okin, for example, has argued that political theory must extend "structures of justice" into the family.[51] As important as Okin's concern should be, she merely reiterates the common conception that what counts as political engagement takes place in the civil, public world, and that true politics consist in developing concepts and applying them to domestic behavior. Such a conception not only misses that the emotional intensity of political life is dependent on families; it even reinforces the opposite idea.

The importance of the family has also meant its continued centrality within governmentality. As governments' concerns with the management of populations have grown, the family has emerged as a central locus of that management. Jacqueline Stevens has produced perhaps the most devastating critique of democratic states' continued complicity with, continuation of, and dependence upon familial structures. In *Reproducing the State*, Stevens has shown how ideas of citizenship descend directly from theories of race, which are reiterated and reinforced by families whose critical function is to inscribe regimes of legitimacy on humans.[52] A child born in Chicago to a Norwegian father and Cuban mother has one confusing but vital set of rights and citizenships; a child born in Addis Ababa to a Sri Lankan father and a Persian mother has an entirely different set. In all cases, the idea that each individual is "truly" one kind of citizen arises from a racialized (perhaps even overtly racist) conception of familial relations. Stevens's arguments are both damning and compelling. But her underlying premise, and optimistic hope, that the role of birth could be decoupled from the practices of statecraft, remains hopelessly idealistic. For if, as I have been arguing, the power of the family arises from its unparalleled importance in quotidian life, no state can hope to surrender that parasitic dependence and survive.

Taking families seriously leads to one clear conclusion: the inadequacy of the presumptions about them within traditional political theory. For the likes of Locke, the existence of the family necessarily means similarity, even absolute sameness. To those for whom the family functions as the basis of identity, the differences within families must be made invisible. A definitive paterfamilias cannot allow dissent, difference, resistance, or correction. This sounds like no families common to us: even the most centralized or authoritarian patriarch must contend with daughters who disobey, sons who subvert, and wives who withdraw. With such an erroneous model of the family underlying liberal conceptions of identity and difference, is it so surprising that we make such poor sense of our commonalities?

As a result, we assume that incommensurability equals the death of community. Most political theories insist that only by drawing together, by discovering, creating, and reinforcing a common identity, can politics continue. But what if we consider that incommensurability and community exist side by side in our everyday lives? What comes of the recognition that the distances between brothers and sisters, fathers and sons, grandmothers and granddaughters are part of what makes those connections so strong? If families really do underpin politics, then community and incommensurability, far from being mutually exclusive, must coexist.

NEGOTIATING FAMILIES

Contemporary political scientists generally, and political theorists specifically, presume that those issues that have what they call "national importance" (or "international importance") are as a consequence the most important ethical issues. In contemporary national and international affairs, debates over globalization and sovereignty, abortion and health care, or party loyalty and economic integrity are considered the real political issues. For academic philosophers, too, ethics either exists in the abstract sphere of logical coherence and formal equivalence or, if more pragmatically concerned, coalesces around such issues as human welfare, social justice, or imaginary moral choices concerning train switches and innocent civilians who hang around on the tracks. What they predominantly fail to address, overall, are the quotidian decisions and choices made by contemporary humans.

This is not to mitigate the importance of such issues—international law or abstract ethics can make the difference between going to war and not going to war, between a dishonest and a reputable business. But as conditioned as we are to assume that abortion, for example, stands as one of the defining issues in the ethical contention of American politics, how often do friendships, partnerships, or other personal relationships fray along those lines? One rarely breaks with a friend or lover over his or her positions on the issues of the day. Instead, the pertinent questions of ethical responsibility in quotidian existence tend to revolve around specific instances of trustworthiness, commitment, and obligation. The negotiations between a parent and a teenager over curfews, bedtimes, and familial responsibilities are far more fraught, far more *important*, than more grandiose and distant abstract ethical questions.

Yet ethical questions these are. What parents and friends think, for example, of opportunities gained or choices made matters far more than how those stack up against holy writ or Kantian reason. We make moral choices according to thick, imbricated social communities, which help determine the inner compasses we measure ourselves against. As such, we more often than not are creatures of specifics instead of absolutes. Absolutism works far better as an abstraction than a mode of life. The fully committed theist is more saint than human; the wholly rational logician is more philosopher than citizen. For most, the ethics of particular situations determine the rightness of the response, and those ethics arise from the connections and commitments of those with whom we surround ourselves.

Chapter 3 | **COMMUNITIES AGAINST POLITICS**

It is not merely the intensities of family living that make families such an appealing rhetoric for those who want to strengthen our larger political institutions and communities. It is also that they promise solutions and closures. In the typical rendition of political prescriptions, families are assumed to "work," whereas larger communities are seen as broken or dysfunctional. That is, policy analysts, columnists, professional politicians, and political scientists all too often operate along the assumption that the dynamics of the family need to be better replicated along macrocosmic lines to solve the difficulties of miscommunication, ideological fracture, and lack of social cohesion that they perceive as the problems to be solved in the greater political realm.

There are two major problems with this approach. The most important, its misrecognition of what families are and how they operate, serves as the subject of the rest of this book. A concomitant misunderstanding must be addressed first, however: such a solution presumes a problem which does not exist. The vision of community that such jeremiads have in mind is an impossible one, a realm of agreement and lack of contestation which is not only empirically inconceivable but also intellectually incoherent. This chapter therefore examines two different interpretive strategies for understanding the demands of community. The first, closely linked to the social sciences and particularly political theory, attempts to develop a normative basis for commonality: a commonality to which everyone can (be made to) subscribe. The second, more closely linked to philosophies of aesthetics, uses judgment as a descriptive analytic to explain the persistence of differences within communities, but lacks a normative prescriptivism. This chapter thus addresses the possibility of community outside of (or without) commonality, and asks why unity is so often falsely presumed to be the precursor to community. It is, above all, an attack on the presumption that communities (be they families, towns, or nations) require commonality, and that incommensurability always threatens community.

The question throughout is, why does commonality, interpreted as sameness, hold such sway over our conceptions of community? The concept proves important to those people who spend their days thinking through ways to improve public life and connect people to political realities. Most of these approaches take the strengthening of community to be a self-evident good, but the universalisms underlying their presumptions make for communities where most forms of dissent or disruption are seen as a threat which needs to be eliminated. In other words, they make for antipolitical communities.

THE APPEAL OF SEAMLESS COMMUNITY

Community, we presume, is a wonderful thing. Whether one is saving the community's children, building a sense of community between ethnic groups, or using working-class consciousness to develop communities, community is the ideal of political philosophers, activists, and politicians across wide swaths of divergent interests. Of course, the *kind* of community that is ideal is often in fiery contestation, but the search for the exemplary form of community is rarely, if ever, questioned.

And it would certainly seem unfeeling to question such an ideal. Community, after all, is about sharing ourselves with others, about working for the greater good, sometimes even at the expense of the self. It is about something greater than ourselves, a connection to other people that allows us each to transcend our individual self-interest and pettiness. It is about acting in concert with our fellow humans, sharing hardships and triumphs communally.[1]

But questioning this ideal is, in fact, precisely what this chapter aims to do. In criticizing our notions of community, some of the most cherished dogmas of contemporary culture must be confronted. But communities themselves are not threatened; they will continue to abide robustly on their own. What should be criticized are the notions of community which remain mostly unspoken, the underlying goals toward which academic and policy understandings of politics have led.

That families serve as the ideal for this unity is telling. The family model that philosophers have long relied upon has tended toward a simplistic model of patriarchal authority. Fathers instructed and directed; wives submitted and served; children behaved and learned. The properly functioning family, in this model, acts as one, with undivided purpose and unitary motivation. Against this, as shown in the previous chapter, stand actual families, collectivities which constantly negotiate differing interests, identities, dreams, and emotional ties. In our lived families, incommensurability exists as often as commonality; the two may even overlap, reinforce, or undermine one another. Families serve as an excellent starting point for investigating the possibilities of a politics of incommensurability, the theoretical senses of connection and contention across human differences.

The families idealized by Hegel and Locke do not exist, indeed have never existed. To expand this interrogation, then, the same question should be asked on a larger scale: "Can there be a political community?" The obvious answer is "no"—an answer dependent upon commonplaces and truisms about what politics and community are. As with the discussion of families, however, this is clearly a false answer: families and communities exist, and serve as important touchstones for almost every human being. And, as with families, the only way political community can be understood as possible is through rejecting the opposition between community and incommensurability.

With the diminution of ideological difference within the contemporary political world, attention has turned to questions of communities: religious, national, cultural, and spatial. This has taken a variety of forms, of course: just within political thought, recent decades have seen conflicts between communitarianism and liberalism, between identity politics and traditional leftism, between secularists and theologists, between republicanism and care ethicism.

Each of these stances either covertly or overtly depends upon theories of community and commonality. In fact, most presuppose a background or an ideal of community *as* commonality, whether statist (as with republicanism) or internal to a group (as in the essence-oriented versions of identity politics). A deep engagement with each of them is unnecessary; the various discussions internal to these debates have already covered much of that ground. More intriguing is what these champions of community centralize in their formulations: the necessity of excluding the dangerous, of determining the proper boundaries of the political actor.

In other words, most of those who celebrate community, however defined, see the exclusion of difference as a necessary precursor to actual community. At whatever level—nation, state, people, or *polis*—they share a presumption that people must share central normative commitments and that those who fail to share those commitments must be excluded from, or at least marginalized within, the political constitution of that community. This move may be overtly stated or it may be hidden, perhaps even from the authors themselves. But repeatedly, this moment of policing exclusions returns.

Arthur Schlesinger, Jr. engaged in a number of these debates at their highest pitch and can serve as an introduction. His popular book *The Disuniting of America* encapsulates a number of these themes regarding community.[2] Schlesinger's argument, familiar to anyone attentive to the "culture wars" of the 1980s and 1990s, is that the increase in identity politics puts the very idea of America in jeopardy. By "identity politics" he of course means attention to ethnicity, resistance to assimilation, and (closest to his heart) critical recastings of historical truths. These sorts of insurgencies alarm Schlesinger: they threaten, he explains, the very idea of an American identity. Any "campaign against the idea of common ideals and a single society will fail," he argues, for each one denies the larger American community.[3] In the persons of what he terms "Afrocentrists," for example, Schlesinger sees an outright challenge to the collective identity that American ideals have historically engendered: the threat that Afrocentrists pose to the cohesion of the country at large needs to be opposed in all its forms.

Schlesinger argues for the necessity of unity in vital interpretive constructions, as well as the invalidation of those interpretive constructions that threaten this unity. These were not particularly novel arguments at the time, of course. But it is interesting to compare Schlesinger's jeremiads for a lost American community with current theorists with greater followings in today's debates about community and collectivity. The "zealots" who Schlesinger excoriates, those who "reject as hegemonic the notion of a shared commitment to common ideals," reappear as different kinds of villains in various forms throughout current debates, repeatedly seen as threatening the very nature of communities.[4]

ANTICOMMUNITY COMMUNITARIANS VERSUS ILLIBERAL LIBERALS

One particular debate, central to political theory at the turn of the century, exemplifies these presumptions: the debate between the communitarians and liberals. A brief excursus into this historical argument can clarify how both sides in a putative opposition in fact rely on the same misguided concept of community.

First, the communitarians: critical of liberalism's focus on individuality, what Alasdair MacIntyre calls the "privatization of the good," communitarians look to the development of norms and guidelines that assist in the development of communities.[5] An unobjectionable goal, to be sure. Their recommendations prove tempting, given their trenchant critique of liberalism as presupposing individuals laughably unencumbered by class, race, creed, location, or nation.[6]

Unobjectionable, that is, until one notices a set of presuppositions common to communitarian thought that are curiously similar to Schlesinger's.

The communitarians, whether their project is a uniform moral code or a society of politesse, propose that an underlying societal uniformity be developed. The cultivation of civic virtues, however encoded, is a necessary prerequisite for the building and strengthening of communities in this view; without a deep level of moral commonality, the sense of common purpose that enables and encourages people to extend their identities beyond themselves cannot exist. In their conception, communities necessarily disintegrate without this unspoken sense of affinity.

This theoretical construction, which says that community arises from shared evaluative senses, emerges from a history of juridical and sociological arguments which say that certain codes of behavior fall below the umbrella of self-awareness.[7] It is because of this need for permanence that Amitai Etzioni can argue, for example, that values should be "handed down from generation to generation rather than invented or negotiated."[8] For theorists like Etzioni, that moral formulations are constant proves more important than the substance of these moral forms; that is, the substance of the values is less important than their continuation. The communitarians are guilty of what they accuse liberalism of doing: placing value on political formulations above the substantive politics within those formulations, and thus celebrating, as it were, substantively empty forms. These formulations, often called "social morals" or "cultural truths," are posited as permanent, unchanging frameworks. Discussions and dissent can happen within these frameworks, but challenges to the frameworks themselves are ruled out of bounds.[9]

This need for such permanence similarly drives the jeremiads of James Q. Wilson. Without common and historical moral codes, he argues, the entire superstructure of any political system is doomed.[10] His demand that the standards of "right and seemly conduct" define the very bounds of community and his location of those standards in the originary, male, white, "preimmigration" (as if such an era existed) American foundation combine to form a cultural identity that cannot, should not, be challenged.[11] Indeed, in Wilson's eyes, those movements that challenge this cultural identity in the United States actively threaten the very constitution of the country.

Michael J. Sandel, though a more subtle and meticulous theorist than Wilson or Etzioni, shares with them this particular desire for permanence. For Sandel, community is openly dependent on universally shared meanings, especially on political issues such as justice. Even when he critiques the universalization of sovereignty (namely, across different communities), Sandel posits smoothly operating communities as the alternative sub-sovereignties which become magically comprehensive. For example, he promotes Catalan, Kurdish, and Québécois communities as alternatives to statehood for those peoples—not suggesting sovereignty per se, but instead merely the ability to create standardized communities under the aegis of the state—as if such goals are desirable to either the insurrectionary populace or the governing nations.[12] He envisions communities (ideally) as safeguards from the vagaries and threats of modernity and capital; but to serve such a purpose, all members of these communities must be united in their efforts and protective of their collective identity.

This is not to say that communitarianism does not come in a wide array of forms, as anyone attentive to the state of political theory at the end of the last century is well aware; indeed, the above examples should indicate its variety. Communitarians may, as in the case of Wilson, attempt to form a statewide civil and criminal regulatory apparatus, or may, as in the case of Jean Bethke Elshtain, want to protect the essences of imperiled communities from the standardization of mass culture.[13] But what each has in common is a desire to reinforce the standards of a community, to encourage its resistance to the kinds of people or ideas that threaten it, be those the demands of "black nationalists," "drug kingpins," or "international capitalism." The discrete and independent community, whatever its size, is their temple, and their motto is *ne vile fano*.

For most communitarians, these threats (whatever they may be) come from the excesses of liberal individualism, a philosophical construct and legal theory and way of life that has increasingly infected American society in their view. Individualism, they argue, provides few if any defenses against these menaces, for it leaves out the standards and regulations of communal meaning which allow for united political resistance. That liberalism does not attempt to instate a sense of "the good," but instead creates a neutral framework where each person can constitute his or her individual "good life," that this is intrinsically different from the communitarian project has by now passed from truism to cliché.

And yet a glance through the central interlocutors on the side of liberalism reveals a project which has vital features notably similar to communitarianism. Both sides, whatever their differences, are committed to the foundation of political identities through harmony with others: liberals through the development of institutions that treat people justly and communitarians through the reinforcement of common values and ideals. Though liberals are (usually) not primarily concerned with developing communities in the sense that communitarians mean by the word, they are profoundly concerned with developing a political culture of fairness and justice. The differing claims of social organization that John Rawls and Robert Nozick and George Kateb popularized in the early 1980s were intended to provide archetypal political systems, that is, a way to envision the construction of a fair society.

Rawls, Nozick, and Kateb have become emblematic liberals in discussions of liberalism (especially versus communitarianism) over the past three decades. All three, famously, valued individual rights over communities, and thus would seem to be entirely at odds with the communitarian project. John Rawls's conception of the just society as one that would be created from behind a "veil of ignorance" about one's own position in that society makes the assumption that all (nonlocated) people within a society would develop a common conception of justice.[14] Rawls's liberalism aspires to be "value-neutral." That is, the formal construction of this society is based on a sense of the just that no longer is fastened to the politics of the merely local. Instead, it attempts to provide a mechanism toward reaching agreement on political priorities: the pretense of nescience allows an ideally removed situation from which to make policies that affect all justly.

For George Kateb, rights-based individualism, found most dependably in constitutional liberalism, provides this foundation. Individuals thrive in conditions of freedom and openness, and a governmental system which protects individual rights from incursions by other individuals and by the government itself must be the precondition for these freedoms. Democratic constitutionalism, in Kateb's view, has the potential to change humans themselves: it makes them more flexible, more willing to believe properly legitimated authority, more committed to others' rights, more normative.[15]

Robert Nozick seems to go even further than Rawls or Kateb: his is the most famous radical construction of individual rights over those of larger communities, at least within the liberal tradition. Nozick's near anarchism privileges individual rights over virtually all claims made on those rights: taxes, for example, or building codes are, to him, an appalling infringement on the right to sell one's labor and control one's property.[16] Where Rawls pushes community to the background and Kateb sees it more as a threat, Nozick attempts to dispose of it altogether.

These liberal approaches seem profoundly different from the communitarian-inflected ones. But upon closer examination, these theorists share many of the conditions (or perhaps more accurately, the "preconditions") upon which their perceived possibility of politics rests. For, fundamentally, does not each liberal approach presume a kind of community, if only a formal one? Rawls certainly presupposes a political community: a set of rational individuals with common conceptions both of the nature of a state and of the appropriately ethical solutions to problematic political questions. While this is not a "community" in the way that Sandel would define it, it shares with the communitarian conception a presumption of sameness, of universal desire to reach a common design. And like the communitarian community, the threat that must be expunged is the shortsightedness of individual preference; the commonwealth must take precedence over personal pleasures.

Not so for Nozick, however; in his argument the needs of the social culture appear to have little force against the rights of the individual. But close attention to his concerns and examples leads to further clarification of Nozick's ultimate goal. In his typology of rights, the right to private property quickly gains precedence over all other political rights.[17] It does so because, in Nozick's world, the rights that humans bear are primarily economic; that is, they have to do with exchange and value. But such a conception of why property rights are important is itself dependent on the establishment of a free market. In Nozick's case, the primary threats to the socius were threats to economic freedom. In other words, Nozick posits a community of material acquisitors, traders, and accumulators: a community of meaning based on possession.

Kateb, like Nozick, seems at first to celebrate an individualism intrinsically opposed to forces of normativity. Katebian individualism is meant to protect the dignity of each human, a dignity under constant threat from the government. Such threats arise wherever the government degrades the individual in the name of communal value or impinges upon personal freedom to promote commercial or political interests. His list of quotidian examples (in the United States) includes a number of governmental actions defended by communitarians: "routine testing for drugs or roadblocks to ferret out drunk drivers; the war on so-called obscenity; the steady erosion of the rights of suspects and defendants."[18] More broadly, issues such as governmental brutality abroad, covert and illegal policies, "manipulation of public opinion," and the threat of using nuclear weapons are large-scale betrayals of the ideals of personal liberalism.[19] Fundamentally, the very idea of governmental membership, at least that which has claim to demand killing and dying in the name of the institutional mechanisms of warfare, is antithetical to Katebian individualism: patriotism, he memorably declares, is a mistake.[20]

But the reasons underlying Kateb's critique of these intrusions upon individualism themselves presume a political community, a normative commitment to a shared set of political formalities. If society oppresses, the solution is a universalist one, a dedication to the exercise of rights.[21] For Kateb, the ontological commitment to rights presupposes political freedom. He, of course, sees nothing "social" about political commitments (even, possibly, about politics itself), but rights-based universalism demands fealty, even beyond national boundaries: "The Constitution [that is, the Constitution of the United States] is a universalist, not a local, document."[22]

Kateb of course recognizes that governments which claim to respect universal claims of individualism have caused evil in the world. At times, such as with the United States war in Iraq, he claims that this is merely a governmental betrayal of individualism. But at other times, this problem rises to the level of incoherence, such as when Kateb wishes to privilege universalist societies above cultures with multiple or nonfoundational sources of morality. We should hold that these latter societies are "still deficient, and that we should not place them on the same level as cultures that possess universal standards, even though cultures acquainted with universal standards have done inconceivably more evil than cultures without them."[23] Kateb hopes to defend the goodness of liberal normativity, even in the face of his recognition of the bloody hands of such universalisms.

A preoccupation with boundaries is central not only to the liberalisms of Rawls, Nozick, and Kateb but also to the political enactments of liberal states. The questions of who can vote or who can own property are emblematic of the perennial problems liberalism faces. Certain boundaries are well policed: excluded are slaves, women (at least historically), children, animals, visitors. Others are less clear: Can someone who retains citizenship in another country still become naturalized? What levels of criminality disqualify? Who decides what level of incapacitation by mental illness qualifies you to have your right to control your property taken away? What all these questions belie is a need to establish a normative "citizen," to exclude those who do not belong to the political community that is envisioned.

Like the communitarians, liberal theorists construct communities, though liberals prefer to avoid the term itself. Rather than "thick" communities, to use Rawls's terms, liberal theorists try to create political organizations. Though Sandel critiques Rawls for lacking a theory of community, Rawls indeed has a conception of what a political community should entail, and what it should not.

"What it should not" is of primary importance here. For in the same ways that political commentators and communitarians decry threats to their communities, liberal theorists decry threats to the political culture. This leads, in the words of William Connolly, to a process of "normalization," where the standards that define political behavior are transformed into stringent exclusions from political engagement.[24] Richard Flathman, himself an avowed liberal (albeit a "willful" one), recognizes liberalism's tendency to claim "to treasure diversities but do so only insofar as [they] are encompassed within or subtended by unity."[25]

In other words, both communitarians and liberals rely on a central dedication to community as the exclusion of differences and the development of a universally agreed upon set of political mechanisms. In their worldviews, evidence of a functioning community comes from lack of argument, agreement on historical narratives, group identification, and collective purpose. As such, they view threats to these commonalities as fundamental rifts within the political system; those who disagree with their frameworks become de facto enemies of the community.

Yet these readings depend on a particular and erroneous conception of agreement. Theirs is a simplistically dualistic view, where one is always torn between opposing choices: either a humanistic secularist or a religious fundamentalist, rightist or leftist, conformist or dissident, white or black. They fail to recognize that agreement is never total, nor disagreement ever entirely oppositional. To explore how agreement and disagreement coexist, I turn here to Immanuel Kant, who can help explain that disagreement always presupposes a mode of agreement, that in fact they must overlap. And yet Kant (and Kantianism), while properly identifying this concurrence, proves inadequate to resolving its political consequence.

DISAGREEMENT

Take, for example, an overtly political contestation which also emerged in the 1990s and remains with us still: that of "gay marriage." This debate not only refers to community norms and liberal self-determination, but is overtly about the forms that families can take in a legal context: can two individuals of the same sex (or gender, as the varieties of national laws apply differently) form a legally recognized union? The appearance of same-sex marriage on the political scene has been relatively sudden and unexpected; in the space of a decade, the idea transformed from being virtually invisible to being a legal reality. Yet despite the sudden appearance of this issue, or perhaps because of it, the opinions about the desirability of same-sex marriage are already clearly drawn.

This particular area of contention proves particularly useful because the foundations of each side have been so firmly established in so short a time. Behind most opposition to same-sex marriage, whether it be couched in terms of nature, reproduction, history, biblical injunction, or morality, is the same essential objection: marriage is crucially an inter-gender affair because that is the way it *should* be. The supporters of same-sex marriage argue basically the same point, with their own twist: that the reasons for limiting marriage benefits to opposite-sex couples in that way are not compelling, and same-sex couples *should* be allowed to marry. In both cases, there is a strong moral component to the issue, and these moral components are in direct opposition to one another.

The argument between the two sides usually goes something like this: A holds that marriage should be limited to opposite-sex couples because marriage is intended for reproduction. B, in response, points out that marriage is not denied to infertile opposite-sex couples. A argues that religious morality necessitates the repudiation of same-sex marriage; B points out alternative religious traditions. A points out that marriage has historically been defined as a man and a woman; B points out the circularity of such reasoning.[26] Ultimately, it becomes clear that A and B differ in crucial conceptions of what marriage, law, and family are. Their notions of what each idea means are radically different, even incommensurable.

Now, this is obviously a very two-dimensional representation of the arguments involved; the reasons for each side's position are far more deeply held, profound convictions of greater importance than this schematic implies. But it is this very strength of conviction that makes this issue both so compelling to each side and so emblematic of collective politics. For A's and B's reasoning (and arguments) come about precisely because so much is actually shared between them: a legal system, of course, but also a community, a language, a sense of morality, and—not incidentally— a commitment to families themselves as intrinsic components of a shared future.

These relationships of political differences to collective political decisions are judgments that are collectively made, but ultimately based on shared grounds external to the issue itself. What are families for? What affections and actions are ungodly, or moral, or private? Are biological children an inherent aspect of marriage? What is the state's proper role in the recognition, perpetuation, and restriction of personal relationships?

Immanuel Kant, famed for his guidance into systems of morality, proves a useful guide along these paths. Yet his overt, moral systematicity serves less well here than his analysis of judgment, his concern in the preconditions for commonality in judgment. And commonality in judgment is precisely what those who expect that there will ultimately be some resolution to the question of same sex marriage are hoping to achieve.

In his third *Critique*, Kant politicized the philosophical realm of aesthetic judgments by emphasizing the centrality of comparison, the comparison between one's own judgments and those of everyone else.[27] It is this politicization that is of interest here, both for the centrality that questions of commonality and community have in political theory and for the difficulties that are raised by this particular goal.[28] Yet for Kant, there is a problem inherent in most theories of political discord and commonality. Issues upon which there is universal assent, the ultimate goal of Kant's aesthetic theory, are in fact *not* political issues: it is the very existence of dissent and dissatisfaction with the status quo that constitutes politics. Admittedly, it is logically coherent to establish a political theory whose ultimate goal is the eradication of politics; it is not, however, particularly satisfying, either as an intellectual aspiration or as a description of specific political contentions. In the example of same-sex marriage, it is unlikely that either of the interlocutors is going to eventually agree with the other's definitions of marriage, and the spaces for compromise are notably lacking.

In other words, there is a disparity between Kant's noumenology and the phenomenon of political difference. For Kant, this difficulty is resolved with the application of correct judgment: the resolution is whatever is consistent with a nature and logic. Ultimately, for Kant, judgments have an essence. Kant's attachment of judgment to nature and sublimity, along with his ranking of compliance over freedom (of action),[29] both serve to attach aesthetics to the constitution of the world, and therefore necessitate the existence of "correct" and "incorrect" judgments. Arendt, therefore, is wrong when she argues that Kant valued judgment and thus the *polis* over truth; Kant actually saw a complex, but mutually reinforcing, interrelationship between the two.[30] In arguing for the universal communicability of judgments, for example, Kant points out that without such communicability, "we could not attribute to [cognitions and judgments] a harmony with the object, but they would one and all be merely a subjective play of the presentational powers," a possibility that Kant clearly finds unacceptable.[31]

Unfortunately for Kant's theory, people in political opposition tend to find their own positions most harmonious with "the object." Both A and B, in the example above, perceive the other as acting irrationally and even perhaps in bad faith. Both A and B suppose that the moral ground upon which he or she stands is clearly more solid than the other's. The conception of the natural order that each holds serves only to reinforce this position; the ideals of Kantian liberalism and formalism are developed by each of them in ultimate support of their own moral outlook.

This proves an insurmountable problem both for pure Kantianism and for many of its descendants. Neither Arendt's agonistics nor Habermas's "universal pragmatics" serve to broker a middle ground between the two sides: the preconditions for agreement are fundamentally lacking. Ultimately, it is clear that A and B are coming from what Charles Spinosa and Hubert L. Dreyfus term "weakly incommensurate worlds."[32] Neither A nor B is willing, or able, to be a part of the other's debate; their senses of what is important about marriage are not shared, and even if they use similar terminology, the grounds upon which they base these terms are radically different. They are not quite using the same grammar or vocabulary; to hope for a "universal pragmatics" is begging the questions that the very issue raises, for in such a case there would be little disagreement after all.

This is not to say that they live in radically different worlds: these two individuals can communicate with one another, indeed they *want* to communicate with one another. Each can convince the other of his or her sincerity, and they can perhaps find common ground on other subjects. But the existence of some shared realities does not denote the necessity of a single reality. Incommensurate worlds are not states of existence that are unrecognizable as human, but are instead narrow realms of mutually exclusive comprehensibility.[33]

That people who share the same political spaces can have intellectually incommensurate worlds should be commonsensical. Evidence for it surrounds us. People who are part of the same political configuration (be it geographical, organizational, or societal) usually do have integrally different conceptions of the good, or the desirable, or the ethical, as liberal theories have long recognized.[34] For a variety of reasons, however, political philosophy often seems either to deny this possibility or to bemoan it. Sometimes this is an avowedly teleological goal, as it was for Plato; at other times it is an attempt at identifying common threads in an otherwise multifarious system, as it was for Marx. But as far apart as Platonism, with its insistence on a universal (but hidden) system of evaluation, is from Marxism, with its insistence on different (class-related) commonalities, both argue that people *ought* to discover a unified worldview. And most successors of these theories, from constitutionalism to traditionalism to progressivism, have continued to urge unity as the highest political ideal.

Arendt is correct, however, in emphasizing that Kant *enables* an ethos that places the community of judgment over and above the regime of truth. In the words of Roberto Esposito, "if the subject of theory is the I, and that of ethics is the Self, the subject of aesthetics is We. Indeed it is We-others, a We that is constitutively open to relations with others."[35] In emphasizing the communal nature of judgments, and thus escaping the traditional debate over objective versus subjective aesthetics, Kant opens the possibility of a political theory based on communities that emerge through agonistics rather than those which presuppose some sort of collective essence. His construction, though based on universal communicability and reason, opens a window to how localized forms of communicability and reason can establish minor communities, worlds that can overlap one another and yet still remain at some level distinct. The clarification of this kind of an idea of political communicability is the ultimate goal of this chapter.

The debate over same-sex marriage, as a political difficulty, resonates deeply with a certain sense of political freedom. This particular sense, though particularly important to Kant, is usually left out of political debates. Most Kantian-based liberal positions on political issues tend to be concerned with freedom as a sense of noninvolvement. Abortion rights, for example, are generally posited as a question of toleration and ability: few abortion-rights advocates claim that abortion is intrinsically good, but instead argue that it is a matter of choice for women. Conversely, abortion foes argue that abortion is not a private matter, but a concern of public interest. In other words, these positions tend to rely on a sense of public and private, and to argue that freedoms are properly based in the private realm and responsibilities in the public.

Kant's sense of freedom has little to say about freedoms that are not public. The public sphere, where intellectual positions are laid out and contested, is by definition the space of the kind of freedom that is dependent on debate. For Kant, freedoms of the individual can only be subsumed under a socially constituted natural order, the "lawful authority within a whole called *civil society*."[36] How civil society is constituted, how the common ways of living are determined through the public use of reason (e.g., debate), is taken as natural and unproblematic. Kant, in other words, holds the idea of private freedom to be oxymoronic.

Yet Kant's idea of public freedom is a robust one, within its own limitations. Though he suggests, for example, that a state has no obligation to grant its subjects what we today consider "privacy rights," and though he is similarly disinclined to defend those who rebel against authority, Kant centrally advocates for freedom of judgment. Most obviously, this includes his championing of free public speech. Human subjectivity and the communities that enable such subjects, according to him, emerge from unfettered deliberation: reason is naturally public and must be defended as such.

Freedom of the public use of reason is the human attribute Kant most defends throughout his works. In "What Is Enlightenment?" Kant promotes the responsibility to *saper aude* and posits public freedom as the hallmark of the modern. In the *Critique of Practical Reason* he makes freedom central to any use of pure reason.[37] In the *Critique of Judgment* Kant gives freedom the most gloried space in the pantheon of concepts: it is not merely the only supersensible concept (i.e., that it "proves its own reality"), but is the only possible groundwork for proving the existence of God and of the soul.[38]

It is well known that this aspect of Kantianism underlies contemporary liberalism; it is equally well accepted in liberal societies that government, for example, should leave expression unfettered. What is less recognized, however, is the degree to which this kind of public freedom is valued only insofar as it helps achieve resolution, as though free judgments are of worth only if they are heading toward a universal settlement. For Kant, and for modern Kantians like Arendt and Habermas, deliberation is useful only insofar as it leads to resolution. Freedom to dissent is allowed in the name of eventual accord; the freedom is thus always contingent upon the possibility of reconciliation.[39] The strength of Kantian theory is the extent to which this eventual resolution is never predetermined, as Arendt makes clear in her lectures on the *Critique of Judgment*. But its weakness, inherited from Kant and persevering in liberalism, is a reluctance to recognize genuine, long-lasting political difference that shows no sign of resolution. This is due in part to Kant's aspiration (and the desire of most liberals) to arrive at consensus, and in part to the inclination of organized bureaucratic institutions to discourage meaningful dissent.

Alternative theories of how political resolution is reached in particularly intransigent cases abound. If it is generational, perhaps the older generations will die off, leaving the paradigms of the younger generations dominant.[40] Another form of resolution may be the forceful overpowering of the adherents of one form, either through overt violence or through rhetorical degradation.[41] Still another form can come about through the privatization of political issues, where a communal issue evolves into a matter of private behavior.[42] But there are other issues which continue to be undecided, waxing and waning over the years in intensity, but never being fully resolved, and these prove problematic for any theory dependent on universalism.

Let us return to the case of same-sex marriage. On the one hand, we have A arguing that marriage between two men or women is immoral, perverse, and at odds with American ideals. On the other, B argues that it is moral, loving, and harmonious with liberal objectives. It is difficult to merely live with this difference, as traditional liberalism would exhort, since same-sex marriage will either be recognized by law within a state's boundaries or will not. The compromise model of political thought is problematic as well for the same reasons: perhaps a separate civil status can be developed for same-sex couples, but the things that make marriage per se so meaningful to A also make it so appealing to B. The Nietzschean model, where one moral system wins out over the other through force, is perfectly adequate descriptively, but is hardly a model for political engagement. To fight to the death for one's moral ideals is a poor prototype for a political engagement sensitive to the needs of alterity. And a traditional Kantianism, where one of these moralities *must be* correct (though we do not yet know which), and thus must be universalized, is not much better; since each A and B are convinced that only one moral position is correct, the other's is seen as not only mistaken but pernicious. Kant's conception of judgment, therefore, is not particularly useful in its entirety.

POLITICAL CONTESTATIONS

Two versions of commonality within community are therefore apparent. The first, that of the liberals and communitarians, is a prescriptive commonality, one leading inexorably toward normative unity. The second, that of the practices of judgment, is a descriptive commonality, one which leads toward multiplicity and contestation. Those enamored of the former are in truth attempting to eliminate the latter form, which threatens both the purity of their utopian visions and the intellectual underpinnings of their ideological commitment. The latter, however, lacks the prescriptive power of the former. It has not the force to compel A to B's methods of judgment, nor vice versa. It thus proves unappealing to those whose goal is normative unity, since it has no mechanism for normalization; in fact, it lacks even an ethic of universalism. One may reasonably ask, however, what the problem might be with communities that are based on normalization. Obviously, people who consider themselves part of a community also consider themselves to have important similarities with those they consider fellow members; what is wrong with a formal kind of unity between peers within a community?

The answers to these questions depend on one's conception of politics. For those for whom politics is a neatly circumscribed realm of differences in matters of civic policy, there is little lacking in such a conception: it lays out the rules of such procedures and provides rationales for excluding those who are unwilling to follow such rules. But for those for whom "politics" means something more, means something like deep-rooted and hard-fought contestations over resources, power, and meaning, such a community looks like an escape from politics, a way to exclude the kinds of battles that might cause discomfort and reflection. In fact, such a community, broadly considered, may even be indistinguishable from a "cult": a system of meaning in which those who challenge its assumptions are castigated and expelled, in which what is allowed to be thought or said has become indistinguishable from what can be properly imagined or conceived.[43]

But isn't a resolution of some sort necessary? Are not political problems meant to be solved? For most theorists, yes. Even Hannah Arendt, the best attuned to the specifically political dimensions of Kant's theories of judgment, certainly thought that resolution was of paramount importance. Indeed, those who are unable or unwilling to participate in public debate (such as scientists, who put too much emphasis on truth) are, on Arendt's account, unworthy of participating in the public sphere.[44] Michael Walzer holds that plurality and uncertainty should never be the basis of politics: "distinctiveness of cultures and groups depends upon closure, and without it, cannot be conceived as stable features of human life."[45]

Such political thinkers generally ignore the ways in which cultures and communities (and, indeed, families) continue and thrive without closure. Debates during the past half century over the existence or nonexistence of a public sphere have highlighted this controversy, as though the lack of a single, unified public sphere would mean the termination of political life. That there continues to be antipathy toward recognizing pluralism in political life is a mark of dread of substantive politics. The enduring appeal of essays and books declaring the "end of" some significant form of discord bespeaks a continuing hope for the ultimate settlement of contention, an ultimately antipolitical ideal.

The fact that humans can and do live in incommensurate ways is the very substance of politics. We constantly engage others and discuss ideas, attempting to convince (and, occasionally, succeeding in convincing) others. We do this across cultures, across religions, and across ideology; we do this in schools, in churches, and in dinner table conversations. We do this from common ground, from indifference, from moral opposition. As Kant shows, we engage with and share some ideas, judgments, and constitutions; to conceptualize humans as isolated and solitary creatures is surely as misguided as insisting that all people share one common culture. That political philosophy ignores this (with a few notable exceptions)[46] is among its greatest current weaknesses.

Conversely, those philosophers who do recognize the possibility of incommensurability often exorbitantly expand this sense of incommensurability. Once anything is incommensurable, this argument tends to go, we have nothing whatsoever in common with one another. For obvious reasons, these arguments tend to promote an image of cultures as monolithic, so that something like Samuel Huntington's "clash of civilizations" becomes the only possible resolution.[47] Even so nuanced a theorist as Alasdair MacIntyre assumes that the most critical questions of incommensurability come from entirely different "traditions."[48] Perhaps the most widely noted attempt to overcome political incommensurability has come from Charles Taylor, whose condemnations of differences of judgment are especially severe. Taylor objects to considering judgments (which he identifies as matters of culture) as though they are in any way politically equivalent to civil rights.[49]

These three theorists share very little, the notable exception being the way they comprehend political difference. Critics of incommensurability habitually posit it as emanating from strong, universal sources, as though controversy emanates primarily from profound ontological clashes. But political, ethical, and moral conflicts more often arise within cultures and ontological frameworks, and such clashes are philosophically more interesting than those that are clearly grounded in different historical and geographical circumstance. A and B can clearly have common opinions about television shows, restaurants, and international relations. That they cannot agree on gay marriage in no way implies that they come from entirely different "cultures" or even "cultural traditions." It is entirely possible that they each share a vehement attachment to Christian values (though each interprets those values differently) or just as possible that they may each reject religious commitments entirely.

"What indeed," asks Jacques Rancière, "is consensus if not the presupposition of inclusion of all parties and their problems that prohibits the political subjectification of a part of those who have no part, of a count of the uncounted?"[50] The excluded, those *nonsubjects* within a formal set of political rules, form the boundaries of the ideo-governmental "community" that both liberals and communitarians have been attempting to establish. Their differences arise from their identifications of those boundaries and their methods of policing them, not from the desire to figure out what kind of person belongs within them.

The most significant split in political science is neither between liberals and communitarians nor even between the Left and the Right but instead between those whose goal is establishing a normative, regulative ideal and those whose goal is something else, something actively political. Slavoj Žižek terms the former "parapolitics": "the attempt to deantagonize politics by way of formulating clear rules to be obeyed so that the agonistic procedure of litigation does not explode into politics proper."[51] If, as the normative unitarians claim, final agreement can be reached on what those rules are (whether universal or localized), then a postpolitical quasi-utopia will arise.

Such uses of the term "community" prove openly inimical to politics: the ideal of a community seems to be the establishment of a normative system of operations that has no room for substantive dissent in its fundamental operations. Such a conception of community is reinforced by popular conceptions of how communities themselves are formed, as though each community was created when a group of like-minded civic individuals laid claim to a particular geographically bounded area and perpetuated their collective identity into an indefinite future. And these conceptions are further fortified by public commentators who perpetuate the conception that threats to community are intrinsic to forms of personal, political, or moral difference. This is why the answer to the question "Can there be a political community?" is "no"; under our current understanding of community such a construction is fundamentally impossible. Where, then, can politics arise? Politics, in Rancière's terminology, comes whenever the accepted system is challenged or disturbed by those who are excluded from it.[52] Alternative theoretical formulations of political community that allow or even encourage agonistic political actions and identities are rare in political theorizing, especially within the contemporary discipline. The common assumption that the goal of political science is the creation of political spaces within which everyone is satisfied (be this a liberal satisfaction with fairness or a communitarian satisfaction with everyone else) discourages substantive politics.

The first and most obvious resistance to communal unity arises from historical practices and theories. The king's two bodies have always had the potential to fight between themselves, but such disagreements seemed to foretell the absolute dissolution of both entities. The fight for democratic representationalism loosed these bonds somewhat, but, as Alexis de Tocqueville astutely shows, it also made any threat to the political corporation also a threat to the very social composition of those citizens around them, increasing the pressures of normativity.

Historically, perhaps the most conspicuous privileging of contestation over community has arisen from Marxism: namely, that dialectical engagement (or put more simply, class struggle) is the necessary precondition for political change and growth. Though Hegel's insistence on the ultimate resolution of all dialectics remains in Marx, the quotidian reality of Marxist practices seems to have escaped the call for universal solutions. To divide societies into different parts whose interests are intrinsically opposed is to conceive of those societies as inherently politicized. Contemporary Marxist theorists thus celebrate conflict as leading to freedom and liberty (and consequently new forms of community).[53]

What is commonly termed "second wave" feminist political thought (and critique) conceived of community in similar ways. As women have been perpetually forced into positions of second-class citizenship throughout the world, the argument goes, they have developed tacit bonds from their common experience. The community of women, in other words, emerged from the ceaseless oppression of females over years and across nations; such a community would not in fact exist were it not for the fact of conflict.

But unfortunately most Marxist and essentialist feminist thought, over the years, has followed Marx's lead in merely moving the locus of community to more specific levels. To be a member of the proletariat, for instance, is to be in constant conflict with the bourgeoisie. But it is also to share an essential sameness with workers everywhere, to be united in your material position under capitalism, which leaves little room for dissent. Similarly, in the past few decades the ascendant critique of essentialist feminism has shown how the assumption of ultimate correspondence between women has shunted aside substantive questions of identity and difference within feminism, ignoring the ways in which feminist theory, for example, has often unwittingly posited the universality of women as white, middle-class, and educated actors. Thus, while admirably instituting conflict as central to political action, these theories have replicated the demand of community as conformity at a more specific level.

A second way to try to avoid these demands of homogeneity that theories of community seem to demand is to institutionalize adversarialism. Anglo-American legal traditions serve as a model for this tradition. In this argument, by institutionalizing conflictual relationships (e.g., in the persons of adversarial lawyers) the subsequent conflict results in more equitable access to the truth. The theoretical equivalent to this is John Stuart Mill's liberal pluralism, which argues that people need free difference to allow progress and the search for the truth to continue.[54]

Unfortunately, such antagonisms are dependent on their own teleology of resolution. The truth will out, it is thought, and the juridical system determines the truth of the matter. The pluralism that such a theory encourages is a temporary one, and one that is subsumed within the assumed puissance and precision of law. There may be two sides to a legal issue, but for that to imply more than one resolution is dangerous to the very essence of law. Similarly, in the case of Mill's pluralism, it is clear that such a community still is unified with an underlying teleology: the search for the truth benefits the whole town, state, or country.

Nicholas Rescher distinguishes empirical "factually constituted communities" from "normatively constituted communities," arguing that the former allow for plurality whereas the latter shut such plurality down.[55] But his very terminology is unconvincing: certainly there are many examples of pluralistic societies, or countries, in geographically bounded areas; each of these makes perfect sense. But he is looking for "factually constituted communities" that act just as the normative kind do: that is, that consider themselves fundamentally alike without actually coercing conformity.

Note what all these conceptions of community, from the communitarian to the liberal to the post-Marxist, have in common: community as lack of dissensus, posited as the optimal and natural circumstance of human existence. There seems to be an underlying teleology that the "unnatural" element of politics is that which prevents the spontaneous creation of community. Community emerges only when there is a "shutting down" of politics—to a greater or lesser extent. Of course, this is represented as the building, reinforcing, and protection of the community.

This building, reinforcing, and protection comes about through the same mechanisms for all these conceptions as well. First, by excluding difference in the name of threats to the community; second, by forming communal identities against these threats; third, by institutionalizing protective mechanisms that develop and reinforce normative assumptions.[56] Taken together, these result in a radical exclusion of political conflicts, except insofar as these can be managed bureaucratically. The term "community" becomes rooted in absolute consensus: a deep-down level of mutability is regarded as essential.

COMMUNITY WITHOUT UNANIMITY

From where, then, can a reengagement with politics which could conceive of the many dynamics of familial life emerge? For a variety of reasons both historical and epistemological, pluralism as a political philosophy would have to be returned to its historical roots to function thus. Even the best liberal readings of social difference fail to acclaim politics, at best accepting contention as a given fact. They do manage to understand diversity as real and normal, look for mutual understanding between diverse people, find respect through a "sensibly managed social system," and hold an interest in "maintaining that peaceful and productive communal order that is conducive to the best interests of everyone."[57] But that management and maintenance has a price, a price that everyone who transgresses the boundaries must be made to pay.

There, of course, are those who have made theoretical strides toward the simultaneity of community and politics. Ortega y Gasset, for example, provides a theory of syncretic community: truth is the unification of all partial and mutually exclusive viewpoints. It is the solidarity of difference that creates validity, out of which can come a larger sense of a political community.[58] But, unfortunately, Ortega did not expand this ontological claim into a meaningful theory of politics.[59]

Closer still was Hannah Arendt's celebration of agonistics, her privileging of human conflict as one of the essential foundations of community. For Arendt, political divisions are not only permitted in a community, they are the necessary conditions of engagement with fellow humans that are the cornerstone of community.[60] These divisions are the basis for equal, considered debate between equals, what Habermas would later term the "ideal speech situation." Arendt's abhorrence of totalitarianism arose from her well-known formulation of authority, in that the former is intrinsically antipolitical, because it is "incompatible with persuasion, which presupposes equality and works through a process of argumentation."[61]

Yet Arendt's personal and theoretical commitments to agonistics were found wanting. Like the liberals she contemns, Arendt constitutes a formal realm of politics, limitations on the political process beyond which she feels people ought not go. In an unarguably Kantian manner, she encourages agonistics only in public spaces; in the private sphere, she argues, such engagements have no place. Nor do people who properly belong to the realm of the private have the right to intrude on political engagement: thus her overt rejection of feminism, and her serious apprehensions and critiques of the American Civil Rights Movement, which had the temerity to consist, in part, of children and other nonpolitical actors.[62] Similarly, other contemporary Kantians, such as Jürgen Habermas, while recognizing the importance of contention, limit such contention either by excluding certain kinds of people from these speech situations or by delimiting what qualifies as legitimate argumentation.

But there are still those who are resources for contention, political theorists who celebrate contestation and argumentation. In the United States, William James (though more famous for his pragmatism) popularized the concept of pluralism as a desideratum for life. Only by testing ourselves against those who disagree with us, he holds, could we find what we truly believe.[63] Today, William Connolly argues persuasively for the "pluralization" of politics: an active engagement with difference that can serve as a constant reminder of the contingent and temporary nature of what people too often see as eternal verities. In a series of engagements with the likes of St. Augustine, Henry Thoreau, and Tocqueville, Connolly has developed a robust sense of the political, one that encourages political critique and dissent.[64] Similarly, in France, Félix Guattari and Gilles Deleuze initiated a philosophical engagement with difference and multiplicity by encouraging the development of a "rhizomatic" politics, lines of political flight that intersect, separate, and reconnect once again.[65] Jacques Rancière's attention to the "distribution of the sensible" encourages a critical reading of the forces that work to shut down peoples' abilities to create political action. And Alain Badiou and Quentin Meillassoux take from Arendt the unpredictability of political events, arguing that true political events arise from their contingent and eruptive nature.[66]

Indeed, there are those who go further, arguing against the possibility of the coexistence of politics and community. William Corlett, for example, utilizes Jacques Derrida in arguing that communities, by their very nature, cannot be unified. Attending to the mechanisms of interrelatedness that arise from such practices as gift giving, for example, Corlett shows how difference (between people, classes, communities) is both the necessary precondition for gift giving and the medium though which community relations emerge.[67] Jean-Luc Nancy, in turn, asserts that to establish community as some sort of common essence amounts to the closure of politics.[68] Nancy takes from Arendt an understanding of politics as a space of articulation of difference, and asserts that the closure of such a space is, fortunately, impossible.[69] In other words, Nancy serves as a reminder that incompleteness is a prerequisite of a political society. What members of a community have in common is one thing only: their distance from one another. So what kind of politics, then, is possible for a "community of those who have nothing in common?"[70] As Nancy points out, the essentially inoperative nature of community means that its bases (such as myths, ideologies, even constitutions), especially those of its creation and founding, serve no single purpose but instead circulate through different nexuses of meaning.[71] Roberto Esposito follows Nancy in arguing that community as such can only result in the dissolution of the individuals it is ostensibly meant to bring together. Community purports to protect individuals, but in fact empties all subjectivity into the common.[72] Even the attempt to think community, to conceptualize what a fundamental commonality might be, leads us to presume it to be a "thing," when in fact it is a "nonthing," a subtraction of the ontological subjectivity of its members to the openness to alterity.[73] Thus the demands of community result in a totalizing normative emptiness in Esposito's reading: the ideal of community collapses into "the void of pure relation" which "tends to present itself in almost irresistible fashion as fullness."[74]

In these respects, there seem therefore to be two challenges facing political theory. The first is that politics needs to be repoliticized, that is, that substantive as opposed to formal contestations need to regain a central location in political science. The second is that the nature of community needs to be reconceived in a way that opens it to politics. We need to discuss community not as an exclusionary system of sameness but as open, multiple, and shifting connections, correlations, and contestations: in other words, more like a family (a real, lived family, not a patriarchially idealized one) and less like an ideological or corporate population. Those who wish to understand community, as opposed to criticizing communities for their divergences, need to attend to how collective identities are developed in ways that are encouraging of contention and political challenge. It is to these sites of collectivity and contestation—our families—that the next chapters turn. Each attacks the putative centrality of unity within families. But more importantly, each also looks to the places where connections and commonalities and engagements actively happen: where we learn how to attend, to care, even to love, across the divides which keep us ever divided.

Political conflicts, identities, and ideologies are negotiated linguistically, language being both the instrument with which humans interact and the means of constructing what it means to be human. That voice and speech are central to the construction of community and political action is practically a truism within political theory. The assumption that language is deployed unproblematically and ubiquitously—that is, that language "just is" and that all people use language identically and constantly—is, unfortunately, just as much a platitude.

Once again, consider how family has been conceived as the archetypal community. A family is made up of disparate individuals, with often conflicting values, commitments, interests, even affections, and yet still (generally) consider themselves a close-knit community. Usually when family is used as a metaphor for a larger community, however, commonality and unanimity is assumed, which essentially fails to even approximate the experience of most actual families. Contrary to the assumptions of such cultural commentators, close relatives no more necessitate unanimity than does national origin; indeed, some of the most brutal and unforgiving conflicts emerge within family structures. Families instead use a variety of mechanisms to persevere. Of interest here is one particular strategy, often used in situations of profound disagreement (religion, politics, sexuality): that of silence. One important though not exclusive way to negotiate such differences is not to speak of them, to allow other, more uncomplicated topics of discussion to form the linguistic medium in which the family exists.[1] These silences need not be total or universal, but they are often a useful strategy to enable domestic continuity in the face of radical discontinuity. This tactic is exemplary, too, for larger communities. Thus, commonalities, both real and imagined, are already based on lack of speech: political, ethical, and epistemological silences which are necessarily backgrounded to establish other, overlapping connections. Silence and power imbricate one another, it is true, but not in the simply reductive way presumed by political science and public policy.

Those who wish to build and reinforce community mention silence only as a threat to community, as a failure and malfunction. Silence is that which is imposed upon marginalized groups, for example, so it is easily assumed that silence must be overcome. Silence is indicative of miscommunication, so a model of community based on an image of language as transparent communication must eliminate silence.

Even if silence is recognized as an appropriate response, it may still be represented as absence. When Wittgenstein famously concludes his *Tractatus Logico-Philosophicus* with the aphorism "Whereof one cannot speak, thereof one must be silent," he supposes that since we cannot achieve truth in nonlogical matters, for example ethics or aesthetics, they therefore have no place in philosophy.[2] Wittgenstein recognizes silence as important (he certainly does not think such issues insignificant merely because they could not be reduced to syllogistic demonstration), but this silence remained a lack. Issues that cannot be adequately addressed should not be addressed at all; they are outside the realm of the proper and therefore rightfully languish.

But in fact silence, as Cheryl Glenn has argued, operates at different times for different reasons.[3] Following Glenn, I am interested here in drawing out the implications of these dissimilarities, showing how silence operates in multiple ways toward (sometimes) divergent ends. If silence, as such, cannot be reduced to determinate purpose, it must be rethought as not only a site of repression but also a nexus of resistance or even as a potentiality for creation. This chapter begins by examining the common conceptions of silence's role through the lenses of communication theory, feminist criticism, and political theory, showing how disempowerment and oppression are the assumed political purposes of silence. Silence, though, can also serve as a refuge from power; the argument thus turns to those fields that recognize the power inherent in silence, whether as a form of subjugation, resistance, or motivation. Finally, I point to the ways in which silence itself establishes private and public commonality, where it is not merely an impediment to connections between people. If silence can be used to create the self, or to create communities, then it is not always something to be feared, eliminated, or overcome. That silence has no preordained structure of power, in other words, makes its potentiality more sweeping. And that silence resists any reductionistic political role denotes a general truth about both language and its lack: similarity in form is not equivalent to similarity in function.

DENIGRATED SILENCE

"Silence is weird" reads the tagline for an advertising campaign in the United States in 2001 for cellular phone service.[4] It is perhaps less surprising that such an approach to silence prevails in contemporary society than that the aphorism declaring silence golden still has wide enough provenance to be thus transposed. There exist, it seems, few states less desirable than silence. Silence is linked to the horror of absence, of aporia; Pascal held that the silence of space "strikes terror."[5] Insofar as communication between people is popularly considered the acme of human endeavor, to be silent means to betray the goals and hopes of humanity, to renounce ties with fellow citizens.

If in popular discourse the idea of silence is denigrated, its fate is hardly better in academe. As the concepts of identity and activity have become increasingly connected to a lingual politics, the existence of silence has in turn been increasingly seen as the subjugation of these identities and activities. If language, in other words, is identity, then the lack of language can only be the demise of identity.

Perhaps the most overt treatments of silence within academic discourse have been recognized by sociolinguistics and the field of communication studies. In examining the role that language plays in the construction of community, ethnicity, society, relationships, ideology, and personality, linguistic approaches have identified many of the vital ways in which language creates and structures human relationships to the world, to others, and to selves. Yet studies of language and society commonly address silence merely as a lack of communication. With a few important exceptions, linguistic theory and studies of communication take silence as their unstated antithesis. Communication is presumed to reside within, or be constituted by, language; words might be demarcated by the lacuna between them, but the words remain the elementary objects of analysis.

Even those few that do recognize silence as a constitutive aspect of language often regard it as merely the lack of sound—perhaps between utterances or as an individual response to certain behaviors. For example, silence may be defined as referring to pauses between words,[6] or "to the failure of one addressee to produce a response to a request,"[7] or as an initial reluctance and delay in reaction.[8] In its most extreme form, the total disappearance of a particular language is metonymically the disappearance of a people, the extinction of a culture.[9]

The sociolinguist Ronald Wardhaugh attends to the use of silence in response to questions that are morally or personally difficult to answer.[10] Silence in such a situation, he argues, is a kind of response (and thus is a proper subject for linguistics), but ultimately remains an avoidance. The appropriate response to rhetorical questions is no response, which is itself a kind of response.

A second analysis of silence has emerged in recent decades from feminist theorists, who embarked on the project of discovering how, when, and why women's voices have been silenced by a patriarchal culture. In some important ways, this approach has overlapped with the linguists'; they criticize silence as a failure or denial of communication, and examine the social and political causes of this aphonia. However, the feminist analyses add a critical distinction: silence is politicized. That some people (women) are encouraged or forced to remain silent can be traced to cultural norms which use silence to deny them agency.

This approach caused a central ambivalence in late-twentieth-century feminist theory: how to both explicate the abusive power relationships that have historically kept women's voices from being heard while also celebrating the work that women have done within the spheres allowed to them. Tillie Olsen's work epitomizes this. In her book *Silences,* she describes and critiques myriad silencings that occur in contemporary American society and the history of literature, and the ways and the times that the voices of women are defamed, ignored, stilled, or precluded.[11] Olsen calls for a rediscovery of women's work that had been purged from literary history, while also advancing a cultural critique of those who attacked (and continue, she argued, to attack) women's voices. If the most talented and original voices among us are stifled, then such systems must impact upon the less resistant even more severely. "What," she asks, do such destructions "explain to the rest of us of possible causes—outside ourselves—of our founderings, failings, unnatural silencings?"[12]

Similarly, Adrienne Rich, perhaps the best-known feminist critic to connect women's experience to silence, argues that women as women have been repeatedly and forcefully obstructed from entering the public realm of speech. "The entire history of women's struggle for self-determination," she argues, "has been muffled in silence over and over."[13] Rich has seen it as her duty to overcome this silence, giving women the voice that has so long been taken from them. Rich, in her refusal of the 1974 National Book Award, dedicated it instead in part to "the silent women whose voices have been denied us."[14]

For Rich, language not only stands closely related to action, it is the way in which action happens, and the modern world—filled with television and pornography—steadily replaces action with passivity.[15] Hers is a combined critique of sexual subjugation and modernity, which celebrates action and speech as the exclusive modes of political practice, and conflates passivity and silence into the realm of powerlessness.

This interpretation of silence as connected to forced absence and suppression transcends Rich's and Olsen's work, of course; it has long permeated the vast majority of feminist readings of silence. One of its strongest manifestations appears in antipornography feminism, where it is often argued that the creation, distribution, and even existence of pornographic materials inherently silences not only those who are depicted within them, but all people (women, children) who are objectified in the process.[16] Susan Brownmiller suggests that rape is a crime not only of sexual violence, but of silences: the publicity and formal categories surrounding rape make the communication and reporting of rape incompatible with societal definitions of femininity as pristine and honorable.[17] And it appears metonymically throughout feminist readings of political life and literature. The marginalization of women corresponds to their lack of words, where (as Mary Eagleton puts it) female "characters not only choose silence or are shocked into silence, but they are silenced in the narrative devices of the texts and consciously so."[18]

Nor is this reading limited to feminist theory. Silence qua absence and powerlessness appears in a variety of political contexts. See it used as absence within history: the lacunae in official archives are termed "silences" in the historical record.[19] See it used as vulnerability in political science: Elisabeth Noelle-Neumann describes the inability to express one's political preferences in the face of contrary public opinion (however slight) as the "spiral of silence."[20] See it used legally as implied consent: not to speak against an action (from a political claim to forced sexual intercourse) becomes complicity with the action.[21] See it used as the opposite of organized political contention: ACT UP's famed anti-AIDS slogan "Silence = Death" intrinsically calls for political speech as action.

Underlying each of these critical conceptions of silence is a model which conflates community, communication, and speech. Silence, whether that of a subaltern group or as perpetuated by institutional mechanisms, represents a threat to that nexus, and by extension a threat to politics. If silence is that which means the lack of articulation, and such an articulation is the primary—even sole—means of creating and continuing community, then silence is incompatible with community and society.

This implicit and explicit denigration infects not just those who decry silence, but also theoretical perspectives that presume the mutuality of community, communication, and speech. Theorists using this model generally either decry a disempowered group's lack of authority within a society (such as the feminist denunciation of silence) who are "silenced," or suggest new strategies to promote equality and democracy by encouraging speech.

Jürgen Habermas's conceptual approach to social power and equality exemplifies this latter approach. Having developed and deployed over the years an ambitious and meticulous critique of the privileging of enlightenment subjectivity, Habermas later began to champion speech as the formulation for democratic practice. Beginning with a rather simplified "ideal speech situation" and moving to more complex conceptions of discursive social space, Habermas's solution to the dilemmas of difference and inequality is resolutely verbal. For example, in his thorough treatment of law and equality in *Between Facts and Norms*, he champions, in turn, "discourse theory," "communicative reason," "communicative action," "communicative power," "communicative freedom," "discourse principles," and his previous stepping-off point, "speech act theory."[22]

Habermas's ideal, a nomologically neutral realm of power, is certainly a valid and laudable ambition. Nor is he wrong in his understanding that speech is a constitutive part of law and fair access to law and remains partially dependent on discourse equality. He certainly has not been the only political or social theorist to reduce freedom and the very possibility of justice to the availability of speech; the vast majority shares this approach. But in reinforcing a normative communicative theory as the ideal formulation of political democracy, he positions silence exclusively on the side of partiality, inequality, and oppression. If linguism is the sole site of community and connection, then fragmentation is inevitable. In other words, Habermas's theoretical approach not only ignores the ways silence figures within people's lives, it makes the grounds of community (which he ostensibly defends) insupportable and implausible.

The idea of the public as normatively locutionary extends to legal and social theorists far beyond Habermas's orbit. That civic political action must be linguistic, for example, is entrenched firmly in jurisprudence in the United States. The shorthand for the First Amendment to the United States Constitution is "freedom of speech," and indeed many justices have argued that alternative forms of expression (e.g., flag burning) are constitutionally unprotected by not literally being speech.[23] Without words, of course, law does not exist.

These various assumptions of words as axiomatic for communication, identity, and politics are popular, widespread, and deeply ingrained. Each serves to make speech and noise normative, and silence deviant; as the sociolinguist Ron Scollon puts it, "hesitation or silences" are thought to indicate "trouble, difficulty, missing cogs."[24] But positioning silence exclusively as absence, and speech as the substantive aspect of these powerful concepts, makes possible a striking set of possibilities. As Foucault argues, "silence and secrecy are a shelter for power, anchoring its prohibitions, but they also loosen its hold and provide for relatively obscure areas of tolerance."[25] The very existence of silence may thereby become a form of resistance, of nonparticipation in these practices of community-building, identity-formation, and norm-setting. Silence, in other words, betokens a rejection of these practices of power.

RESISTANT SILENCE

In its most moderate understanding, silence is seen as basic withdrawal, whether from a conversation or from the business of modern life. Silence is a ceasing of participation, a discovery of self by cutting off external stimuli, whether it be the creation of "a time for quiet," a spatial or temporal retreat, or a particular venue in which to read, think, or relax. Silence, in this conception, is as much metaphorical as literal. The "silence" of the wilderness, for example, is not really a literal quiet, as anyone who has spent a night camping in it well knows. Instead, it is a figurative slowing down, an escape from the quotidian pressures of its imagined opposite, city or suburban life. Yet this metaphorical quality prevails precisely because silence is seen as a rejection, however temporary, of those metaphorically noisy practices which are being escaped.

Contrary to popular assumption, silence is not the precondition of sleep, of thought, of meditation, of artistic appreciation; a great number of the world's people do all these things without absolute quiet. But silence is perpetually posited as their prerequisite. Of course, it could be argued, one *can* sleep next to noisy streets, farm animals, elevated trains, or church bells, but one does sleep better without those distractions. And yet those who sleep near these noises often find it difficult, or worrisome, to sleep without them. Similarly, those noises which would keep some people awake by their very absence, sounds such as ticking clocks, bullfrogs, or another person's breathing, are essential for others' slumber.

If silence is not privileged as imperative for personal growth, then, why does it have this reputation? The answer lies in the metaphorical position it holds: if silence is a form of withdrawal, then those aspects of life which require a degree of withdrawal from the assumptions and involvements of that life are metonymically linked to silence. Silence, in other words, functions as a representation of withdrawal; the assumed tranquility of silence bars the nontranquil involvements of the outside world.

This does not, however, constitute a particularly overt power of resistance, even if it implies a form of disavowal. Linked to the withdrawal conception of silence is a more overt refusal to participate in the normative linguistic practices of a state or society. Silence can prove to be powerful not only as isolation, but for the social function of self- or group-withdrawal as a resistance, an "exercise of silence" which Thomas Dumm says "suggests a reverence for the self that is self-owned."[26]

The sociolinguist Perry Gilmore gives one familiar example: that of the student whose silence in the classroom serves to resist the authority of the teacher, whose power in turn cannot force an answer.[27] The studied silence, or "sulk," can be used against a teacher's attempt to settle, understand, or appropriately punish a student; in refusing to speak, the student resists participating in the linguistic management of a classroom. Gilmore notes that while teachers may refer to persistent silence in a variety of ways, such as "'pouting,' 'fretting,' 'acting spoiled,' 'being rebellious,' 'acting nasty,' 'having a temper tantrum,' and so on," in each case it is seen as a threat to the normative standards of a classroom and usually causes a teacher to respond and pay attention to the silent student.[28]

Silence can serve as resistance to any institution that requires verbal participation (as virtually all do). In the face of forced speech, to "speak may be to justify what is unjustifiable."[29] On a macroscopic political scale, states often require such participation and subsequently employ a variety of means to compel it. The state-sponsored requirement to take an oath is a particularly overt form of obligatory speech. Loyalty oaths, public recantations of heresy, self-incrimination, enforced pledges of allegiance, and required judicial affirmations all oblige certain well-circumscribed speech acts. The work of Haig Bosmajian illuminates a profound trajectory of the ways in which coerced speech has been used to control, imprison, and even kill those who dissent, from Thomas More and Galileo to the victims of the United States House Un-American Activities Committee and employees forced to sign oaths as a condition of employment.[30]

Most notably, these institutional forces consider silent dissent threatening; declining to support a king's or legislative body's activities is judged tantamount to opposing the nation. Silence as nonparticipation threatens institutional forces in that silence resists whatever demands are made without necessarily opposing. In the cosmology of language, it is equivalent to heresy. For the Catholic theologian Max Picard, for example, the primary value of silence is, paradoxically, this lack of value. "Silence," he argues, "does not fit into the world of profit and utility . . . it cannot be exploited."[31] As absence, it lacks substance; as nonresponse, it resists interpellation.

Jane Campion's film *The Piano* meticulously captures and illustrates this role of silence. The protagonist, Ada, played by Holly Hunter, is mute; early in life, she says, she decided to stop speaking: "My father says it is a dark talent and the day I take it into my head to stop breathing will be my last."[32] Her silence weighs heavily on her husband Stewart (who selected her by mail order), but his inability to listen carefully to the silence in which she lives distinguishes him from his blunt, illiterate, but ultimately more responsive neighbor Baines, who learns to treat her as a fierce, independent, full person. Ada's silence adds to her humanity in that she demands more from her noninterlocutors; yet her silence clearly demonstrates a constant defiance rather than any sort of passivity.

The silence of a nineteenth-century woman is not an uncommon affair, especially as represented by the strain of feminist criticism epitomized by Adrienne Rich. But Ada, unlike the archetypal silenced woman, uses her silence to discomfit those who regulate social behavior with speech. Her primary communication through the eponymous piano is available only to those with the ability or will to listen; that she does not speak seems both the literalization of the norms of her society and her rebellion against those norms. One way of viewing the relationship of silencing and being silenced is as a "self-contained opposite," where silence can be reclaimed from the mechanisms of power to be used as a practice of self-creation.[33] By demanding unexpected relationships, Ada's silence serves to reinforce her individuality, the aspects of her person that make her different as she engages in power struggles with her husband and her lover.

Yet Ada's refusal to speak has its own aggression. Silence can be used against others, not merely to resist. To see such usage as merely wresting a tool from an oppressive system, as nothing more than a self-contained opposite, is to miss that silence's power extends beyond resistance. Silence, both as withdrawal and as pointed avoidance, can be used to manipulate, control, and harm others just as easily as to protect the self.

To turn to children to understand its uses, their deployment of silence against one another shows a silence which itself does violence. The "silent treatment," the calculated withdrawal of communicative words from an unfavored member of that societal group, can be devastating.[34] Importantly, this does not literally silence the individual in the sense of negating that person's attempts at speech, but attacks by revoking accepted social forms of recognition. Similarly, so-called passive-aggressive behavior, using silence to punish someone who relies on verbal interaction within a relationship, also wields silence to castigate and discipline.[35] In each case, silence operates on an exoteric register.

In each of these cases, silence is not something that is done to one, but a practice which one aggressively performs. Active and reactive silence does not fit well into the predominant model of silence as powerlessness. However, this is not to say that silence as power is better, or more often true, than silence as denigration. Indeed, insofar as normative speech structures both, discourse equally constitutes both models, since each works with and against the norms of speech. Wendy Brown points out that these conceptions, far from being oppositional, are in fact mutually structured: that it is possible for silence, she argues, "both to shelter power and to serve as a barrier against power."[36]

Yet before moving beyond this dialectical relationship, one more model of silence as power exists, one which is not reducible to a passive, a resistant, or an aggressive posture: that used on the analysand. Professional psychotherapeutic relations are premised on an evocative silence, yet one that is certainly far from neutral in the way it is structured by organizational power. The therapist's silence, at least relative to the client, intends to promote, or even provoke, disclosure.

Similar situations include a professor's use of silence to draw out a class, a journalist's to encourage elucidation, a priest's to hear a confession, or indeed any interlocutor's to induce conversation. In each of these cases, silence functions as a demand, not for silence in return, but for narrative participation. Silence thus evokes nonsilence: it incites interaction without demanding it. Even Susan Sontag, renowned for her opposition to the authoritarian nature of Freudian psychoanalysis, recognizes that this use of silence contains an "element of wisdom" within it, where it "keeps things 'open.'"[37]

If silence can function to provoke a discursive subjectivity, then, its power is neither defensive nor aggressive. It may operate in both registers at once, as in Jean-François Lyotard's description of the "differend," speech which is simultaneously demanded and impossible, such as by those who demand eyewitness accounts by victims of genocide.[38] It may operate on neither, as in the case of evocative silence. It may be that *silence has no predetermined structure of power at all.* If this is the case (and it is my contention here that it is), silence can play an infinite variety of roles in social, political, and linguistic networks. If it can be destructive, defensive, and evocative of selves and social relations, then it can also contribute to the constitution of these identities. The remainder of this chapter therefore examines some ways silence operates at this formational level, particularly emphasizing its use as a strategy to negotiate the competing realities of incommensurability and community.

Silence can operate in multiplicitous, fragmentary, even paradoxical ways. The politics of silence, in other words, are not reducible to any particular political functionality; even more than its putative opposite, language, silence resists absolution. As Lisa Block de Behar explains, "silence remains subject to the interpretations of the receiver to whom its message is addressed."[39] The difficulty of articulating silence, she continues, arises because there is "no guarantee that an interpretation occurs of a discourse which is not uttered, of an intention which remains unknown, and which may not even exist."[40] Insofar as silence cannot be literalized or universalized, it is not reducible to one singular function. If silence were strictly resistant, or oppressive, it could be neatly categorized as salutary or sinister; instead, it both embodies and transcends these neat categorizations.

Condemnations of silence, especially in institutional contexts, arise from this very indeterminacy. Gail Griffin describes how classroom silences are experienced by the college professor thus: "A stretch of silence may mean any number of things. It may mean 'We have no idea, as we have not yet even glimpsed the frontispiece of this text.' Or 'You appear to be operating under the naïve delusion that we care.' Or 'I will never drink orange vodka again.' Or 'If she doesn't call me tonight I will throw myself off the chapel tower.' Or 'If you'd just break down and tell us the answer, we could all go home and sleep.' Very often it means 'I am a cretin in a classroom of geniuses.' But teachers, often bad translators, usually interpret it as follows: 'We despise and loathe you.' "[41] Griffin clearly means to remind teachers that silence is not necessarily to be feared, but her multitude of meanings is not quite so reducible to the moral lesson she intends. For the classroom silence may well mean loathing; its very irreducibility to any of these territorializations makes the lack of speech threatening to those organizational structures and their representatives. Teachers are often justified in distrusting silence.

This particular capability significantly differs from the customary political roles of silence, even among those discussed above who recognize some of its potential kinds of power. If silence is solely a lack, communication becomes impossible; if it is limited to force, either as resistance or as aggression, it separates and partitions relationships. If it can function within, for example, families in various ways, both to create divisions and to resist power, then the nature of silence is in fact that there is no intrinsic nature at all.

That silence has no necessary form, however, leads to an unexplored and unacknowledged capability: it can also enable and produce. Silence, in other words, can be constitutive. It can create identities and sustain communities. It can, in the words of Cheryl Glenn, "engender," "witness," "attest," "command," even "open" us to the world.[42] Once understood as freed from interpretive structures that necessarily condemn (or celebrate) it, the unlimited aspects of its multiplicitous functionality are freed for their creative and productive capacity.

Nietzsche, as Zarathustra, conceives of silence as the method for the most profound individual changes. An anthropomorphized Solitude welcomes him from the world of men, the "world below," where "everything among them speaks, everything is betrayed."[43] To the "fire-dog," the creature of the underworld, he argues against the cacophony of the "world-changing" events. "The greatest events—they are not our noisiest but our stillest hours. The world revolves, not around the inventors of new noises, but around the inventors of new values; it revolves *inaudibly*."[44] Zarathustra, in a parable he calls "The Stillest Hour," explains how he changed from comparing himself with other men to creating himself. Repeatedly, "something" spoke to him "voicelessly," helping him realize how to escape his childhood, his pride, his shame, and his limitations imposed upon him by society.[45]

As Sonoda Muneto (the foremost Japanese translator of *Thus Spoke Zarathustra*) has shown, the centrality of silence to Zarathustra's self-origination is remarkably akin to that of Buddhism, especially that of two books on the Buddha's achievement of enlightenment that Nietzsche was reading at the time of writing *Zarathustra*.[46] The profundity of the role of absence of language within Buddhism extends far beyond the ken of this book, but individual silence and meditation figure centrally within the process of Buddhist enlightenment, especially its Zen (Chan) and

Madhyamika forms.[47] (The ascetics of monkish silence likely also served as a model for Nietzsche.) Zarathustra's embrace of nonlinguistic forms of communication (dance, music, singing) ultimately does not depend on silence, but Zarathustra's trajectory exemplifies how the rejection of language can help a new self transcend the limitations of the old.

Zarathustra's conception, Zen meditation, and monastic asceticism all point to silence as a constitutive element of the overcoming self. These models are intrinsically individualized; each characterizes subject-centered creation. As such, they are akin to (though not identical to) silence as a resistant form of power. For Zarathustra, for example, only after he renounces language (the language of others) does he find a new mode of being. Ultimately, however, these are silences which reinforce disparity and discontinuity, whose archetype is that of withdrawal.

Yet if silence can be constitutive of individual subjectivity, it can also serve to constitute commonality. The very existence of social silence depends upon its acceptance. Silence must always be a collusion, as Deborah Tannen points out; social silence cannot be limited to one side.[48] Silences between two or more people must be actively maintained as such.

That any communal silence must be socially preserved is obvious, especially when cases of those who disturb it are taken into account, for example, during a theatrical production or symphony. Noise, be it speaking or mere rustling, is seen as disruptive to the experience of the performance; an audience member who cannot learn silence is commonly seen as failing in his or her place. Nor is this limited to those moments where dialogue emanates from the stage or sounds issue from instruments. An audience member who speaks loudly during a tense emotional standoff in a Harold Pinter play or applauds between movements in a Mozart concerto implicitly breaks an alliance of silence, an alliance to which other audience members (and occasionally venue staff) are deeply invested.

This is of course a partial silence, one on the part of the audience instead of the performers, but it is instructive nonetheless. The audience members recognize the necessity of silence on their part for the experience they desire, and go to great lengths to protect it. In doing so, they create a particular kind of audience, with norms and mores: a community.

Yet this is a limited example. To better explore this aspect of silence, I turn to two cases which actively and overtly use silence to constitute a community, instances where silence plays a far more active and recognized role than in the familial example with which this chapter began. These two illustrations, traditional Quaker meetings and the famed John Cage piano piece 4′33″, show silence bringing together disparate people in common experience.

Quaker worship is famed for being conducted, for the most part, in silence. Friends, as Quakers call themselves, were not the only Christian group to promote silent worship; even within the Catholic Church the long-present apophatic tradition gained strength in the late seventeenth century in the quietist movement led by Miguel de Molinos.[49] But Quakers are the best-known historical and contemporary sect to worship in this way, and the centrality of silence in their worship and daily life is overtly justified as conducive to theological truth and community creation by Quakers themselves.

From the denomination's beginning, this form of worship drew considerable attention and criticism. In his *Apology*, an explication of Quakerism written in 1678, Robert Barclay spends considerable time defending silent worship, especially once he declares that "there can be nothing more opposite to the natural will and wisdom of man than this silent waiting upon God."[50] Barclay saw silence as a method of diminishing the automatic demands of the self, allowing the word of God to emanate instead. Speaking thereby became representative of all activities of the body, which could through practice become secondary to listening to God's voice.[51] For Quakers, silence has long been the foremost way to allow the overcoming of the egocentric mind. In the words of a pamphlet from 1805, "there is no exercise whatever where self is more shut out."[52]

This is not the silence of constantive individualism; like most religious ceremonies, it is practiced as a community. This silence must take place communally, Barclay argues: it is the "duty of all to be Diligent in assembling of themselves together, and when assembled, the great work of one and all ought to be to wait upon God."[53] The Quakers considered congregation vital, even, as with their convention, in the absence of a central speaker, priest, or minister. When "these who came together, to meet after this manner in Silence, so that they would set together many hours in a deep Silence and Quietness," they practiced silence together, as a community.[54]

Those who attempt to theorize silence often remark on Quaker practice, but its communal aspect remains consistently overlooked. Even Richard Bauman, in his admirable treatment of the interplay between speech and silence in seventeenth-century Quakerism, treats silence as something ultimately individualistic.[55] However, the literature of the period, though primarily concerned with the overcoming of self in the service of "the Light," continually refers to the necessity of assembly. Even in the twentieth century, Quaker theologians take pains to differentiate the experience of individualized silence from the authentic communal worship: silence, argues Violet Hodgkin in 1919, must arise not from "each soul alone, but united as a community."[56]

Silence, in this social role, creates the community. It provides emotional, theological, and political sustenance in many of the same ways any denominational organization does. But rather than sharing a literal symbol as the organizing principle of their association (a Torah, a crucifix, a minister), the symbolic unifier in the Quaker case is the absence of symbol. Silence functions as shared experience, but one whose meaning is not necessarily (or even likely) shared. Silence's "primary object is group unity"; the unarticulated yet contiguous experience of silence itself forms the community.[57]

John Cage's famous piece 4′33″ invokes similar experiences. A performer sits at a piano for four minutes and thirty-three seconds without touching the keys; an audience hears what would usually be considered incidental noises instead of notes from the piano. While not silence in the sense of absence of sound (Cage held there is no such thing as absolute silence), Cage's piece throws all sound into stark relief.[58] In doing so, it encourages the audience to consider the nature of music (the most common interpretation of 4′33″) but also, more importantly, to become aware of itself as an audience.

Cage's study of the role of silence within Zen Buddhism convinced him that music's ideal role was not to unilaterally communicate emotion or ideas to listeners, but rather to create awareness of surroundings: in this case, the surroundings of the performance hall.[59] Cage's interest in the creation and reception of music serves as testament to this focus: his dislike of recordings as "the end of music"; his insistence on a score, page turnings, and note durations for the performance of 4'33"; and his fundamental interest in the art of everyday experience.[60] As Susan Sontag points out, the dialectical nature of the silence that Cage created necessitates a surrounding fullness of response in the audience.[61] It is as though the silence constitutes the awareness of the audience *as such*, both within its self-awareness and in the arrangement of its relation to the "music."

The audience, therefore, transcends its assumed identity as passive recipient and actively partakes in the piece. Cage's is not a form of performance art that primarily relies on shock, or even on transgression. Instead, the surprise of 4'33" emerges in its uses of silence to enable the recognition of the audience as integral to performance, as composing the piece as much as the composer or performer. Silence, in this role, does not distance, resist, or overpower; it forms the artistic and intellectual basis for the recognition and constitution of communal identity. Indeed, even those who dislike or resist the silence of the performance become part of a community of engagement: intentional harrumphing or even stalking out of the hall become part of the pluralized audience's performance. For Cage's musical composition, as for the Quaker theological tradition, silence creates community.

These creative productions, from Zarathustra's self-creation to Barclay's theological assembly to Cage's communal experience, make singular interpretations of silence's functions problematically simplistic. If silence cannot be fixed to the singular interpretation of powerlessness or of resistance, then neither can it be easily and clearly constitutive. No sure way exists of determining if all members of a community are affected by silence in ways that actually create community; no silence is indisputably formative or reactive.

A search for *the* politics of silence, for the determinative classification of the power dynamics inherent within silence, is consequently doomed to fail. The multiple, fragmentary, and overlapping dynamics of silence can be iterated, investigated, and explored, but they cannot be fixed or predetermined. Indeed, the implications of this impossibility may well have more to do with how politics gets conceptualized in contemporary theory than with the particularities of silence. Power itself, like silence, is radically indeterminate, open to processes of domination, emancipation, and resistance which can never be fully contained, represented, or comprehended.

It is silence's simultaneous resistance to and eliciting of interpretation that acts in ways profoundly troubling to those who demand explanation. It can be disturbing for moral and ethical reasons; Martin Heidegger's lifelong silence about his attitude toward National Socialism remains a disturbing provocation both for those who wish to defend him as an insightful genius and those who try to reduce his thought to a pro-Nazi solipsism.[62] It disturbed those surrounding the Quakers, who as late as the twentieth century would invade Quaker houses of worship and shout at the gathered Friends.[63] It disturbs those institutions and institutional executors (including teachers) who demand verbal interaction as evaluative mechanisms. It disturbs parents, who see family communication as the parroting of instructions. It disturbs precisely because the ideal of transparent speech is the presumed mode of participation in our cultural practices, a standard to which silence is not reducible.[64]

Both the creation of community and the disruption of organization are among silence's constitutive aspects. Each of these forms is linked to silence as oppressive or resistant power, but silence does not ultimately or necessarily perform any one of these functions. Or, more properly, silence does not perform only one of these tasks in only one way. Silence functions as a negotiation of the disparate and the common, but like any true negotiation it takes more than one path and more than one meaning. In silence, as in few other mechanisms, individuality, incommensurability, and community coexist.

The predicament: your dog's life is in danger, and you have to decide whether to spend a significant amount of money and time on a remedy. One alternative, among many, is to spend an equivalent amount to help, even save, a number of human lives; the International Red Cross or a United Nations relief fund could use that money to feed the starving or rescue disaster victims. Will you, to put it most pointedly, choose the life (and comfort, and even luxuriance) of your dog over that of human beings? Though one alternative is clearly virtuous, and the other questionable, you—like most North Americans facing this choice—will likely choose the latter. And the choice you make, interestingly enough, calls into question the basic principles of ethics, political philosophy, and human primacy.

Confronted with this question, especially a generalized version about what the proper response should be, there seem to be two predicable answers. The first is an aggrieved "Well, I have a dog, would do many things for him/her, and refuse to accept such a judgmental interpretation of those kind of actions." The second, oppositional response is "How can anyone value animal life over human life? Such people have lost their moral bearings!" and presumes that to rehabilitate a dog in some way betrays humanity.

Neither of these responses is particularly interesting. It would be easy enough to explore the defensive psychology of the first or attack the naïve humanism of the second. Yet neither explains the gap between the two views, how one person can feel so strongly about an animal that another cares very little about. Rather than attempting to definitively resolve this predicament, which perhaps cannot be answered satisfactorily, this chapter instead uses it to ask particular questions about the presuppositions and causalities within political theory.

This takes place in three different ways. The first of these investigates how the relationships and connections between humans and dogs bridge profound differences, examining how those are individually and historically constituted. The second calls into doubt the assumed compulsory force of logic within political philosophy, especially the status of logical demands. The third looks at different ways of investigating the intellectual and ideological stakes, eventually arguing that fiction may be more attuned to the everyday complexities of these relationships than other explanatory forms.

That an individual might well prefer to spend money on dog food or veterinarian bills than on helping refugees, victims of natural disasters, or the poor is problematic for political philosophy; indeed, it can logically be extrapolated within most theoretical systems as not only radical injustice but a betrayal of humanity. The value in this relationship escapes political theory. Virtually every democratic theory holds that equivalence and formal equality, both of which are dependent on deep levels of mutuality, are the necessary precondition of just political relationships.

The centrality of equivalence and formal equality is misplaced, in part because any theory that insists on a rejection of some of the most important of human affinities is bound to fail both empirically and ideologically, and in part because these connections provide ways in which humans learn to care for and attend to the world around them. The failure of these theories is in their insistence on the commensurability of political actors, the necessity of "being understood" across the multiplicitous edges of worlds, and their exclusive privileging of logical formalism. On the contrary, we can learn from those who love their pets that communication is not limited to abstract thoughts or human speech, but can and does happen in startling places and across surprising boundaries.

CANIS FAMILIARIS

William James describes the incommensurability and unintelligibility between people and dogs at an everyday level: "we to the rapture of bones under hedges, or smells of trees and lampposts, they to the delights of literature and art."[1] Humans and dogs live in fundamentally different worlds, where the very methods of communication and connection are so disparate that they are untranslatable. A human, in other words, finds insensible much, if not most, of what is interesting to a dog, and vice versa; the two can communicate only through the most rudimentary of language, and even that often seems limited to command and obedience.

Yet, James argues, dogs and people can rely on, develop trust in, and even love, one another: "our dogs and ourselves," he writes, are connected "by a tie more intimate than most ties in this world."[2] That people and dogs cannot understand one another's interests has little to do with their bond. Each fills needs in the other, for caring, companionship, physical and emotional affection, fun: that is the basis for their allegiance. Certainly these needs play out differently in each species and in particular contexts; certainly the needs of food and protection and shelter are paramount, and yet the emotional attachment is not reducible to those needs. Dog (and human) affinity continues beyond the ability to meet those wants. A toothless guard dog often remains part of a family.

Is proof really needed that what people feel for their dogs is actually love? Of course, such a claim is impossible to prove to those who would deny that such a complex emotion is appropriately applied to pets. But let a list of various behaviors, institutions, and items stand in for such a verification. Some are familiar and others strange, some are common and some rare, some are reported as outrages and others as paeans to humane behavior. Such a list would include, among other evidence: pet cemeteries; people leaving property to dogs and cats in their wills; canine health insurance; cultural and emotional prohibitions against eating dog flesh; neighborhood flyers pleading for the retrieval of lost pets; the history of dog portraiture; pet therapy, including drug treatment; ceremoniously burying and memorializing dead dogs; books and poems "written" by dogs; sleeping with dogs (literally, though bestiality also belongs in this list); pet organ transplants; furniture designed for dogs; attempts to replicate dead pets through cloning; the bestowing of names upon animals; and popular depictions of dogs as central to children's lives and emotional maturity, such as in *Lassie* or *Where the Red Fern Grows*.[3] All these practices, whether conventional or unorthodox, show the different (but often central) loves that people have for dogs.

That a wide variety of people love dogs is obvious. This love transcends class, race, gender, sexuality, ethnicity, education, intelligence; it is limited by almost none of the subterranean fault lines that permeate the society of the United States.[4] People do not (usually) love dogs to the exclusion of all others, though some instances—such as when a last will and testament renounces human offspring in favor of Rex—come close. The love of dogs does not usually replace the love of others, but is often thought to encourage it. Marjorie Garber, for example, argues that it is through the love of dogs that we become fully human.[5]

Yet such canine conceptions are relatively recent. Historically, dogs were commonly set up as models of morality, not as objects of human love: their fealty was representative of the highest of human aspirations. The connection between Fido and fidelity is an ancient one, reaching at least as far back as Argos in *The Odyssey* (who is left uncared for while Odysseus is away and happily dies upon his return). John Adams praised those who have "a Fondness for Dogs," for such feelings show "evidence of an honest Mind and an Heart capable of Friendship, Fidelity, and Strong Attachments . . . [which are] the Characteristicks of that Animal."[6] In the eighteenth century, the faithfulness of dogs became the model for children's poems and books, wherein children were encouraged to reproduce the virtues that dogs naturally possessed. Yet this did not translate to their desirability, except for pragmatic reasons. Keeping them solely as pets was limited virtually exclusively to the extremely wealthy, at least until the late nineteenth century.[7] To be able to keep an animal that was ultimately "useless" (in utilitarian terms) was reserved only for those who wished to mimic the behaviors of the upper classes.

But by the nineteenth century, dogs began to be seen within American and European cultures in a different way, as virtuous actors rather than insensate embodiments of abstract virtues. James Turner describes how the Victorians intellectually shifted from merely teaching children to note the steadfastness of dogs to making the claim that dogs were manifestly virtuous.[8] As the Victorian preference for emotion over abstract intellectualism emerged, animals began to be conceived of as morally superior to humans. A dog did not need to remind itself to be loyal and courageous, as did a man; it merely responded with its essential qualities. Moral actions were attributed to dogs: the ideal canine is one with the human ideals of compassion, loyalty, and bravery. If children could overcome their human susceptibilities, the Victorian romanticism asserted, they could approach the glory of dogs. Dogs, it was argued, "posses incontestably all the qualities of a sensible man," whereas "man has not in general the admirable qualities of the dog."[9]

For the Victorians (and their pet-loving contemporary descendants), the very goodness of dogs was seen as bred into them. The prolonged domestication of dogs as work companions, whether for mushing, hunting, or herding, had eliminated their natural ferocity and given them an inclination toward virtue. It was a triumph of humanity: the brutal, wild nature of the wolf had been remade into an inborn—one might even say "natural"—obeisance. At a time when, thanks to Darwin, humans were increasingly seen as members of the animal family, dogs embodied the best of human creation; to love them was to love human mastery of animal nature.[10]

Thus loving a dog began to be seen as an intrinsic good, with such love thought of as evidence of a caring, kind, humane soul. The emergence of associations for the protection of animals in Britain and the United States and the development of the Audubon Society into a full-fledged political organization joined the emergence of pet ownership for the middle class as examples of the proper concern for the natural and the care of the dumb: such concern, it was thought, elevated the humans who acted appropriately.[11] People who care about animals and nature, those who transcend their narrow self-interests in the service of the beasts who cannot even speak, such people were understood to be finer than those whose concerns are solely for themselves.

Much of this perspective remains in contemporary society, of course. There is even a commonly understood correlation between the treatment of pets and the treatment of other humans. For example, the skills and patience required for the proper training of a dog is popularly thought to be partially analogous to the skills and patience needed to raise a child. Caring for a dog is commonly seen by young couples as preparation for children; men walking puppies are hoped to be (or themselves hope to be seen as) prime candidates for fatherhood; people whose dogs are well behaved are assumed to also properly discipline their children. Often, too, the companionship offered by a dog is understood as a credible replacement for the departure of grown offspring. In all these cases, the dog functions as an ersatz human in the sense of an object of care giving: a repository for affection, guardianship, and love.

However, the love that people give to their dogs is not universally admired. While there are few who deny that this emotion is experienced as "love," such love is often denigrated as an inferior imitation of true human emotion. Even some of the great defenders of animals suspect that such affection can border on the pathological. Konrad Lorenz, for example, held that a person "who, disappointed and embittered by human failings, denies his love to mankind in order to transfer it to a dog or a cat, is definitely committing a grave sin, social sodomy so to speak, which is as disgusting as the sexual kind."[12]

Even those whose antipathy does not run quite as deep as Lorenz's may still feel grave misgivings about allowing the love of pets a status equal to "true" love. In response to those who would judge the love one feels for a dog as a humanizing experience, Andrew Sullivan argues that such a relationship "is an inferior one, because dogs offer unconditional fidelity . . . and thus offer a much easier and less virtuous relationship than difficult humans."[13] That is, because of the unrestricted nature of a dog's affection, it need not be earned in the same way as a human being's, and therefore lacks the arduous (and therefore superior civic?) negotiations that mark interhuman compassion. Needless to say, Sullivan ignores whatever similarities this may have to a parent-child relationship or to other relationships marked by unequal power or sentiment differentials.

Even within less stringent criticism, a tenuous suspicion remains that the emotional affinity between humans and dogs does not measure up to the standards of true *love*, that the term itself connotes an intensity of emotion that might better be termed "affection," "attachment," or "fondness." But the emphatic term "love" is, I believe, unavoidable. The energy, attention, and sacrifice that people give to their pets bespeak a far stronger affiliation than the other terms imply. In addition, that people themselves choose this term is telling; not only is the iconic phrase that serves as a title for this chapter familiar to all, but children and adults alike usually overtly profess love when speaking of their dogs. Finally, I can think of no other term which makes sense of the intensity of these relationships. People who claim to love their children or spouses or parents are trusted to best understand their own feelings; why deny this to other equally felt claims? The emotion that people have for their dogs should be called by no other name.

And so the love of dogs ends up in a tenuous spot in contemporary American society: known as vital to many human lives, sacralized for some, dismissed by others, cheered by the culture at large (witness the sales of Elizabeth Marshall Thomas's *The Hidden Life of Dogs*),[14] roundly derided by the culture at large (witness the standard filler newspaper article snickering at the new dog-oriented store, trend, or drug), while— above all—the affections for these animals in our midst endures. Fully assessing what to make of humans' love of dogs seems virtually impossible, but one thing is clear: dogs are loved.

POLITICAL SUBJECTS

Rather than speaking of dogs specifically as pets (though the subject will return), let us turn to the human side of the equation. Political philosophy, in investigating the creation and legitimacy of power, must necessarily address relationships between human beings. Political philosophers intend to ascertain the moral and logical underpinnings of these kinds of problematic questions: what, actually, are the political connections that people owe to one another, and what are the limits to these connections? So in this section I also turn to two fields related to (some would argue subsumed by) political philosophy: ethics and animal rights. The first restates the fact of human attention to dogs as a moral question: *ought* people treat dogs better than people? The second asks a similar but slightly different question: *ought* nonhumans have moral and legal standing? But, ultimately, the answers that these approaches give are unsatisfactory, for the answer in both cases (though there may well be one, or many) does not necessarily resolve anything.

Michael Oakeshott took the problematic nature of political thought seriously, positing a fundamental rupture within its very essence. In his essay "A Philosophy of Politics," Oakeshott notes that political philosophy "must be a reasoned and coherent body of concepts," that its very existence as philosophy is dependent on its claims to logic and rationality.[15] On the other hand, he notes that political philosophy has another standard to meet: that of conforming "to the so-called 'facts of political life,'" those empirical aspects of human reality that are, after all, the object of its inquiry.[16] For Oakeshott, these two charges will often be in conflict, splitting political philosophy against itself; when this happens, he argues, the responsibility of political philosophy is ultimately to the latter. Unlike pure philosophy, which is not bound by relevance or tangibility, any adequate theorizing about politics must primarily be about the lived, human experiences of the political realm.

To follow Oakeshott here, then, in trying to understand the ethical and political constitution of people, it is more important to attend to how they behave than how they think they should behave (or, especially, how theorists argue they should think and then behave).[17] One of the implications to be examined in the following pages is that such behaviors are not necessarily logically integrated and causally ordered by the political actor. This is not to say that they are necessarily oppositional: many people would not see support of their pets as contrary to the safeguarding of human life. But their actual comportment shows that they may often choose the former and disregard the latter.

Yet many, if not most, political theorists continue to treat the function of philosophy as though a politically responsible and ethically coherent conscience follows a careful pattern, first creating a hierarchy of ethical commitments, then correlating those to possible behaviors, and finally acting appropriately. What becomes apparent from a range of them is the overwhelming degree to which this logical causality is presupposed. From basic economistic theories to complex ethical systems, this presumption underlies virtually all conceptions of how logic, evaluation, politics, and ethics work together.

Of course human actions and attachments fail to follow these sorts of logics. To return to the example with which this chapter began, people are not unaware that the time, money, and energy that they spend on their dogs could make life better, or even possible, for human beings somewhere in the world. Nor is it the case that they hold an abstract conception that dogs are more deserving of concern and comfort than humans, as though they only need the truth of morality to be spelled out for them to behave in a properly principled manner. Even with this knowledge, they commit time and resources to nonhuman animals, overriding their supposed obligation to the human race. If indeed universalized ethical commitments were the absolute determinants of human behavior, such people would be committing grave errors of omission, and would readily change their behaviors once the proper ethical course was pointed out to them.

Political theory, by Oakeshott's standards, should be concerned with people's actual choices rather than those a philosopher thinks they ought to make. And yet, for all the practical criticisms of ethical philosophy from a political standpoint, most of these critics methodically, even painstakingly, construct the same instrumentalist conceptions of reason and action. These include, but are not limited to, liberalism (such as that of John Rawls), utilitarianism (as presented by Richard Brandt), and libertarianism (as propounded by Robert Nozick).[18] In each of these cases, the philosophical construction of the ethical system is logically sound, more or less, and yet leads to conclusions that, while analytically following from the premises asserted, are profoundly antithetical to the everyday ethical standards of virtually all people. Admittedly, it is intellectually interesting to conclude, as Rawls does, that the principle of "desert" (e.g., whether people get the incomes they deserve or the punishments they deserve) should have no place in politics, or to conclude with utilitarians that it is logical that "our duty to our own children is not fundamentally different from our duty to all children," but such stances directly conflict with political and ethical life as understood by the vast majority of people.[19]

In fact, political philosophies qua philosophies assume that the analytical aspect of the "reasoned and coherent body of concepts," in Oakeshott's words, are more important than the experiential disconnects between those concepts: that syllogism trumps reality. Indeed, as Michael Smith has convincingly shown, even when people make certain moral judgments, such judgments do not necessarily motivate such people to act in accordance with them.[20] For example, even if one strongly believes that humans are more important to protect than are dogs, one may not necessarily act that way. That someone thinks (or even argues) for a certain behavior's rightness has no essential correlation with that person's actions.

G. E. Moore, noting this distinction, argues that logic therefore has nothing whatsoever to do with moral actions; for Moore, logic is best left solely as an academic puzzle. In response, Mary Midgley has shown that Moore was wrong, at least within everyday life: people can and do use rationality to change their emotional states.[21] But the fact that they *can* do so (and actually sometimes do so) does not mean they *must* do so, nor even that they do so often; and without such a normative directive, each of the forms of political philosophy noted above fails. Bernard Williams attacks the notion of ethical behavior as categorical—that is, he does not think that philosophical considerations can (or should) lead to the conclusive governance of behavior. The fact that historical and societal conditions authorize certain ethical outlooks above others provokes skepticism, admittedly, but it is "a skepticism that is more about philosophy than it is about ethics."[22] If, as Williams holds, the rationalistic standpoint of philosophy and the lived experiences of ethics are not necessarily commensurate, then there appears to be an inherent problem in the common and academic view that logic underlies ethical contention.

A brief reiteration of a certain aspect of a well-known animal rights debate can highlight this problem. Peter Singer, among others, has pointed out that the grounds for any specific claim to rights based on a specific attribute of humanity are intrinsically problematic; there is no specific quality such as intelligence, language, or self-awareness which is felt by all humans (including newborns, those with mental impairments, and the terminally ill: what have become known in animal-rights discourse as "marginal cases") and which is not in some way exceeded by some animals.[23] Since it thus follows that humanity as a whole is not a privileged category, Singer concludes, humans owe some degree of consideration to nonhuman animal existence. Some theorists who disagree with Singer point out that such a position could justify the breeding of humans with brain capacity adequate only for minimal bodily functioning; under Singer's view, they argue, there could be no ethical opposition to the sale of the meat and organs resulting from this breeding. That we find repellent the eating of human flesh, even from mentally defective humans, they argue, logically compels us to privilege all forms of humanity over the nonhuman.[24]

This is, of course, a highly simplified version of this debate, but it will suffice here for my concerns. For I am less interested in which side has a legitimate argument (both seem to) or the conclusions each draws (both seem drastic and counterintuitive) than I am in examining the use of philosophical deduction in each. The role of logic for either viewpoint, and a host of others in this debate, is seen as the absolute condition upon which concrete public and personal decisions must be made. Both sides understand epistemology as fundamental to ethical behavior: you believe X, of course, and as Y follows logically from X, you therefore must believe Y. Though you think you believe Z, it is shown that Z is incompatible with Y, and therefore you do not, cannot, truly believe Z. Plugged into these syllogisms are various claims about animal rights, human morality, and infant justice, but the causal nature of the logical argument is simply assumed.

Some in political philosophy have tried to avoid this dominance by displacing or at least reapportioning the station of logic in human judgments and evaluations. Jürgen Habermas, for example, dismisses the notion of humans as discrete, unencumbered political and social beings; instead, he privileges intersubjectivity in his theory of communicative action.[25] In doing so, he places human relations, not abstraction, as the central constituent of existence. The reasons he does this, and the criticisms of those reasons, are well known. Most profoundly, Habermas humanizes ethics and politics by emphasizing the personal interactions that can make up communities, norms, and standards. And yet this solution does not solve the ethical conundrum of the money spent on veterinary medicine any more than does the formulation of a transcendental ethics, for Habermas's intersubjectivity is always and necessarily human; there can be no intersubjectivity unless there is a basic recognition of the self in the other. "Subjects," he argues, "who reciprocally recognize each other as such, must consider each other as identical [as subjects]; they must at all times subsume themselves and the other under the same category."[26] Without the primacy of the subject (that is, without the category of the human that supersedes all other claims), intersubjectivity lacks the ability to stake a moral claim on people. This arises, in part, from the dominance of universalism in his thought, as well as that of his followers such as Seyla Benhabib.[27] For by making all subjectivity equally applicable to all humans, he and they must in turn profoundly differentiate the human from the nonhuman.

Can any philosophies, then, help make sense of this question of dogs? There are two twentieth-century strains of philosophical thought that encourage an escape from these limitations.[28] Not coincidentally, both of these trajectories move away from analytic deduction and toward experiential location.

The first, the loosely associated classification of "existentialism," understands the subject as grounded not in its self-identity but in the conditions of its existence. For this approach, the relationships within life provide the ultimate formulations and adjudications of meaning, truth, and ethics. In the thought of Karl Jaspers, for example, "the 'thrown' or irreducibly situated character or our being-in-the-world and our being-with-others is the guarantee of, rather than the obstacle to, our existential freedom."[29] Selves, always in relation to others, are created by (and themselves create) significance from acts of care and consideration. Heidegger situates care at the center of his philosophy. In *Being and Time*, he posits "care" as the "formal existential totality of *Dasein*'s ontological structural whole."[30] Jean-Paul Sartre, in emphasizing the ethical implications of such an orientation, concludes that our own freedom is possible only with our struggle for widespread human freedoms.[31] And Arendt finds the very "condition" of humanity in its activities with the world: work, labor, and action.[32]

The existentialist's concept of existence, however, remains firmly wedded to the human. For each of these authors, the character of the world, however it situates and is in turn situated by human existence, is important exactly insofar as it relates to human existence. Human relations, after all, are the subject at hand. And to that point each privileges the interhuman interaction over the "thingness" of the nonhuman.[33] Martha Nussbaum, who goes even further in recognizing the centrality of love in the constitution of identity in connections, still must rely on the final word in the following quotation: "Love is not a state or function of the solitary person, but a complex way of being, feeling, and interacting with another person."[34] The existential focus upon the located nature of being does allow for love's central place in ethical outlooks, but limits the recognition of being to other humans.

The second group of philosophers who have profoundly challenged the limitations of universalist subjectivity—and those who have come closest to the question at hand—have been feminist theorists, especially those from the strain of feminism influenced by Carol Gilligan's and Nel Noddings's "ethic of care."[35] Like existentialism, such philosophies begin from the epistemological assumption that the located nature of subjectivity is primary to human existence, but add that such located natures are realized more completely (at least in most instances in Western societies) within the experience of women and girls, especially the giving and receiving of nurturance.[36] Gilligan, for example, contends that when people are identified primarily in terms of "self-discovery and self-recognition," "the language of relationships is drained of attachment, intimacy, and engagement."[37] When the concepts of care and attachment are seen as fundamental, instead, humans become communal creatures, reliant on trust and connection above autonomy and self-interest.

Such an approach is not specifically antirationalist (at least not usually); in large part, it is the opposition between reason and emotion that is being critiqued.[38] That reason excludes emotion, that its most ardent defenders see emotional connection as threatening the very basis of rationality, has historically eliminated these emotional qualities from the ambit of philosophy.[39] Instead of conceiving of analytic rigor and universalized moral rules as the goal of philosophy and ethics, these critics argue, we need to discover and discuss how "commitments occupy a deeper stratum of our moral psychology than do moral obligations."[40] Nor is the ability and consideration of care necessarily determined by gender. Joan Tronto explicitly decouples any essential link, noting that even though the majority of caring values are associated with "the feminine," caring can include a wide, diverse range of practices.[41]

Yet, similar to Habermasian communicability and the varieties of existentialism, humans remain the objects of virtually all renditions of care ethics: family members provide the archetypal examples, followed closely by friends and group members.[42] Taking other, nonhuman forms of care into account is rare.[43] One exception is notable, both for taking pet relations into ethical account and for its subtlety. Chris Cuomo and Lori Gruen overtly theorize human relations with "companion animals" and parallel many of this chapter's themes by arguing that friendship is often an essential component of these relationships, and that moral and political traditions ignore and deny the reality of those friendships.[44] They argue that by attending to such relationships, feminists can see the similarities between oppressive gender binary relationships and oppressive species binary relationships.[45] Ultimately, their goal is to overcome "moral distance" by recognizing the correspondence between the animals we love and the animals we eat: that we can "learn to see nonhumans as beings that deserve our moral perceptions, . . . shift from viewing them as background or mere food to seeing them as enablers of our own abilities to bridge moral distance, to cross boundaries, and to expand our moral orientation."[46]

In other words, even those who are most interested in theorizing the relationships between humans and animals continue to seek logical lessons from those relationships, and to apply those lessons in particularly normative, even obligatory, ways. If we do indeed love our pets, to continue this example, we must stop eating animals which are essentially similar to them.[47] That is, we are obligated to these experiential understandings and logically extrapolate them to the larger world. Even when specifically about care of animals and the environment, the implications of such outlooks are judged insofar as they fit a generalizable necessary change. Certainly to do so is admirable and no doubt ethical. But what becomes of such an argument if its logic fails to command obeisance in human behavior, if people can and do love certain animals and eat others simultaneously?

DOGS, ANIMALS, HUMANS

There seem to be two primary responses to the dilemma with which we began, the insufficiency of which these specifically philosophical approaches illuminate. The first (call it the "humanist" critique) is to excoriate the dog owner for misunderstanding how a personal allocation of resources in favor of a dog's health betrays responsibility to other human beings. Choosing a dog's veterinary care over human life, it is claimed, equals failing to fulfill necessary political and ethical responsibilities. The second (the "animal rights" critique) extrapolates from the responsibility felt by the pet owner to a sense of responsibility to animals in general, or at least to animals of comparable cognitive status. That one can recognize the worth of a dog means that one must therefore also recognize the value of the animals constantly slaughtered for no higher purpose than culinary pleasure.

What both of these approaches share, as I have argued, is the erroneous presumption that abstract categorical expressions of ethical responsibility must predominate over personal and quotidian emotional existence. Or, to put it more simply, that logic trumps love. When Singer or Tom Regan hypothesizes conflicts between animal life and human life, even these militant defenders of animals argue that, philosophically, human life must take priority. In this they agree with those who dismiss the possibility of animal rights.[48] And yet as our veterinary example shows, this is not necessarily the case; people may well choose their pets' lives over the lives of distant and unfamiliar humans.

It may well be, logically, that those who eat meat should indeed have no compunctions about eating dogs, even their own dogs. Of course, such an argument will prove attractive only to those whose affinity for logic exceeds their affinity for dogs. Those whose love of pets is genuine and fervent may well recognize the logic of one or more of these arguments while continuing to love their dogs, eating meat, and showing relative indifference to abstract humans (and, not irrelevantly, showing even more indifference to the other animals killed to make dog food). How can we—as writers, as readers, as political theorists—make sense of these logical disconnections? The final pages of this chapter attempt to uncover how such love can coexist with humanity (and humane-ity); what is it about the love of animals, in other words, that can transcend both the rigors of logic and the demands of the vast majority of political and ethical philosophers?

One way to begin to answer this question is to note the attitudinal differences toward dogs that are pets and dogs in general. The tenor of affection toward a particular animal is far more intense than it is toward a generalized category of animals. The specific connection between an owner and a pet can be so intense that it overwhelms linguistic and spatial boundaries. The ethnographers Arnold Arluke and Clinton Sanders, for example, have studied the ways in which different sets of humans reinforce or break down the divide between humans and animals.[49] One set may reaffirm it (e.g., animal researchers) while others see it in necessary but problematic ways (e.g., shelter workers). Arluke and Sanders note how pet owners often transgress this division, for example, when deciphering symptoms to veterinarians. These elisions of the distance between pet and owner can be subtle, as in explanations of a pet's moods ("She's upset that we have a new baby"), or blatant, as when the dynamic between them is spoken for dyadically ("We aren't feeling well today"), or even transposing speakership from the human to the dog ("Oh, Doctor, are you going to give me a shot?").[50]

On the other hand, it would be misleading to assume the likelihood of a similar connection with distant or previously unknown animals. People virtually never feel that dogs in general are equal to humans. There is an important and popular endorsement of the distance between dogs generally and particular pets. Many people support the efforts of animal shelters to decrease the numbers of feral dogs by euthanizing (that is, killing) them; few would support similar treatment of homeless and impoverished humans.[51] Not that they want their particular pets killed, but they do regard a (random, unowned) dog's life as inferior to that of a (random, unconnected) human being.

Of course, these conceptions are not totally separate; dogs as pets and dogs as animals bleed into one another. For many, dogs have a semisacred position below humans but above most other animals. Contemporary reluctance to recognize dog flesh as meat exemplifies this. This ambiguous stature has been in place for many years: witness Captain James Cook's reluctance to eat dog when it was offered to him by Tahitians (though, after consuming it, he was gracious enough to allow that the taste of "South Sea dog was next to an English Lamb").[52] Thus the European prohibition against dog eating in the eighteenth century was not a full-blown *tabu*, but merely a common presumption. In the contemporary United States, however, this status is most clearly seen when it is violated. When a Hmong immigrant sacrifices a puppy to save his wife from evil spirits in Southern California, he is arrested for felony charges of animal cruelty.[53] Greyhounds may be used for racing (and killed when they are no longer serviceable) but this practice is under increasing pressure, outlawed by populations untroubled by horseracing.[54]

These examples point to a curious aspect of dog love: its particularity. To outlaw their consumption or their racing is to treat dogs as a class different from other animals. Clearly, a kind of generalization of the category "dog" as different from, say, "pig" has occurred in American culture. But dogs are not usually loved in general; in the veterinary example beginning this discussion, it is the specificity of a particular dog that is loved. And yet that specificity leads to general implications which outstrip the specific example: dogs exist not only as individual beings, but as a classificatory category. One does not need to describe *why* one loves one's dog; that it *is* one's dog is enough.

The specific relations of dogs to humans also complicate the political nature of their social position. As pets, as owned animals, they are necessarily in a servile position within a household. A "natural" order of domination is always at play in the relationships between humans and dogs. There is clearly an imbalance of power inherent in pet ownership; that one party controls access to food, the timing of exercise, and the propriety of play (both temporally and spatially) bespeaks a clear domination. Indeed, the language of control seems troublesome for many who want to exalt the relationship between people and pets. Such exaltation often results in the rhetorical reversal of ownership, recourse to terminology such as "companion animals" and "guardians," and the understanding of pets as mystic and transcendental.[55]

Many have been happy to connect the imbalance of power between canines and humans with other, equally "natural" forms of authority between humans. Racial and gender analogies are less common than they used to be fortunately, but there are still plenty of commentators who draw similarly fatuous parallels: "the dog clearly flourishes in a regime in which he is 'dominated'—kept in order, like children in school, which many psychologists as well as teachers and the children themselves will explain they prefer: they want to be controlled."[56] Such a justificatory theory premises far too much about both children and dogs. But without entering the territory of exculpation of dominance, we can indeed note its presence in pet ownership.

Thus one way, albeit a dangerous one, to think about the role of dominance in pet keeping is to recognize the possibility, variety, and validity of love within and throughout severe imbalances of power. That such a conception of love is politically troublesome does not mean that it has no legitimacy in human's lives (it clearly does) nor that those ethical and philosophical systems that want to exclude such a relationship from the proper channels of meaningful relationships are right to do so (they are not).

The questions of whether or not the human domination of dogs is "natural" or "right" or "necessary" are not the ones that are so threatening for traditional philosophy; the language of ethics and political subjectivity are designed for precisely these kinds of questions. Perhaps, as against the liberal traditions which underlie contemporary Western politics, equality in most respects may be neither possible nor optimal. Liberalism famously particularizes citizenship to a strange, socially disembedded, competent, and rational adult (who is also usually presumed to be white, male, autochthonic, and educated). The ideals of republicanism, similarly, presume nondomination as a central goal of governance and politics.[57] What makes the humanist and the animal rights approaches seem to be the only traditional answers to the veterinary dilemma is the unwillingness for philosophy to recognize the emotional connections between humans and their pets. That such strong connections exist across the registers of powerful and vulnerable, human and nonhuman, is troublesome not merely for the role of domination in these relationships, but for the ways in which they put the very idea of a privileged human subjectivity into question.

Clearly the humanist position rejects the strength of these connections, dismissing them as sentimental or even anthropomorphism. But what is surprising, and indicative of the stakes involved in such a discussion, is the extent to which the animal rights approach dismisses it as well. Peter Singer, for example, disclaims any interest in love. He goes so far as to state that he does not love animals, that his arguments for animal rights rest entirely upon reason, which is "more universal and more compelling in its appeal."[58] Love for an animal, in other words, is not reasonable in that it cannot command obeisance to its conclusions in the way that (he assumes) rationality does. This is not to say that Singer does not love animals (or that he does not hate them), but that he finds such emotive registers irrelevant to ethical arguments and, hence, to ethics.

The idea that caring for an animal can so strongly affect humans (even those humans who are philosophers) intrudes upon the primacy of reason, and thus on humans as reasoning beings. The moment when Nietzsche throws up his arms about a horse being viciously beaten and starts to cry, it is commonly believed, is the beginning of his descent into madness. Peter Singer thinks he knows that logic, not love, compels people to act and to sacrifice. Deprived of its coercive force, logic would be something else, something less powerful, something that would not demand action. People may recognize logical specifications and yet still make choices that slight those specifications; this common practice has long been the bugbear of normatively inclined philosophy.

Additionally, recognizing that animals may take preference over humans at certain times also profoundly disturbs the centrality of mutuality in the presumed conceptions of political subjects. For the essential tenet of liberal politics (as well as virtually all antiliberal politics) is the primacy of the citizen. Those marginal to the status of citizen provide the grounds of debate over issues of equality, rights, and political participation, for example, past questions about women and slaves and contemporary questions regarding minors and the imprisoned. Yet these debates concern the boundaries between the human and the citizen. How much more dramatic are the debates over the boundaries of the human?

The problem common to these approaches is simple: all presume that logic drives action and ethics, that ethical and political theories should strive above all for analytic internal coherence. If philosophy, even (or especially) ethical and political philosophy, provides little help in answering this question, then other types of writing may prove more useful. An easy reversal, however, will not do; merely assuming that dogs are equal to people would not help understand people's political commitments and behaviors either. The spoony narratives of pet owners, for example those who refuse to speak of their "ownership" of animals or who look to their pets for spiritual guidance, are just as amblyopic as those who deny the love of animals entirely.[59] Instead, I turn to the novel, specifically a novel which dramatizes the connective, even redemptive, powers of dog love.

When J. M. Coetzee's novel *Disgrace* begins, the protagonist, David Lurie, is a university professor incapable of love; by its end he is an unemployed volunteer at an animal shelter whose main responsibility is the disposal of dog's bodies.[60] In the pages between, he undergoes humiliation, assault, incomprehension, and ultimately a kind of rebirth. Coetzee, a novelist for whom relationships between humans and animals are central moral concerns, places his protagonist in the metaphorical position of a dog in his world, a location from which he can learn what it means to love.

Lurie sees himself as a clear-thinking, righteous, and self-contained human; occasionally bewildered by his urges, it is true, but with a categorized understanding of the order of the world and an articulate moral outlook. He is, in other words, a fully rational being. And he is not prone to transformation: in the beginning pages of the novel, he is convinced that his personality is "not going to change; he is too old for that," his "temperament is fixed, set" (2).

It is not until his world has ceased to make sense to him on his terms that he begins to realize the tenuousness of his identity and existence (at the same time, not coincidentally, as the "rise of lawlessness" in post-Apartheid South Africa). Dismissed from his job for seducing an undergraduate, Lurie goes to live with his estranged daughter Lucy in the provinces, where both of them are attacked by unknown local men. Lucy is raped and impregnated. His rationality has led him to a position where he no longer comprehends his daughter, his neighbors, humanity, or himself, where his disgrace is complete: "I am living it out from day to day, trying to accept disgrace as my state of being" (172).

Coetzee repeatedly draws parallels between this disgrace and the lives of dogs. Canines are not privileged here; Lurie and Lucy are forced to recognize that their state of disgrace is not a redemption. Before they are attacked, Lurie likens being controlled by desire to the situation of a dog, a dog which "might have preferred being shot" (90). By the novel's end, as Lucy puts it, they must learn to live with "nothing. No cards, no weapons, no property, no rights, no dignity." To which Lurie replies, "Like a dog" (205).

But Lurie becomes involved with exactly such animals, dogs in an animal shelter where he volunteers to help put them to death. The dogs for which Lurie ends up caring (in all the complexity of that term) are not exactly alive, but neither are they dead. Within his life, the pragmatic purpose of dogs has proven ineffective. The guard dogs which are meant to protect him and his daughter have failed. Working at Animal Welfare, however, he discovers a need to care for the dogs being killed; not to keep them from death, but to make their last moments as pleasant as possible and to care for their bodies beyond what is necessary. Rather than merely leaving the animals at the dump, for example, Lurie incinerates the bodies himself. "He may not be their savior," Coetzee writes, "but he is prepared to take care of them once they are unable, utterly unable, to take care of themselves" (146).

It is precisely the particularity of the dogs that Lurie begins to notice and care for. He considers himself an antisentimentalist, and the novel is far from a sentimental one, but this caretaking becomes central to his meaning, to his identity. If Lurie is to be saved, Coetzee implies, it is not through grand gestures or even art; it is, instead, through the tending of others, nonhuman others.[61] Emotionally, Coetzee has crossed what Ian Hacking calls the "species boundary," where he has become attuned to the possibilities of "sympathy between some people and at least some animals."[62] By the end of the novel, this is all the choleric, superior, and self-centered protagonist has learned, and yet it may be enough: "He has learned by now . . . to concentrate all his attention on the animal they are killing, giving it what he no longer has difficulty in calling by its proper name: love" (219).

In Coetzee's work, dogs are both the debasement and the expiation, at least in this final possibility of love. In these cases, dogs are neither political actors nor subjects of politics. They are, instead, *actants*: nodes of love where the intersections of love, intensity, proximity, belonging, and interspecies relationships interwork one another.[63] But is it only the love of dogs which upends the presumptions of human centrality? How far does our recognition extend? What if, in other words, these attitudes are not limited to our affection for dogs? Perhaps they extend to things that seem even more distant from humans than dogs, not merely those species with whom we share our homes, but also those with which we share other things: attitudes, appetites, even space. Might we, following Christopher Stone's groundbreaking legal work, even need to ask if trees and other natural objects should have legal standing, if political recognition should transcend humans and human constructs?[64] That we give legal recognition to human abstractions such as states and corporations shows that absolute individual humanity is not a necessary prerequisite for political, legal, and ethical status, he argues. So what prevents the recognition of other entities which can be equally important, both to humans and in their own right?

Moreover, it is easy to doubt that such emotional connections are limited to organic, living beings. Some theorists of animal rights have drawn critical parallels with the human interest in cars: cars are certainly valued by their owners, who may well value the qualities of some cars more than others.[65] As troubling as the line between our selves and our dogs, then, is the line between our selves and our things. Fanciful as it may seem, however, the idea of constitutive and identity-related political theories about things is not inconceivable. Timothy Kaufman-Osbourne, for example, has investigated the ways in which objects at specific historical and cultural times actively gender those who "use" them.[66] To see politics in the use of a tire iron or the wielding of an eggbeater in mid-twentieth-century American suburbia is indispensable to feminist theories of power. Similarly, Jane Bennett has explored the politics of what she calls "enchanted objects," those material things in quotidian life which literally embody promises of transformation and dynamism.[67] Bruno Latour has explicated the means by which even the things we care virtually nothing about, such as a doorstop, are themselves part of our social beings; they can even be said to have their own sociology through their literal transformation of political geography and attachment.[68] And all three of these theorists are indebted to Donna Haraway's conception of the human body as already a cyborgian organism.[69]

If, then, it is the very surroundings of humanity that makes up humanity, why pay any special attention to dogs at all? Why, in other words, not pay equal attention to all things that envelop us as political actors? I do not doubt that one could, though to do so would seem even more outrageous than to recognize dogs as such. But humans and many dogs continue to share one trait that is central to this discussion, a diffuse, difficult-to-comprehend thing, to be sure, but one that goes by a single name: love. It is love, Coetzee's protagonist recognizes, that allows him to overcome his distance from a world around him that he no longer recognizes. And it is love that convinces a pet owner that the pet should be cared for, even at great expense, even at the expense of another human.

What, then, does attention to the love of dogs provide political theory? Certainly the attention to familial relations in this book does more than merely plead that love needs to play a serious role in political theory. Exploring the reality of these relationships brings up three more interesting approaches. First, it brings into focus certain complexities within political connections: the unacknowledged possibilities of relations between humans and animals, the unattributed importance of particularity in ethical commitments, and the underappreciated effects of distance and proximity in relations. Intersubjective relationships, even those of an ethical and political nature, are not limited to those between humans, nor can the specificity of the object of love (the importance of one actual dog as opposed to another) be ignored. Second, it encourages the uncommon recognition that the political implications of imbalance and inequality, even incommensurability, are not necessarily pernicious. The complex history and specificity of the role of dogs within Anglo-American culture shows that compassion and community can and do coexist with control and disparity. Finally, it can help to overcome the naïve assumption that political and ethical philosophy's relationship to behavior should be normative, that excellence in logical composition has direct compulsory results. People's love of dogs does not necessitate them, or anyone else, to stop eating other animals, to give dogs equal legal and civic protections, or to place the suffering of distant, unknown humans above their pet's needs and pleasures. To treat reason as coercive is as absurd as treating it as irrelevant.

These are not claims that the political overcoming of distance is impossible, even of the "moral distances" described by Chris Cuomo and Lori Gruen. Nor should indifference be embraced, especially in those cases which make thoughtless cruelty possible, allowing for banal evil by encouraging mechanized obedience. Often we do care about those who are radically unlike us, those whose spatial locations or ethnic affiliation or class status or racial identification we see as remote and of little relation to "us," whoever the "us" may be. These claims instead point toward a recognition of the legitimacy—an embattled legitimacy but a legitimacy nonetheless—of the kinds of love which attach humans to animals.

| **THE SPACES OF DISABILITY**

The spaces we inhabit are not inhabited equally. Differences in physical and mental ability result in dissimilar encounters: instructions written in English, a cobblestone street, or a ringing telephone cause profoundly disparate experiences for those generally considered "able bodied" and those considered "disabled."[1] Yet, these spaces remain the same; excluding radical solipsists, people agree that those physical objects, spaces, and events are held in common even while they are experienced differently.

Family life, when life is lived in part for others, necessitates a pluralization of space—the ability to experience it through the experiences of an other. These locations provide an exemplary site through which to understand the interlinked nature of commonality and incommensurability, particularly as encouraged by familial relations. (Though here I focus primarily upon physical disability, similar arguments could and should be made regarding mental and psychological disabilities—they too should assist in remapping the normative universalities we too often presume.) This exemplarity arises not from the physical changes that a disability causes, nor necessarily from the changes in lifestyle that a disabled person undergoes, but from an abstract expansion: the corporeal and conceptual pluralization of spatial experience that disability produces. The individuals for whom this happens are not necessarily disabled themselves. Indeed, this multiplication may exist merely as background for those with congenital disabilities. Instead, it is predominantly found in those in the process of learning about disability, be it their own or others'. In other words, the focus herein is not to figure out "what to do" with or for disabled people, nor how society has treated or created disability, nor even how to improve conditions for those with disabilities; each of these projects has been (and continues to be) addressed and discussed and debated elsewhere. The focus instead is on how we, disabled and abled (or "temporarily able-bodied," the term favored by many disability activists), can learn from the experience of disability: that our world, our space, operates both universally and particularly, all at the same time.

As in the previous two chapters, the aim here is not merely to show that interdependence and incommensurability are "already there" in our lives, but also to point to the ways in which we—both as thinkers and as human beings—can learn from those who have most deeply thought about and acted upon these realizations.

EXAMINING DISABILITY

Disability studies, as a field, has predominantly taken one of two forms.[2] The first, which generated the possibility of disability as a social and political approach, strove to build common understandings between disabled people for intellectual and political purposes. Emerging from activist organizations and social justice concerns, this branch of disability studies has emphasized the overcoming of institutional impediments for the disabled. By highlighting the difficulties faced by people with seemingly dissimilar impairments, activists and scholars created the conceptual alliances necessary to argue for equality and to attack discrimination. In the United States, the Americans With Disabilities Act, which nationally mandated access to public and commercial space, stands as the grand achievement of this first approach.

The second, which emerged more recently but now constitutes the majority of the discipline, examines the various ways in which disability is constructed through the social citation of normativity. A society, theorists of this camp argue, institutionalizes particular and dominant modes of transportation, sensation, and information technologies. In doing so, it *disables* those particular people who do not meet its criteria. Culture, in this view, privileges certain approaches, making any deviation from them seem extreme or even insurmountable. By positioning certain bodies as normative, cultural practices position other bodies as inferior, bizarre, or in need of supplementarity and control.

Various intellectual traditions have discovered different but overlapping evidence for this second analysis. One method highlights historical examples where deaf or blind people or others who modern Western culture would consider disabled were far better integrated into their communities than they would be today, one could even say "fully" integrated.[3] Another examines specific methods by which contemporary societies demand and inscribe norms: speech, or reading, or even climbing stairs are made to be the necessary preconditions for full personhood.[4] A third looks at the ways the meanings of disabilities have been variously constituted as representative or endemic within different societies while others have been naturalized.[5] Each of these approaches show how cultures, and not people, cause incapacity.[6]

While the particulars of disability and the politics of space in this chapter do not correspond neatly with any of these traditions, it remains indebted to them. One commonality between these two arises from their coincident recognition that the social can be critically politicized through the transformation of our understandings. The first wants to reconfigure our collective space into one which is inviting or at least functional for those with disabilities, the second to transform our collective understanding of the social to recognize the inherently oppressive nature of "normality."

In both cases, interestingly, the subject of the discourse becomes not "the disabled body," as it has traditionally been positioned in medical and remedial discourses, but "society": how those without disabilities should change (laws or presumptions) to better welcome "the disabled" (as they are commonly represented) into their midst. It is "others" who are addressed, who are entreated to transform, a profound distance from the cultural positions that accept (or even celebrate) the disabled depending on how well they can achieve normality. Both approaches are also "normative," however, in the academic sense of the word: social presumptions and laws should be like this, not that, they say.

The purpose of this chapter tends more toward the descriptive than the normative. The attempt to change prevailing social attitudes, while admirable, will be extensive, and if history is any indication, political philosophers will be far more likely to follow than to lead. But there are those who go through such a shift on their own without following societal pressures, and discussing their experiences can provide tremendous insight. In fact, two groups of people do this, the first more obviously than the second: first, those who become disabled beyond early childhood and must learn their worlds anew; second, those who are the close friends and family of people who become or are born disabled and feel the need to figure out the world from their loved ones' perspectives.

This latter group proves particularly interesting for the purposes of understanding pluralized spaces. For these people, whom I term "caregivers," the experience of disability is real yet removed—they continue in the experiences and bodies to which they have become accustomed, but to be effective they also must imagine themselves into another's experiences and body. Concentrating on caregivers, however, causes an interesting theoretical difficulty, for such a focus seems not to be about disability at all. The changes undergone by a person who loves and cares for a disabled person are not physical or bodily, nor are they cultural or societal. They continue to live in the same bodies and the same large-scale society as always.

This experiential doubling implies certain philosophical dynamics. Those who are affected by disability without undergoing it through their own bodies or minds often find their relationship to the world utterly transformed, without concomitantly experiencing any change in their material, physical being. Materialism cannot explain this at all, since the concrete manifestation of particular physicality does not change. Nor does it fit neatly with the philosophical presumptions of phenomenology: the "thrownness" of the world, in Heideggerian terms, does not fundamentally change, and yet the being-in-the-world that is thought to result from this thrownness is profoundly altered.[7]

Instead, these individuals bring disability's aesthetic dimension to the forefront. If what changes is their *judgment* of the world, not their *experience* of the world, then the category of the aesthetic makes sense of this shift. Aesthetics, of course, should not be seen here as "mere" aesthetics, but rather as "taste" in a post-Kantian sense: as a communally created yet individually responsive set of interpretive lenses which form the very possibilities and groundworks of judgment.

At times, the aesthetics of disability are clearly laid out, such as with the proliferation of "ugly laws" in nineteenth-century North American cities (many of which lasted well into the latter half of the twentieth), which criminalized the public appearance of visibly disfigured people.[8] At other times, conceptions of normality and abnormality almost entirely obscure the aesthetic component, such as when the main hope for disabled people (from strangers, from their families, and even from themselves) is to achieve ordinariness, to "be like everyone else."

The aesthetics of disability become central for a variety of reasons. First, an aesthetic approach highlights the contingent and political nature of judgments. Second, aesthetics also enact the communal and collective nature of judgment, openly depending on social dynamics to reach collective conclusions. Finally, most people view aesthetic conclusions as malleable and non-ontological in nature, readily allowing for change, critique, and evolution.[9] In other words, both the disabilities themselves and the experiences of those who care for those with disabilities are aesthetic.

EXPERIENCE

Especially for those who are not born with a disability or those who have not developed an awareness of themselves as disabled (e.g., an individual who finds he or she has a late-onset genetic disease), this experience is particularly pronounced: suddenly the world looks a far different place, with obstacles where none had previously been. This transformation, while basically cognitive, depends on physical experience. Lived incidents underlie this intellectual transformation; trying to imagine various disabilities cannot replicate experiencing life with one.

The empirical ways that many people begin to deal with issues of physical disability illustrate these creative locations. For most, such issues are raised by the experiences either of their own disabilities or of those close to them—usually family members (though, again, the definition of family remains wide). Envision, therefore, the process that members of this latter group experience. Your wife develops diabetes, leading in time to partial blindness. You give birth to a deaf son. Your daughter's doctor diagnoses her with multiple sclerosis. A sports accident paralyzes your sister. Your elderly father begins to require a scooter or a walker to move outside the house. Your brother has an epileptic seizure and must decide whether or not to give up driving.

First, you probably view this event as a tragedy: the contingency of the disability, the necessary arrangement or rearrangement of care, the profound *unfairness* of it while so many others continue their lives unscathed. And not only does this seem unfair and tragic, but the larger world seems inexplicably indifferent to this calamity: institutions, buildings, transportation, arrangements your mother depends on suddenly are inaccessible to her. Distances, tasks, even everyday cleaning and care are magnified to the point of impossibility. At times, physical space itself seems the enemy.

Eventually, he or she starts to adjust, however well or poorly, depending upon the local environment, friendship and kinship networks, and social and institutional responsiveness to this particular disability. New routines become established; certain pastimes remain possible; previously unfamiliar technologies take their place in the household; a new kind of life is lived. You, too, are changed: you have started to see the world differently. Now, entering a coffee shop, you notice front steps that had been invisible to you before. You internally criticize the distances between bus stops. You realize that the local elementary school's emergency information system depends entirely on sound. You notice that the local library's physical layout is crowded, with no room for a wheelchair. Airports seem even worse.

Actually, you probably do not notice each and every one of these. What you attend to are those specific impediments to your loved one's life. But you start noticing these barriers everywhere. Your world has been transformed. It has gone from a relatively supportive, manageable system to a somewhat antagonistic one. Where once there was nothing, now you see long distances, physical obstacles, or insufficient information.

You know that this antagonism is not directed at you. Unless you are with your sibling, you can negotiate the subway and the supermarket just as well as before. The critical difference is your ability to see through eyes not your own while, simultaneously, you are seeing your old world. While living in your particular and individual spaces, you also imaginatively live in different ones, ones far less cooperative with your family member's physical abilities.

To those who go through these experiences through their own bodies, especially those with congenital or developmentally early disabilities, this seems unremarkable. They of course share your double vision. Even though she cannot see, a blind person has developed a conceptual version of "sight," the sensual system that others have. A wheelchair user knows very well how easy it is for others to board a bus. But to you, who has unthinkingly assumed a normative, universal body, this pluralized physical world comes as a shock.

To make sense of this experience, however, one cannot simply conceptualize physical disability as a problem that some people have and others do not. The relationships described above rely on three interlinking complexities, none of which are properly taken into account by the received wisdom that conceives of disability as identical with impairment. These complexities are the relations of care, the social nature of spatiality, and the meanings of embodiment. For each I turn to different conceptual and intellectual conceptions, arising from feminism (care ethics), social geography (the particularity and historicity of space), and body politics (the centrality of corporealism). Each of these fields, of course, far exceeds in complexity what can be briefly sketched here, but each plays an important role in understanding how and why our physical worlds can be so radically multiplied by the practice of caretaking.

Precisely how such a realization comes about likely depends on inter-related factors, dependent on the kind and degree of care and also on the personal relationship between the family member and a person who desires or needs care. Those who care for a parent gradually descending into confusion will find a notably different set of obstacles than will the young parent caring for a child with myalgic encephalomyelitis. And the antagonisms within a sibling relationship may be exacerbated or rendered moot when one is diagnosed with multiple sclerosis. All may have in common a mix of gratitude and frustration toward medical personnel, a transformed outlook on government, and a new relationship to caring, but the precise dynamics of each will depend on myriad encounters, feelings, and problems. So what if anything can be said about care overall? Does caring in and of itself have a common cause or effect?

The decades-old debates emerging from the feminist discussions of "care ethics" may lead one to believe not. The idea of care as a set of practices and attitudes deserving of serious philosophical inquiry arose from an insight by Carol Gilligan and has been developed through the writings of Sara Ruddick, Nel Noddings, and Joan Tronto.[10] Though they differ in certain important respects, the overall point of their contributions has been to emphasize how "ethics" as a philosophical subdiscipline has delegitimized the everyday experiences of care. This, they convincingly argue, has resulted from a combination of sexism, the attractions of Kantian formal logics, and a dismissal of the quotidian aspects of human (and family) life. Each in turn argues for a centering of care in ethical understandings, pointing out that most people make their largest efforts and sacrifices in their quotidian concerns, not in logic games concerning trains on tracks. Ethical resolution already surrounds us, and one need only look to those (usually women) who make those decisions to understand care.

For Ruddick, this example is to be found in the maternal caregiver; for Gilligan, in the way girls are socially formed. Whether or not women come to care as a result of social pressures or natural causes (e.g., "maternal instinct") has become a central aspect of the debates over care ethics that have emerged within the feminist literature. But for the particular issue of caretaking being asked here, concerns about foundationalism prove far less important than the transformational nature of caregiving, one that disappears and reappears in these discussions.

That transformation is, namely, the process of coming to care, the alteration of the self that caring entails. For these theorists, and the many who have followed their insights, the person one becomes though care generates a wide variety of new ethical outlooks. Care transforms one's ethics, one's engagements, one's very understanding of individualism and community. Raising a child can make one far less supportive of military actions which result in death, especially if there is a risk to one's child.[11] It can make one particularly aware of power and authority, and force one to develop skills of attentiveness.[12] Noddings puts it thus: "When I care . . . there is also a motivational shift. My motive energy flows toward the other, and perhaps, though not necessarily, toward his motivational ends."[13]

In the experience of caring, the self is changed: not physically nor analytically, but emotionally and aesthetically. Admittedly, the vast majority of these discussions focus more on the good that caring does for those being cared for, but the dynamic and profound changes that the caregiver undergoes serves as a constant refrain and undercurrent. And while these philosophies also tend to focus on care for children rather than for siblings, peers, friends, or parents, virtually all these theorists hope for an expansive and widely applicable notion of care.

Three other important points emerge from taking care ethics seriously. The first arises from the sometimes implicit, sometimes explicit assumption that an inability to care, whether institutionally or personally, serves as a necessary precondition for evil. Hannah Arendt points to an extreme case: the inability of Eichmann "to *think*, namely, to think from the standpoint of someone else."[14] (As Maurice Hamington has pointed out, it is precisely Arendt's ability to intuitively enter Eichmann's experience, her skill at imagining his inner life, that makes this insight possible.)[15] This imaginative alterity, Arendt insightfully argues, serves as one necessary precondition for ethical behavior. One must dislocate the self from its Archimedian centrality to the world before one can see what ethical behavior and judgment entails.

The second point concerns the relation of care to justice. From its inception, care ethics has been presented as an alternative, oppositional ethical outlook: feminine, instinctual, and undervalued, where justice is masculine, formalized, and overvalued. As a result, some feminists read care as an alternative way to experience relationships, others as a superior methodological approach, still others as a necessary supplement to "justice ethics" though insufficient on its own grounds. Even for this last, amalgamating point of view, care and justice are seen as intrinsically oppositional, needing to be brought together.[16]

A third and final point emerges when care discourse bumps up against disability: the terminologies of care turn out to have negative implications. The general uses of the term "care" emphasize its unfreedom, its responsibility, which positions caregiving as a selfless, almost saintly practice. Popular discourse and media can allow for the possibility that care could have its own rewards or necessarily be part of life when it comes to children, but not nearly so readily when it comes to those with disabilities. As Jane Stables and Fiona Smith have shown, children with disabled parents intensify this effect: stories of children doomed to care for their family members universally bemoan the destruction of an innocent childhood by the circumstances of disease and disability.[17] Caring, in other words, smuggles a set of negative political connotations under cover of sunny optimism.

And yet these relationships can, on the other hand, become idealized by the very theorists who celebrate them. Though misrepresenting care as unending and unrewarding obligation has certain untrue and depoliticizing effects, so does misrepresenting it as unalloyed joy. Caretakers often feel frustrations, anxieties, even rages. Those being cared for also feel intruded upon, controlled, and delegitimized. Individuals clash in most circumstances when something important is at stake. What stakes are greater than control over a life? To ignore such passionate conflicts romanticizes caretaking, rendering it shallow and undemanding.

Thus, the linguistic locale of "care" remains unsettled, in ways both provocative and troubling. The incommensurability inheres within the word (and the concept) itself, between the caregiver and the person cared for, and, in many families, between caregivers, who must make decisions for people incapable or unwilling to make decisions on their own. Precisely because of their importance, the conflicts and undecidabilities within care and caregiving are not only unsolvable, they proliferate new and varied kinds of oppositions.

Yet, while important, these points remain conditional. One productive formulation of care ethics could emphasize neither the ability to care nor the desire to care. It could accent, instead, the transformative power of caring itself. The experience of caregiving in turn gives new abilities, new sights and sounds, new appreciations and criticisms. The locale of the self is no longer bound to the strictures of singularity: one becomes more than one, one with another's interests, one imbricated in another. Care ethics, in emphasizing interaction over self-sufficiency, enables a view of the self as multiple and engaged.

PARTICULAR SPACE, HISTORICAL SPACE

Space itself makes up a second component of the rewriting of space highlighted by care for someone with a disability. In traditional discussion of disability and its relationship to space, constructionality (or reconstruction) serves as the common denominator: problems get identified by an author, and solutions are suggested to solve those problems. Be it stairways and ramps, signage and sound alternatives, or bathrooms and bathtubs, the barriers faced by the physically disabled are authorially transformed into possible solutions (and costs and benefits).

But these discussions depend upon, even reinforce, a particular conception of space, one which itself helps disable. That presupposition is that space is "empty," merely a concept always waiting to be shaped into something by walls, people, objects. Things are assumed to have material reality, whereas space merely responds to those things.[18] Space, in this view, is normatively meaningless: eternal, universal, vacuous, and ahistorical.

This conception arises not from the uses of space but from a self-anointing vantage point. In *The Practice of Everyday Life*, Michel de Certeau attacks the universalist presuppositions of the "space planner urbanist, city planner, or cartographer."[19] These people, he argues, approach space as though they could be gods, seeing-all and totalizing space as finite and mapable. Their scopic drive leads them to prioritize concepts over practices, formulations over techniques, and organization over life. In their conception, cities are inert, even cadaverous; only their own omniscience can comprehend such space. Sentient beings must control and formulate empty space to make it useful.

In contrast, Certeau celebrates the "ordinary practitioners" of a city, who walk in, participate with, and make use-networks of the varieties of city space in which they live. "They are walkers," he writes, who "make use of spaces that cannot be seen; their knowledge of them is as blind as that of lovers in each other's arms."[20] By engaging with spaces in all their complexities and partialities, Certeau contends, they *enunciate* space: they make it their own, with a range of meanings, connections, and locations. Here and there, rather than abstractions such as north and south, specify and locate these walkers.

His positively charged metaphor of blindness was not accidental—he overtly refers to the Descartian tradition of sensory doubt, wherein vision misleads.[21] Such nonseeing results in continual and plural meaning creation; a place *here* becomes linked to certain experiences and sensations, as well as another place *there*. For the city planner, not only are these associative, sensate connections absent and even nonsensical, but the relationships *here* and *there* can have with one another are limited to the adjacent.

Certeau's overarching theme, to note how people redemocratize the spaces and meanings that are assumed to be fixed, has been shared by others. Guy Debord, for example, published a map of Paris that became an iconic representation for the Situationists. Unlike most maps, however, *The Naked City* is "composed of nineteen cut-out sections of a map of Paris . . . which are linked by directional arrows printed in red."[22] For the Situationists, space is partial, lived, and filled with chance. Their map subverts the cartographic imperatives of totality and completion. It is "predicated on a model of moving; . . . it organizes movements metaphorically around psychogeographic hubs."[23] For both Certeau and Debord, only by emphasizing the lived and contingent natures of space can its democratic aspects be understood.

A tradition of Marxist and post-Marxist thought has similarly emphasized the historicity and politics of space, though for different reasons. Spatiality, theorists such as Henri Lefebvre, Edward Soja, and David Harvey have shown, arises from specific historical and economic trajectories.[24] Instead of embracing the particularity and specificity of space to which Certeau was attuned, these theorists (and many who followed them) emphasize the social forces which construct the abilities and limitations space creates for people. In Lefebvre's words: "The space that homogenizes thus has nothing homogenous about it. . . . It subsumes and unites scattered fragments or elements by force."[25] Capitalism, especially, serves as the mechanism by which certain people are forced into specific spaces: disallowed from some, isolated by others, mechanized into still more.

Using diverse methods, these analyses sometimes transcend attention to class to reach a variety of critical postures. Each shares a common objection to received spatiality; each critiques what Neil Smith and Cindi Katz called "absolute space."[26] For this generation of geographers, the idea of space as normatively empty hid a vast range of oppressions: not merely of owners over workers, but also of whites over nonwhites, men over women, straightness over other sexualities, even the imperial empires over the rest of the world.[27] In these analyses, space operates to exclude or privilege. The distinction between public and private, the idiom of travel, the language and metaphor of distance, the meanings of housing, and the proprietorship of locale: all are structured by relations of political power within contemporary society. By examining the historical development of what counts as "absolute space," these critics have examined how these forms of oppression have come to be normalized and thus invisible in our everyday social relations (often implicating coetaneous systems of globalized capitalism).[28]

Attention to these two understandings of spatiality—one might call the first "the particularization of space" and the second "the historicization of space"—clarifies the theoretical possibilities of pluralized spaces. Multiple modalities of spatial experience have always been available, whether actual, as in Certeau's celebrations, or closed-off, as in the post-Marxist critiques. Thus, the different ways that the physically disabled experience space and the similarly varied conceptualizations of their caregivers show that space has always been, and can always continue to be, both communal and plural. These experiences, more than the abstractions of urban planners, serve as reminders to all, disabled and temporarily able-bodied alike, of the potentials within space.[29]

EMBODIMENT

The encumbrances of physical disability result from engagements with spaces, as determined by the specificity of the body's interactions. A remembrance of climbing a mountain by Eli Clare encourages attention to this dynamic. In his antinormative reclamation of abusive terminology, Clare describes himself as "a gimp, a crip, disabled with cerebral palsy."[30] For Clare, the oppositional nature that space can have for a mobility-impaired person poses both an opportunity and a threat. Opportunity arises from the pure pleasure of movement, of hiking for example, but this pleasure can too easily fall into the trap of what he calls the "Supercrip" narrative, the disabled person who is celebrated for performing "just as well as a normal person." Access, mobility, social pressure, and concepts of normality all help construct his everyday experiences of space.

Clare's climb illuminates this complexity. Hiking Mt. Adams in Massachusetts, reminded at each step how cerebral palsy limits his access, he interrogates his own motivations for the endeavor. Is he attempting to be a disabled person whose primary purpose is to achieve what passes for normality (even though many if not most nondisabled people actually do not hike mountains)? Is he enjoying the hike on its own terms, or attempting to summit the mountain for the sake of achieving it? Do the reasons he gives for hiking meet the standards of this particular trip?

These questions do not arise from generalized and universal bodily challenges of hiking (which he enjoys immensely), but from the implicit and particular challenges of *this* hike in *this* body on *this* day. The specificity of Clare's journey defines the meaning of the spaces through which he travels. The mountain, this particular negotiation of acceptance, overcoming, purpose, and pleasure, belongs to Clare alone. In describing this experience, however, he raises similar questions for other bodies on other journeys.

It is too easily forgotten that care does not take place between ideas, concepts, archetypes, or ideologies, but between bodies. Our intentions and wills interact, cooperate, resist; our bodies do the same. Interpretations of (or engagements with) disability must account for the material existence of bodies. Otherwise, abstract histories and the theoretical conceptualization of disability risk becoming entirely abstracted from the people with whom they are ostensibly concerned.

This is not to imply, as the disability theorist Tobin Siebers wrongly does, that the human body escapes its social formulations, that it provides one "side" in opposition to theoretical thinking's other side.[31] But Siebers correctly diagnoses in social constructionism a reluctance to take on the specificity of bodies (e.g., the reality of physical pain as opposed to metaphorical pain). In this, his attention to functionality requires our attention to specificity: "people with disabilities want to be able to function: to live with their disability, to come to know their body, to accept what it can do."[32]

It is the specific nature of various types of care—the lifting of bodies, reading of words, cleaning of catheters—from which the concrete interrelationships between people arise. Theoretical renditions of caretaking tend to forget or elide this.[33] That is, many academic treatments of caring do one of two things, both of which displace particular bodies: they allow one form of disability to synecdochically stand for all (e.g., the way in which many public and academic discussions of disability access unintentionally focus merely on wheelchair users), or they generalize a universally "disabled" body (as the opposite of the "normal" body, since normality is presumed universal).

Of course, the particularities of each personal narrative contain multitudes. It is difficult to insist upon the specific delimitations between physical disabilities and other sorts, for example. Many born with physical disability also suffer from congenital mental impairments; sudden-onset physical trauma often leads to changes in emotional state (which themselves cause difficulty in caregiving).[34]

Each caretaker, just like each person who suffers, must take these specificities into account. For one person, bandages will need to be properly applied and stretching techniques imparted; for another, the things around the house must be moved; for still another, proper methods of chest physiotherapy treatments must be learned. The caregiver who generalizes care, who assumes that one body is much like the next, fails in his or her responsibilities. Good care must respond to the particularities of each body's needs, and pains, and desires. Regard for the specifics of a particular body is just as important as the general knowledge of the disabilities attendant to that person.

The physical presence of bodies, a critical understanding of geography, and the insights of care theory: each of these seems dissimilar, perhaps unduly abstruse on their own. But together they provide the conceptual framework that helps explain what you have already discovered in taking care of your loved one: the physical world is a pluriverse, filled with overlapping spaces which are contradictory but communal.

THE DYNAMICS OF MULTIPLICITY

Many approaches to the topic of disability seek to develop a sympathy for those who "suffer," often for emotional or therapeutic reasons. Other treatments encourage identification, seeking access to equality through political change. Both these approaches are important, but as has likely become clear, neither serves as the goal of this chapter. Instead, the focus here has been on how the experience of caring for someone with a physical disability expands the conceptual overlaps of differing spatialities, how it develops the ability to recognize the incommensurability of the communal.

Yet two key questions remain: How have we lost sight of these pluralized spaces in the first place? And how can we learn to see them again? The answer to the first question has as much to do with epistemology as with disability; the answer to the second touches on imagination and pedagogy.

Western culture developed the very idea of normality relatively recently. Lennard Davis points out that the concepts of "normal," "norm," "average," and "standard" did not develop their current usage until 1840.[35] Previous to this, all corporeal things were assumed to deviate not from one another, but from the nonexistent ideal (e.g., Plato's forms or God's archetypes). The development of statistics and collectivity, however, encouraged the idea of a common standard, around which certain variations can be measured.[36]

In this bell-curved world, disability is parasitical on normality. Without the assumption that an average both exists and is desirable, the idea of disability makes no sense. All bodies, so long as they are earthly (that is to say, corporeal), fail to approach perfection. If perfection serves as the ideal body-type, our current dividing line between the able-bodied and the non-able-bodied makes no sense. Theologically, all on earth is imperfection, whereas statistically, perfection surrounds us.

Of course, this popular conception arises from a misunderstanding of statistical reasoning, but one often shared by statisticians as well. Neither "the average" nor "the most common" (in, say, a bell-shaped distribution) should imply "the normative." But within the modern socius, the average becomes confused with the rule or the ideal. In the rule-bounded nature of the normative, profound divergences from the norm must be described in terms of that divergence rather than on their own terms. Not only does this tend to conflate all extreme forms of deviance from the norm into one category (in this case, "the disabled"), but it also incorrectly implies that a universalism of treatment, of renorming, should and does exist.

In turn, no perfect standard of care could exist (much as some would like to use one, for example, to sell guidebooks). Care must always arise from context—what is pernicious at one moment might well be desirable at another. Noddings uses an example from mothering, where a general rule boundary (for example, no sundaes before dinner) can be temporarily superseded by viewing the event though the perspective of the other: "We see the desired sundae with our own eyes and with the child's. If our own view reveals nothing very important and even seems a bit stuffy, we turn to the child with eyes brightened and refreshed with delight."[37] Only through attentiveness and flexibility, combined with a long-term concern for another, do we reach these realizations.

These variations may have been lost, but can they be found once again? If so, how? The example of the caregiver shows one method through which they can be regained, though not one most people will be happy to experience. Short of caring for a loved one with a disability, two methods come to mind.

The first method, often the default position for academics, entails overt pedagogy. As disability studies emerges as an interdisciplinary field of study in the academy, its presuppositions and definitions continue to be debated, often intensely. As college students enter those debates, issues of judgments, performances, and enactments of disability, and thus of the pluralization of social spaces, repeatedly emerge. Margaret Price, for example, argues that studying disability allows students to clarify the implicit relationships between language and power as well as between ideology and practice.[38] Analyzing the usually unacknowledged presumptions contained within disability discourse, law, and practice, she argues, encourages attention to one location where boundaries blur and possibilities multiply.

This dynamic will emerge even more strongly as disabled teachers themselves appear in the classroom. Students spend their days figuring out what motivates their teachers: the experience of learning from a disabled instructor will ingrain the variability of experience almost as strongly as caring does. This depends on the continuing training of disabled teachers, of course. Schools of education might well begin to see disabled people as potentially better teachers than the temporarily able-bodied.[39]

But overt pedagogy is only one method of awakening our recognition of the multiplicity of space which surrounds us. Another, which this chapter has attempted to evoke, arises from imaginativeness. What if your father, your sister, your lover, or your child found his or her life irrevocably changed, and yours changed along with it? This need not happen for it to be imagined; indeed, its happening may well overwhelm your ability to theoretically conceptualize the event's political and spatial implications. People do take a great amount of care, after all.

Families differ profoundly, yet the terminology of family proves strong enough to encompass their wide arrays of relationships. This final chapter returns to language as the source of these strengths (and potential weaknesses): what dynamics of terminology and representation closely mirror the energetic, restrained, and agentic aspects of familial life and, to extrapolate further, of political life within and between communities?

This connection between familial relationships and linguistic theory emerges in part from the problematic similarities and incommensurabilities that language allows; both contain many of the same false oppositions of freedom and rules, commitment and creativity, community and difference. Internal rules or grammars of language teach something about familial roles and political logics. One kind of utterance having a normative and significatory coincidence with another (though each may point to entirely different regulatory and policy ends) illuminates aspects of intention, collectivity, and individuality that exemplary cases of family have already highlighted.

This connection also draws upon and revives certain contentions within political theory, laying out the phratric likenesses between contentions within 1970s social philosophy and the arguments so far made in this book. The debates that emerged from the recognition that both politics and philosophy take place within and through language are neither dead nor gone, but oftentimes merely forgotten. That language participates in what J. L. Austin memorably termed "speech acts" was recognized as a social and political claim early on by theorists such as John Searle and Charles Taylor, but what became of those recognitions remains implicit in many of the continuing debates concerning methods and empiricism.[1]

Finally, it remains important to remember that community and difference already always exists within language: languages are communal and collective, and yet they allow, even encourage, original and strange perlocutions and illocutions. How we create these relationships depends on a creative combination of bodies, silence, communication, motions, judgments, and, yes, language. Language, state, and family remain in whirling, complex, and unpredictable networks of meanings; the infinite task of understanding these meanings and the relationships between them can often best be illuminated through their difficulties and disorders. Thus, we begin with a linguistic apologue.

"IT DEPENDS ON WHAT THE MEANING OF 'IS' IS"

Once upon a time, a president of the United States had the temerity to state that the same word can have different meanings to different people, sometimes in the same sentence. This particular linguistic incommensurability, the president's critics quickly recognized, leads to a number of difficulties for many who want language to unproblematically represent specific political projects. In this case, he overtly argued that words, which we expect to always mean the same thing, in fact function in parallel or even divergent ways, especially when the stakes are greatest. The president faced strong criticism for his contention that what appeared to be the same word could have different denotations, depending on the context of its articulation; critics felt that such an assertion also implied acceptance of the dictum that words "can mean whatever anyone wants them to mean." Such an idea—that the same word, the same idea, could have entirely different meanings to different people depending on their backgrounds or objectives—was considered hazardous and threatening to a country whose historical unity is popularly thought to rest not on racial commonality, or collective history, but on the very words of the Constitution. That the president of the United States implied this linguistic pluralism made his contention all the more egregious.

This contention, of course, refers to a speech by Abraham Lincoln. In the Baltimore Address, made at the height of the Civil War, Lincoln described the problems that came from using the same word to different ends. "The world," he began "has never had a good definition of the word 'liberty,' and the American people, just now, are much in want of one. We all declare for liberty; but in using the same word we do not all mean the same thing. With some the word liberty may mean for each man to do as he pleases with himself, and the product of his labor; while with others the same word may mean for some men to do as they please with other men, and the product of other men's labor. Here are two, not only different, but incompatible things, called by the same name—liberty."[2]

For Lincoln, clearly one of these definitions of "liberty" held moral superiority. But his larger point, that the term and the concept worked as justifications for both sides, remains. Lincoln's understanding of the rhetorical use of this word highlights a particularly problematic issue in the political uses of language. Lincoln recognized that both sides in the Civil War were fighting for "liberty," but whereas one side emphasized the individual and political liberty of enslaved black Americans, the other side struggled for the personal and legal liberty to continue to enslave those same people. Both sides could (and did) argue that liberty stood central to the very Constitution of the United States, and both would be (and were) right. Both could contend that the causes of the war arose from their attempts to defend or promote that liberty, and again both would be right.

This is not merely a difference in grammatical usage, or meaning, or definitions. "Liberty" means "liberty," and liberty itself is worth going to war for; everyone, Lincoln included, agrees on that.[3] The fact that these definitions differ does not keep the word from being used. Or, in other words, the reality that each side seeks a different result does not negate the fact that both sides are fighting for liberty. Similarly, these fictional interlocutors agree that the threat to human liberty has caused the Civil War. But that the South and the North both fought for liberty clearly does not mean that they were in agreement.

This last chapter turns to the example of linguistic incommensurability because of its direct (though only occasionally causal) relationship to theoretical dynamics which the examples concerning silence, dogs, and caregiving highlight, and which this book has tried to emphasize as having important political consequences. The first of these, already obvious, is that language serves as a location where incommensurability already always exists. That different meanings emerge from similar words delegitimizes and fragments language no more than the differences between family members make them less of a family. The second concerns the familiarity of these debates: unlike the demands of the mainstream of political and ethical philosophizing, linguists have long recognized these fundamental indeterminancies. To note that language operates in multiple ways in different contexts has proved far less contentious than the idea that community connections can vary and diverge, but it has been argued over nevertheless. And the third restates the error of the presumption against which this book aims: that all forms of community arise from identical experiences, judgments, interpretations, and ideals. Communities, in this erroneous view, only exist when all of their members see and hear things precisely the same way. The claims here about families are not entirely new; they in part relocate linguistic theory to quotidian practices.

These practices take place in our lives, within our moral formulations; no degree of incommensurability between persons obscures the fact that we usually consider ourselves part of ethical systems. Were that not the case, the emotions that come out of political and moral debates would not be so raw. We care deeply about moral formulations, which are after all the places of meaning in which we *dwell*; on the other hand, it is vital that our regard for our own historically arbitrary accidents not get in the way of conceptualizing alternative possibilities.[4]

Linguistic differences, in other words, constitute relationships: relationships internal not only to words but also to the people living in those words' worlds. The very connections between them are their very differences; the power of a word rests not in its isolation from others, nor in its universality, but in its reverberances and resonances alongside others.

These relationships are not polysemy, where a seemingly identical word has related but different meanings. Nor are they identical to (though they are partially based upon) the idea of "essentially contested concepts," introduced by W. B. Gallie in 1955. For Gallie, and those social scientists who later applied his ideas, the contestation internal to certain concepts leaves them indeterminate but also underpins the moral dedications people have to them. For example, one interlocutor could mean by "democracy" a formal mechanism whereby voters appoint and remove their governments, while another means equality between all citizens, while a third means the "continuous active participation of citizens in political life at all levels."[5] In examining the particularities of contestation, Gallie points to the conditionalities of language—the necessary openness of certain terms to strategic usage, pragmatic considerations, and conceptual idealization. Gallie also recognizes the importance of adscititious effects upon language: while empirical events and logical arguments do not make concepts uncontested, they can have a "definite logical force" which refigures the notional playing field.[6]

For many political and social theorists, Gallie's insights served to politicize language. Both William Connolly and John Gray, for example, see Gallie's charges as necessitating new conceptions of linguistic politics, the former celebrating its encouragement of critical modes of life, the latter subtly decrying it as leading irreducibly to an incoherent liberalism. For Connolly, conflicts over the uses of "partly shared appraisal concepts are themselves an intrinsic part of politics" and should be recognized as such by social scientists; for Gray, contestability cannot be about criteria but must be exemplary of "conflict between adherents of mutually unintelligible worldviews" and should be discouraged as erosive of community.[7] Both, however, recognize that Gallie's thesis depends both on a level of linguistic incommensurability and a mode of intersubjective communication whereby each contestant understands the claims made by the other. For Gallie the importance emerges from this interrelationship; the fervor of the disagreement arises from each understanding the differences.[8] Defining "freedom" in profoundly different ways (such as "freedom from want" and "freedom to vote") makes such words not contested but merely different.

They are different because they are thought to point to different things. Their valences divaricate, and no contestation results. The common distinction in semiotics between "reference" and "meaning" (e.g., "New York" and "the Big Apple" prove dissimilar in their connotative meaning, but not in the city to which they refer) is not the topic here. Instead, it is those times when two groups of people think they are using a word in the same way (a "correct" way, needless to say) and yet fundamentally disagree about the term's substantive implications. Such oppositions constitute disagreements about both meaning and referentiality in a larger sense, that the same term may hide the fact that different groups may know and understand the nature of "New York" in incommensurable ways.

In an earlier chapter, disagreement over the commonality of a concept —namely, of the term "marriage"—caused political disjuncture, but here the different implications of the same term conjoins community and incommensurability in another way. This chapter addresses the stakes in a claim such as Lincoln's "we all declare for liberty." These stakes are especially high in a country such as the United States, whose founding and continuation are widely conceived as textual and documentary, and where these texts and documents require explication through institutional means (for example, the courts). The import of words literally comprises the definitions which constitute the United States: laws, policies, administration, and contracts are all composed of words whose meanings remain (at least potentially) contested. The problem of overt difference in meaning thus becomes fundamental for politics in such a society, particularly for those who want to map language unproblematically onto epistemology to master constructions of law and policy.

One approach for resolving this problem has been, simply, to argue that one of these meanings of "liberty" is fundamentally, absolutely, definitionally wrong. The South, one could argue, was not making true claims to liberty, for any political system based on the enslavement of human beings can never occasion liberty. Liberty must always mean the same thing in an objective and universal sense, or else a political order founded upon liberty cannot continue. Differences in definition are fundamentally errors—whether moral, logical, lexical, or interpretive.

This kind of linguistic universalism, which asserts words as having true and integral meanings, explains Lincoln's dilemma in two different ways. Both approaches are common and dependent on a widespread comprehension of language usage. The first of these understands words as directly and clearly referencing things. The second, recognizing that what appears to be the same word can be employed in different ways, argues that usage and context are the final arbiter in language and sees those particular language functions as being performed by fundamentally different words. This second approach is somewhat dependent on the first (and is more complex as well).

In the most basic and common (though wrong) interpretation, the learning of language is seen as learning the proper names of things. Language forms a representation of the external world: one sees a chair and (after a period of learning) soon learns to associate the word "chair" with the seen object. As a theory of language, this assumption has one notable virtue: it is simple. It holds that words have referents, and the deciphering of proper objects presents the only difficulty of interpretation that might arise.

By the nineteenth and twentieth centuries, this approach became known, in Gottlob Frege's and Wittgenstein's terminologies, as the "referential theory" or the "picture theory" of language. For most people unfamiliar with the complexities of linguistic theory, this theory tends to model the relationship between words and meanings. It does hold true for most nouns, usually (though mistakenly) thought of as the most archetypal kinds of words; the annals of linguistic theory are full of discussions about "this desk" or "that chair." But turning to other words, the troublesome nature of the picture theory quickly becomes apparent.

Picture theory's paradigmatic explanatory power of all language has deep and intractable roots. It emerges, as J. L. Austin argues, from the confusion of words with names, as if those tall, woody plants have been baptized "trees."[9] The human naming of things and creating of words seems to denote the managerial role of language. Indeed, the originary power and primacy of the picture theory of language emerge from the passages in Genesis where Adam takes possession of the world and language simultaneously by being given the responsibility to name "every beast of the field and every fowl of the air."[10]

Matters of law and policy thus often presume that words have a true, direct, pictorial meaning. Made up as they are primarily through language, such overtly political sites of interpretive contention become a battlefield of linguistic theories. If a correct, true, and intended meaning exists "behind" (as though there is a spatial relationship to language) a law or Constitutional amendment, then courts' and editorialists' interpretive questions have ultimate answers. There will be correct and incorrect meanings, not politically contested uses of language.

The attempt to discover and recover "original intent" proves paradigmatic in these cases.[11] Underlying this interpretative approach is the idea that, with enough historical, psychological, and excursive information, one can determine the precise and absolute meaning of words. A question of Constitutional doctrine? Then the answer lies in the state of mind of the Constitution's framers. A query concerning the current application of a law? Then one must look at the intention of the congressional committee that drafted it. By simplifying the search for meaning and locating it solely in the author, one is told clearly where to look. A significant disadvantage is that the author may be inaccessible: dead, as in the case of the authors of the Constitution, or a conglomeration of authors that cannot ever be reconstructed, such as a congressional committee.[12]

Original intent involves manifold and legendary problems, which prove distracting here.[13] But one must note that its underlying appeal comes from the possibility of discovering an unarguable authority. Placing the ultimate responsibility of meaning in the hands of the author solves the ambiguity of language by discovering a source of authority external to the words themselves. It thus presumes a correct and apolitical interpretation, equally discoverable and distinguishable to all who do the proper research, and thus displaces the search for these references from traditions and personal motivations.[14]

Metaphor openly and obviously threatens direct referentiality. Simile, metonymy, synecdoche, irony: these tropes, bitterly contested in semiotic theory, all share the problem of substitution. Indistinctly defined words challenge the picture theory of language, because they often appear to transfer meaning in particular or even contrary ways. Moreover, there appears to be no direct purpose for them; a metaphor, for example, more cumbersomely refers to something than does a directly connotative word.

Universalists have long identified metaphor as a specifically political problem. In *Leviathan*, for example, Hobbes argues that using words "metaphorically; that is for a purpose other than what they are ordained for" is an abuse of language equal to lying or slander.[15] Language, in Hobbes's conception of a rational social system, creates the necessary foundation of order. Fundamentally used to remember and transmit ideas and information, it must be defended against those who would undermine that transmission by confusing its substance. As in the semiotic theories of Hobbes and Frege, such tropes today loom as disruptive to law and policy. Laws by their very nature lack irony or metaphor; such constructions undermine the transparency to which law allegedly aspires. If the best policies ought to be straightforward, coherent, and direct, more complex theories of language threaten politics.

It is difficult to disagree with this perspective; an ironic law would cause unending grief.[16] The concern is not that judges, for example, will miss the metaphorical aspects of laws, but that they will assume a straightforwardly representative nature for legal language. Such an arid model of language misses how language actually works, and is based on an ideal of what words do that (even were it possible to achieve) would be thin and uninteresting. This model is not only wrong, it blinds its adherents to the constitutive nature of language. If words merely reflect a given, pre-existing reality, then those using those words merely put into language the truths which surround them. Criminals, heroes, governments, states, morality, violence, law: language and the people who wield expressions assume that they merely refer to already existing things in the world, rather than conjuring and commissioning them. And who can differ from the implications of words and phrases such as "terrorism" or "the legitimate use of force" and be willing to support the former or oppose the latter?

But one can still hold that words have universalizable, intrinsic meanings without subscribing to a picture theory of language. (Even if a theory where words directly reference things is rejected, a theory supporting the primacy of usage and context can still explicate meaning as "true.") One can deny that either of those people using the word "liberty" is using the same word at all. One can insist that a word's only real meaning emerges from the precise way in which it is used, and because these two sides mean different things by the term "liberty," they actually employ the word in two fundamentally incompatible ways. Because a word can refer to a variety of mutually exclusive ideas, it follows that each of these various usages has its own meaning.

This is another way of fixing the relationship of meanings and words, though unlike the previous method it does not insist on an unambiguous definition. But it does share with the linguistic fundamentalists the idea that singular, universalizable meanings exist. Each definition maps directly onto a word; the complexity of this second approach lies in the recognition that more than one meaning can be affixed to the same word.

The logical positivist A. J. Ayer, for example, argues that using the word "is" in differing ways proves unproblematic once it is realized that there are actually many different words that are spelled and pronounced "is" but are in fact profoundly different.[17] The incommensurability of meaning becomes, in Ayer's reading, merely a case of incommensurable words that people too often confuse merely because they are spelled the same and used in similar but fundamentally disparate ways. The point of philosophy becomes, for Ayer, distinguishing these various kinds of meaning and straightening out the various usages of the word.

Others of the Vienna Circle, following Ayer, argue that words and sentences that cannot be made sense of in this way—that is, that cannot be either proven analytically or corroborated by measurements from the nonlinguistic world—lack meaning.[18] This form of positivism, which defines meaning as verifiable truth, seems at first profoundly different from the idea that meanings are ultimately determined by the author, as do those theories which argue that words are similar to names or that there is a singular, coherent "original intent." But like those theories, words and statements are measured by absolute standards. These positivists hold that words are ultimately universal, and that the scientific approach that they employ locates the ways in which language is congruent with logic, method, and the unarguable truth of the "real world."

The normalization of the subjective and specific uses of words creates a major problem with universalist and positivist theories of meaning (of both the referential and contextual variety). Linguistically constituted objects of inquiry are treated as epistemologically unproblematic: violence in international relations or domestic violence in the United States are considered uniform, definable categories removed from specific social, historical, and political forces that define and circumscribe them as linguistic entities.

Michael Shapiro has demonstrated how unacknowledged linguistic presuppositions have shaped common public understandings of identities, behaviors, and ethics. By presuming language's representational character—that "criminal behaviors," for example, somehow exist outside of a language system—users of a language system naturalize and effectively disclaim responsibility for a system of social order. If language merely denotes a preexisting reality, those who use language are accountable only for describing reality, not for participating in it. Shapiro identifies the central problem of such speech: that "the idea that we can speak *correctly* about objects and situations is predicated on an indefensible theory of meaning" and is thus "a misleading way to represent the relationship between speech and phenomena."[19]

Of course many theorists have searched for ways to analyze and undermine these conceptions of meaning. This reaction, especially prevalent in the twentieth century, rejects conceptions of words as directly representational. Instead, these semiotic theories locate a word's use within larger systems of social and linguistic structures. Words, therefore, do not refer to objects, but to organizations and systems.

Ferdinand de Saussure famously theorized that the structures of a language give meaning to its mere words. For Saussure, and subsequent linguistic structuralists, the relation is not between a word and an object (in the language of semiotics, the "sign" and the "signifier"), but between the sign and the system of other signs which impart significance. In language, Saussure argues, "there are only differences, *and no positive terms*."[20] The "picture theory" idea of a direct, positive linkage between word and object should be replaced, for Saussure, with an understanding of the relationships between words, or, more exactly, of the relationships of the differences between words.

Saussurian language is a system of classification, one with a necessary underlying order. Structuralism replaces the investigation of the representation of words and objects with an examination of language's underlying kinds of order. Word usage is seen as dependent not on objects themselves but on systems of language and society. Various forms of structuralism emphasize different classificatory systems; a Marxist analysis, for example, would emphasize the materially productive while an anthropological analysis would focus on the cultural.

This approach develops from the recognition that language, always social, must emanate from a selection of already existing possibilities. That words and meanings are constricted is commonsensical: if a word could mean "whatever you want it to mean," it would no longer function as a word in a society and would become an entirely private language. This, Wittgenstein reminds us, is an impossibility. Language, in Shapiro's reading, is "usually a matter of giving voice to discursive practices that represent a selection from a fixed set of practices permissible in the language."[21]

The structuralist argument demands that one must look at the practices and selection processes that make a language possible.

Language is thus deterministic. The existence of syntagmas, the structuralist argues, is testimony to those systems outside the phrase itself that serve as the medium within which such a phrase or sentence has potential meaning. Stanley Fish's assertion that the mere dominance of certain political and economic forces determines the "truth qualities" of statements exemplifies this assumption.[22]

Feminist critiques of linguistic theory provide a specifically political example of this structural understanding of language. Robin Lakoff's groundbreaking work on the dynamics of gendered power underlying word usage, for example, shows how socially reinforcing relationships can cause the same words (or the lack of words) to be utilized in different ways depending on the hierarchical status of the speaker, a status contiguous with sexual difference.[23] For Lakoff, the same word, phrase, or sentence has different uses depending on a society's social and sexual structures (namely, in her case, American society). The acceptability of speech strategies based on gender results in certain articulations having radically differing connotations depending on the speaker's sex: forms of speech that are allowed for one gender and not for another, or that are weighted differently depending on the sex of the speaker.

Many feminist and queer linguists have followed Lakoff in studying how gendered societal forces form language, showing the intrinsically political nature of the battles over the meanings of words. The terms "feminism" or "rape," for example, serve as sites of contestation for cultural and political battles over the proper roles of (and relationships between) men, women, and society.[24] The variety of meanings attributed to these words bespeak political and social differences; the words themselves are practically buried beneath the divergent meanings. Other feminists have reemphasized Lakoff's focus on the identification of language and language patterns according to the social status of those who hear and use the words. Deborah Tannen, the best-known popularizer of Lakoff's linguistic theories, interrogates how words are used, heard, and understood divergently by men and women.[25]

Catharine MacKinnon provides one of the most ardent of these structural linguistic interpretations. MacKinnon's antipornography activism has led her to construct a legal theory that breaks down the ostensible division between language and actions. Against a purely formalist reading of the First Amendment of the Constitution of the United States, which protects language from legal restrictions, MacKinnon describes the ways in which language acts—how it supports systems of power inequality.

MacKinnon argues that courts readily recognize multiple exceptions to the First Amendment. Words that are libelous or overtly incite dangerous actions or fix prices are clearly not sheltered by freedom of speech principles. MacKinnon strives to add pornography to this category. Pornography is, in her words, "masturbation material. It is used as sex. It is therefore sex."[26] In identifying certain kinds of words (and images, of course) as a form of sex, one that she posits is intrinsically based on the domination and enslavement of women, MacKinnon insists that they should be legally recognized and legislated as actions.

Most important to her reading is how these particular words participate in the maintenance of patriarchy and gender violence. For MacKinnon, pornography reflects and reinscribes these social relations. "Social inequality," she argues, "is substantially created and enforced—that is, done—through words and images."[27] Pro-egalitarian laws and social policies, therefore, must target such words and images, since they create the infrastructure upon which societal inequality is perpetuated.

MacKinnon's theory allows no room for ambiguity and multiple connotations. Like both the representationalists and the positivists, hers is a reading of language which sees words as ineluctably reducible to a specific meaning. But for MacKinnon this meaning rests not in what these words "say" (i.e., represent) but in what they "do" (i.e., enact). And they do what they have to do; as words in an oppressive, sexist, and racist society, they reflect and reinscribe that oppression, sexism, and racism. Their intelligibility to us proves this: MacKinnon explains that words of assault would make no sense in an equitable society.[28]

By shifting the location of meaning for words in spaces outside the relationship between words and objects, structuralists and structural feminists such as Lakoff and MacKinnon help explain how social arrangements distinguish and differentiate words.[29] This, in turn, can explain why Lincoln's Northerner and Southerner seem to be using the same word to different ends; they use languages based in differing and incompatible structures. That one lives and works in one culture, and the other in another, implies that they cannot use the term "liberty" in the same way." The early Wittgenstein suggests the same idea, stating that "the limits of language . . . mean the limits of my world."[30] But none of these universalist approaches explain a vital (perhaps *the* vital) question in Lincoln's suggestion: how do these people recognize one another as using the same word?

The underlying attempt of structural accounts of language remains the same as that of the positivists: to affix and explain meaning through a directly correlative account of words, whether the correlation be to a system or to a thing.[31] In other words, language models something else, a mapping of social or physical reality. This approach explains the incompatibility of the two terms both spelled "liberty." But, crucially, it does not explain their sameness, their familiar likenesses.

WORDS MATTER

To claim meanings as universal is to demand agreement. If I can *prove* a word's direct and unarguable conjunction to an object or a system, you no longer need to interpret, and you owe nothing to a larger interpretive community. Those who are attempting to build a ubiquitous system of meaning (of both the referential and contextual varieties) make a central, underlying claim: through a system of determination, whether semiotic or scientific or historical, words' meanings can be worked out in such a way that they demand agreement. If the real sense of "liberty" can be determined, even if (as the postitivists and structuralists argue) real meanings make up different definitions of a word, then their signification can be fixed *and shared*. Claims to universality, in other words, are commands.

But words do not reflect an ostensibly nonlinguistic reality in these ways. They are neither (as in referential theories) indicative and purely representational nor (as in contextual theories) exhibitions and indicators of superstructural political relationships. Words, in other words, are pluralized: there are always "other words." While words can engage, cajole, seduce, inspire, dismiss, teach, injure, and captivate, they do not necessarily *demand*. They could demand only if they held a directionally simplistic relationship to exteriority. If they did, if words could only represent things or systems, then they would indeed be impotent and not particularly worthwhile objects of study. Studying the objects or the systems themselves would make more sense.

Instead, words have complex registers, varieties, and meanings. Charles Taylor provides a useful example of how words are not directionally simplistic. Saying to a fellow traveler "Whew, it's hot" neither imparts information (he or she is already aware of the heat) nor encourages the formulation of a linguistically inaccessible idea (it is not a particularly difficult concept to conjure).[32] Rather, it attempts to bridge the fundamental distance between people, to create a realm in which conversation and connection, however limited, become normal and acceptable.

Language, then, does something more complex and multidirectional than the previous conceptions would have it do. The reflective or structural models do not hint at its potential to establish spaces for human experiences such as community and creativity. The formative capacity of language has occupied a central place in twentieth-century linguistics— namely, how can a word hold more than its "meaning"? When does a word go beyond in its purely locutionary sense?

J. L. Austin described the effectuation of language in *How to Do Things with Words*, explaining the impossibility of separating speech from action. In his description of illocutionary "speech acts," those utterances which by their very articulation cause events such as "I now pronounce you man and wife" or "I christen thee" or "I promise," Austin identifies the ways in which language acts upon the world. Discussing the perlocutionary aspects of language, he identifies language's effect on people. This is a complex outcome, for when one person says "This film is boring," the locutionary force (describing being bored) is obvious; the perlocutionary force (the reaction on the part of another to the implied request to leave) is not.[33]

In describing these ways in which language operates, Austin is doing more than depicting unusual alternatives to the universalist models of meaning. He instead provides an entirely different understanding of what language does. To focus solely on the relationship between words and objects, for example, is to miss the everyday use of those words. The "ordinary" aspects of language interweave with these creative, constitutive uses.

Wittgenstein, in his lecture series known as *The Brown Book*, conceives of a language (or, more properly, a "language-game") made up purely of nouns used as commands: a builder calling to his assistant "brick" or "slab" depending on which physical object the assistant will next bring him.[34] Such a language has immense simplicity, and seems to be directly representational. But Wittgenstein highlights the ways in which communication and action are decisive aspects of language: "slab" ends up meaning not only the thing, but also the bringing of the thing, the ordering of the work, even the relationship between the builder and the assistant.[35] Even one word contains multitudes.

The political difficulty with this pluralization in more political contexts is that these separate meanings are incommensurable: liberty cannot mean both the perpetuation of slavery in certain states and its end in the United States. More precisely, these two meanings can *no longer* remain in the peaceful proximity they enjoyed before the Civil War. The complexities historically concealed in the term "liberty" have been revealed; the word has become politicized. Its ability to work as a simple uncontested term has disappeared and the different functions it can and does serve have been made apparent.

Two major strains of post-Austinian language theory presume that words exceed representation. The first accepts the structuralist conception of the ineluctable bonds between language and power, but rejects this as a unidirectional causal relationship. The second develops a pragmatics of language, accepting Austin's and Wittgenstein's notions of language as active and differentiated, and expanding these insights to the ways in which words activate identities and pluralities. The first of these strains is most closely identified with Michel Foucault, the second with Gilles Deleuze and Félix Guattari.

Academics have debated Foucault's genealogical projects for decades now, yet they rarely address language's central role in his philosophy.[36] But language proves central: overtly at times, such as in his extensive discussion of discursive practices in *The Archeology of Knowledge*, but also in his later examinations of the history of self-constitution in "Technologies of the Self."[37] The capacity of language changes over the course of his intellectual development, to be sure, but the ways in which words serve as a political and social focus of regimes of knowledge do not. Foucault specifically views the philosophical emergence of a focus on language as fundamentally and centrally transformative of all of French political thought.[38]

Forget semiotic theories of reading; Foucault does not argue that there are underlying meanings to systems of language which work subterraneously and require extensive methods of translation to discover. Like Austin and Wittgenstein, he envisions meaning within language itself rather than hidden beneath it.[39] Foucault considers it therefore obvious or articulated; he showed that an investigation of language that ignores or deemphasizes language in favor of other, "more real" systems is, in fact, not about language at all. The object of linguistic study, for Foucault, should be how language and power are linked in the use of words.

Why should such imbrication not be obvious to those who use language every day? Foucault's systematic focus on linguistic prescriptions and constraints shows how various functionings of power mask themselves through the normalizing forces of the mundane uses of language. Early in Foucault's career, he primarily examines such disguises. The uses and meanings of words are not accidental but surrounded by institutional and societal mechanisms of reinforcement.[40] This may not sound very different from structuralist theories, where social forces determine language. But Foucault further argues that these prohibitions help constitute social practices that themselves depend on power formed by particular linguistic usages. These regimes of power—what Foucault called, at various times, *épistémé* or disciplines—do not and cannot exist outside of the linguistic practices of those who live within them.

Later in Foucault's career his focus changed from the proscriptive concealments of language to its prescriptive characteristics. In his histories of sexuality, for example, he notes that after the (alleged) Victorian prohibitions on overt sexuality, the twentieth century saw a radical outpouring of words on sexuality. Yet this deluge justifies itself as a reaction against restraints on discussions of sexuality, which depend on a theory of repression that is disproved by its own existence.[41] What, Foucault asks, does such a language of liberation entail?

Part of the answer is that it justifies, almost necessitates, speech. Confession and interpretation become necessary parts of social life because they assert truths that would be less supportable were there not a "history" of subjugation against which they ostensibly strive. This results, Foucault argues, in a system of justification that conceals and rationalizes power, where those who bravely fight against the alleged silence achieve what he called "the speaker's benefit: the interrelated discourses in which sex, the revelation of truth, the overturning of global laws, the proclamation of a new day to come, and the promise of a certain felicity are linked together."[42] In their pretense to authenticity, marshaled against tyranny, words "produce truth": this effect, Foucault contends, arises from the distinction Plato makes between philosophy as truth telling and politics as the field where truth is tested.[43]

Across his work, Foucault presents a linguistic theory of language and power as coterminous, where power and words circulate in social, institutional, and political structures. Such an analysis of language entirely rejects universalist notions of meaning. Words do not mean "things" or represent "structures"; instead, they constitute relations of power themselves. Not exclusively, of course; Foucault clearly does not underestimate the power behind prisons, armies, or police. But he emphasizes that such institutions are profoundly dependent on the discursive practices that constitute the institution itself. A prison cannot function outside of a legal and discursive system that determines why some words (and actions) that are tolerated or encouraged outside the system are forbidden within it.

Contemporary theorists such as Judith Butler and David Campbell have applied Foucault's linguistic theories to specific political questions. For Butler, language is both the site of the making of gendered subjects and a location where such subjects can exceed (some of) the constraints of power.[44] This, she argues, makes language always partial and always contestable, though it is also the reason that words have such power to constrain, limit, and produce our selves. David Campbell identifies similar ways that the uses and effects of language work by examining its role in the relations between national and state identities. For example, Campbell identifies linguistic formulations of difference which form the groundwork of the foreign policy of the United States, where danger and threat are displaced onto those who are rhetorically defined as most un-American,[45] or how political identities can be lexically transformed from discordant coexistence to radical violence.[46]

A second Austinian linguistic effectuation rejects the very notion of language as meaning, turning instead to what language does.[47] For Gilles Deleuze and Félix Guattari, linguistics is the investigation of acts. Language, they argue, "is neither informational nor communicational."[48] It is, instead, "the transmission of order-words, either from one statement to another or within each statement, insofar as each statement accomplishes an act and the act is accomplished in the statement."[49]

A Deleuzian conception of language primarily arises from the perlocutionary, to use Austin's terminology. Deleuze and Guattari focus on what arrangements of language both *generate* and *transform*.[50] Words form a part of larger structures—here they too agreed with Saussure. But Deleuze and Guattari also point out that Saussure conflates difference and opposition when he moves from claiming that "in language there are only differences" to the unnecessary corollary that these differences "are without positive terms." In doing so, he denies those times when language is positive, creative, and different all at once.

Words can be positioned differentially without being oppositional for Deleuze and Guattari.[51] This critical approach to the words of law, policy, or politics shows that words have an empirical, material reality, not in the sense that they exist as corporeal objects, floating about through the air, but in the ways in which they effect changes, affect people, and reconstitute the world. At first this may seem the same as MacKinnon's project; after all, she too is interested in what words enact rather than what they "say." But for MacKinnon what words do—at least the words which interest her—is oppress; they are intelligibly direct appliances of subjugation. For Deleuze and Guattari, conversely, words can oppress, but they can also do many other things, both salutary and not, even simultaneously. The mistake, they believe, comes from thinking that "content determines expression by causal action, even if expression is accorded the power not only to 'reflect' content but to act upon it in an active way."[52] Language can certainly be used by one person or institution to act upon another (for example, the kind of language known as "law"), but it can also reconstitute relationships between people and other people, things, and organizations.

Language, in this picture, is not *about* the world but is *of* the world. If language represents the world, that is, if it reflects things or structures, then using language empties the world of meaning, it replaces the identity of things and structures with depiction. But language in fact does no such thing; instead, it is elemental to and formative of the human world. It is not a tool to be employed by people so much as it is an ontological component of people. For Deleuze and Guattari, it constitutes a composite articulation: "Enunciation in itself," they argue, "implies collective assemblages."[53]

Jean-Jacques Lecercle calls this Deleuzian moment the move "from the body of the individual to the body politic."[54] One can conceptualize these assemblages as collectivities and communities of people; this presents perhaps the simplest formulation. Language must be communal. Speaking, as Foucault asserts, subverts the assumption that humans are disparate, discrete, and fully individuated beings.[55] Only those whose identity has been constituted within at least one social nexus can talk.

But these assemblages are also accumulations of language, accretions of implications. For Deleuze and Guattari, words and sentences are in constant relation to the world and to other linguistic assemblages, a "regime of infinite debt, to which one is simultaneously debtor and creditor."[56] Nor is this a singular regime; language is multiplicitous, with currents of slang, eddies of other languages, tides of usages. A Deleuzian reading of language emphasizes linguistic intensities, learnings, and flows.

These quotidian aspects underlie both the power and the pragmatics of language. Deleuze and Guattari emphasize the transformative nature of language: words, they show, turn "prisoners" into "criminals," "passengers" into "hostages," and "workers" into "a proletariat." This transformation is not corporeal; it is actual. A criminal fundamentally differs from a prisoner. The former kind of person embodies evil and guilt; the latter exists in a particular sort of situation. Language can change identity, create meaning where none was before, and reorder the material reality of the world.

What do these post-Austinian theories (of both the Foucaultian and the Deleuzian variety) say about Lincoln's understanding of "liberty"? They show that the word differs when used by a Northerner or a Southerner, but it is not purely located situationally. Rather, it forms part of a chain of variation, where the different "effectuations" in which Northerner and Southerner participate continue through one another.[57] Employing the word in service of different ideals of freedom does not mean that they use it in antithetical ways. As in families, difference is not reducible to opposition in meaning.

It does mean an enactment of identity, an enactment upon common bases (the word itself) to differing states of being—violently so, lest the brutal Civil War be forgotten. "Liberty," even though a central component of identity, shifts and flows, referring doubly and oppositionally.

PUBLIC POLICIES, PUBLIC LANGUAGES, PUBLIC FAMILIES

Linguistic incommensurability has tangible consequences, for example, in constructing public policy and understanding the nature of law. The central linguistic problem in jurisprudence and public policy, as many see it, emerges from the perceived need for words and sentences to have clear and overt references. Such approaches strive for clarity and agreement; once clarity has been achieved, political problems become solvable.

But wouldn't we have figured out how to do this by now? In fact, attempting to universalize meaning and referentiality proves impossible. Even the problems that form the objects of policies are politically defined and contested. Thus the very conceptual foundation of this book—the idea of "family"—can never be clearly determined nor delineated. It can only be argued over and reconfigured, over and over. Do two gay men and their children make up a family? A childless heterosexual couple? Three roommates in the big city? And who is in this family: children and grandparents certainly, but what about second cousins, or dogs and cats? A divorced, and thus no longer legally related, child's spouse? Friends who often stop by for dinner? The inhabited physical structure?

Political and policy processes, determined in part through these arguments, profoundly act upon those families. Clearly, questions of legitimacy and inclusion affect members of transnational families; health care involves children and partners in gay and lesbian relationships; anti-poverty programs constrain nutritional choices and medical decisions. Here the incommensurability of language and the determinacy of policy prescriptions collide most dramatically.

The terminology of "poverty" exemplifies these clashes, where language and policy draw together through the erroneous presumption of universality. As Sanford Schram has pointed out, the language of poverty—its presumptions, applications, and logical consequences—profoundly shapes its political support and efficacy, while perceptions of its efficacy and constituency simultaneously affect what counts as poverty.[58] Language effects poverty, Schram argues, and the social sciences' presumptions of linguistic neutrality serve to mask not only poverty's constructions but also to naturalize its effects.[59] For example, attempts to change the fundamental understanding of poverty are smuggled in public policy arguments. A study published in 2004 by the Heritage Foundation attempted to show that poverty in the United States is far less widespread than popularly presumed. Among its evidence: 78 percent of families living in poverty have VCRs or DVD players; 97 percent have a color television; more than half have a stereo; over 33 percent have an automatic dishwasher.[60] More recently, assumptions that cellular phone ownership could never be compatible with true poverty have made it difficult for social services agencies to equip homeless families with such phones.[61]

Most if not all people in the United States would acknowledge the possible coexistence of systematic and structural economic hardship in modern American life alongside the ownership of a thirty-nine-dollar Toshiba DVD player or a ninety-dollar Sony television. As Adam Smith recognized, a linen shirt may not be a necessity of life (Greeks and Romans having lived without one), but it may become "a necessary of life" at particular historical periods, even for the poorest of the poor.[62] This kind of claim highlights the difficulty of arguing for the necessity of antipoverty programs to those for whom historically bounded versions of material wealth decide and delineate "poverty." If poverty and televisions are mutually exclusive, then poverty has been largely eliminated in the United States; if poverty can coexist with television ownership, then the statistics on color televisions do not necessarily inform the poverty debate.

This does not mean that a final definition of poverty should be properly established. "Poverty" as a concept remains an essentially contested term; it cannot be reuniversalized. The very question of a "word-having-meaning" (as Austin puts it) ultimately cannot make abstract sense. No meaning of "liberty," "pornography," or "poverty" can transcend their usage.

Words are not, however, interchangeable within the same contextual and situational circumstances. "Liberty" represents an ideal worth fighting (and dying) for; "the continuance of slavery as a way of life" is far less compelling. It takes very little effort or thought to oppose "pornography" or "poverty," at least insofar as those concepts are deployed in contemporary discourse. They remain easy opponents.

The idea of marriage has become political precisely because its meaning is shared, yet access to the institution remains contested. Liberty, for Lincoln, proves political for the opposite reason: it has incommensurable meanings, although all agree on its necessity, even so far as justifying war. In both these cases, the public uses of the terms remain vital and celebrated as their politicization causes difference and strife.

In both examples, the popular presumption remains: we should reach a uniform and common agreement regarding the meaning and uses of these languages as the foundation for the very basics of public, common life. In other words, the incommensurability of terminology must be overcome before community can return. But the ongoing engagement over the terms, the very debates that make each approach and usage coherent, proves that communities of meaning already exist, either in spite of linguistic incommensurabilities or (possibly) as a result of them. The attempt to elide or eliminate these differences implies the antipolitical and the anticommunity.

IN CONCLUSION

Families constantly explode the putative opposition between community and incommensurability, thus disproving the conceptual assumption that connected togetherness can never coexist with radical differences in outlook, affect, or ideology. The immediacy and intensity of familial relationships, the inconclusiveness and distances between people who love one another, the shifting emotional tenors, legal connections, and temporal responsibilities that make up the modern family: all show that even a small community is complex and irreducible to easy sloganeering about "connection" and "sameness."

The particularities of these relationships should not be forgotten, especially if political communities are modeled upon or against families, as they were for the list of political philosophers listed in the second chapter. Families connect closely to politics, these theorists intuit, precisely because families constitute sites where conflicts and desires of independence, belonging, and responsibility hold strongest: they are the locales where people feel their relationship to power, obligation, rights, privilege, autonomy, and dedication most intensely.

What, ultimately, do these recognitions mean for political understandings of community? One solution, which makes little empirical sense, would be to call for a disappearance of felt community, to argue that in the face of profound differences the affective ties of nation or state or neighborhood have been falsely created and should be eliminated or ignored.[63] The opposite solution, wrong rather than merely unfeasible, would argue that differences within families prove minor and unimportant compared to large-scale, "real" political differences. But the persistence of domestic violence and murders, of monies spent on health care for parents, of emotional energies expended between couples or between parents and children disprove this commonly held assumption.

Instead, attention to families illuminates the real and quotidian incommensurabilities between people tied together by accident of birth, lines of affiliative affection, or choice, while also revealing that such incommensurabilities need not be pathologized or rejected. Families contain differences, but this does not require working out the proper hierarchy, or demanding absolute and total equality at all times, or building a legal system which coordinates all families in the same ways, or dismissing the entire familial project altogether.[64] Families indicate the ways we already coordinate, contest, and overcome the most important divisions in our lives. They provide models of love and anger, respect and regret, connection and independence, life and death.[65] In its best moments, such recognition can create what Jean-Luc Nancy calls "a generosity of *ethos* more than an ethic of generosity."[66] Our forms of life ought not disappear, nor need they merge: such a politics requires only magnanimity toward different, overlapping forms of life.

This is something we do every day. The practices of everyday life necessitate that we dwell in weakly incommensurate worlds. Business, family, academics, and entertainment all have varied contexts that we juggle, overlap, and negotiate daily. We already possess "at the same time the different skills required for dwelling in several weakly incommensurate worlds and hence [we] can occupy more than one identity at a time."[67] These multiple roles and worlds and responsibilities and emotional tenors enfold and produce the kinds of people we are.

The human subject is always part of organizational, institutional, and collective identities, but this does not mean that we must subsume ourselves in these identities. They make up parts of us, important parts, but subjectivity also emerges from the contestations, the aporias, and the overlaps of these communities. The whole of who we are, our individual life worlds, involves the combinations of these judgments: combinations which always conflict with and depend upon others' ways of making their own worlds. The lives we lead emerge from the negotiation of these common but incommensurate communities of judgment.

These communities crystallize at their most intense locations, where our quotidian lives form our identities. It is the family—the realm of the intimate, the personal, the interrelational—where people always already negotiate dynamics of interplay and interaction. Where we love, argue, engage, think, care, and act. Where we likely spend more time and energy than in any other relationships. Where the vast and insurmountable distances between us coexist with our knowing other people as well as they know themselves. Where, in other words, our communities emerge from our incommensurabilities.

If the family serves as a model for political understanding, it should not be as a form or an archetype. No *polis* can be shaped as a family, since the intimacies and intensities of families cannot be transferred to organizations of unknowns. But our family lives can help us understand important aspects of political life: that difference does not foreclose community, that incommensurability does not threaten collectivity, that the techniques of familial living, when they work, can balance the competing pulls of dissimilarity and solidarity. These recognitions, while never faultless, prove both sufficient and necessary for life with others. Families, while themselves imperfect, provide reason for most of us to change ourselves on their behalf. To take that implication seriously—to commit to work on ourselves at the same time we work on those around us—proves the precondition to being both dedicated and engaged citizens and participatory and responsible family members.

CHAPTER 1: FAMILIAL INTENSITIES

1. There are exceptions, of course: hermits, holy figures, and others who find isolation helpful for their purpose. Some people with autism or who fall within the autism spectrum find the emotional requirements of familial life overwhelming and intolerable.

2. I do not mean the institutional structure of the family here. The positivist institutionalism of the 1960s paid considerable attention to the institutional frameworks of state and family, in the guise of political science, anthropology, and sociology. See, e.g., Ernest W. Burgess and Harvey Locke, *The Family, From Institution to Companionship* (New York: American Book Company, 1960). Long before that, many political scientists and sociologists explored how families serve to form citizen and cultural networks: Joseph Kirk Folsom and Marion Bassett, *The Family and Democratic Society* (New York: John Wiley and Sons, 1934).

3. Among contemporary critiques, I have found most helpful: Carol Smart, *The Ties That Bind: Law, Marriage, and the Reproduction of Patriarchal Relations* (London: Routledge and Kegan Paul, 1984); Gerda Lerner, *The Creation of Patriarchy* (New York: Oxford University Press, 1986); Carole Pateman, *The Sexual Contract* (Stanford: Stanford University Press, 1988); Susan Okin, *Justice, Gender, and the Family* (New York: Basic Books, 1991).

4. Emmanuel Levinas, *Humanism of the Other*, trans. Nidra Poller (Champaign: University of Illinois Press, 2006).

5. Thomas Kuhn, *The Structure of Scientific Revolutions* (Chicago: University of Chicago Press, 1970).

6. Charles Bazerman and René Augustín De los Santos, "Measuring Incommensurability: Are Toxicology and Ecotoxicology Blind to What the Other Sees?" *Rhetoric and Incommensurability*, ed. Randy Allen Harris (West Lafayette, Ind.: Parlor Press, 2005), 424.

7. Nola J. Heidlebaugh, *Judgment, Rhetoric, and the Problem of Incommensurability: Recalling Practical Wisdom* (Columbia: University of South Carolina Press, 2001); John O'Neill, "Value Pluralism, Incommensurability, and Institutions," *Valuing Nature? Economics, Ethics, and Environment*, ed. John Foster (London: Routledge, 1997), 75–88; J. Donald Moon, *Constructing Community: Moral Pluralism and Tragic Conflicts* (Princeton: Princeton University Press, 1995); Elizabeth Anderson, *Value in Ethics and Economics* (Cambridge: Harvard University Press, 1995).

8. Isaiah Berlin, *Four Essays on Liberty* (London: Oxford University Press, 1969); "The Incompatibility of Values," *Ethics in an Age of Pervasive Technology*, ed. Melvin Kranzberg (Boulder: Westview, 1980), 32–33; and *The Sense of Reality: Studies in Ideas and Their History* (New York: Farrar, Straus and Giroux, 1997). Recent political discussions of Berlinian value pluralism include Joseph Raz, *The Practice of Value* (Oxford: Oxford University Press, 2003), and *The Morality of Freedom* (Oxford: Oxford University Press, 1988); William Galston, *Liberal Pluralism: The Implications of Value Pluralism for Political Theory and Practice* (Cambridge: Cambridge University Press, 2002); and George Crowder, *Liberalism and Value Pluralism* (London: Continuum, 2002).

9. John Gray, "Where Pluralists and Liberals Part Company," *International Journal of Philosophical Studies* 6, no. 1 (1998), 17–36.

10. Michel de Certeau, *The Practice of Everyday Life*, trans. Steven Rendell (Berkeley: University of California Press, 1984); Thomas L. Dumm, *A Politics of the Ordinary* (New York: New York University Press, 1999).

CHAPTER 2: THE FUNCTIONING FAMILY

1. C. C. Harris, *Kinship* (Minneapolis: University of Minnesota Press, 1990), provides a general overview of this history.

2. Geoffrey S. Nathan, *The Family in Late Antiquity: The Rise of Christianity and the Endurance of Tradition* (London: Routledge, 2000), 57–58.

3. Ibid., 60.

4. Ibid., 27.

5. Ibid., 17–18.

6. Augustine, *de bono coniugali*, I. *"Prima itaque naturalis humanae societatis copula vir et uxor est."* Quoted in Nathan, *The Family in Late Antiquity*, 76.

7. Augustine, *Confessions*, trans. Henry Chadwick (Oxford: Oxford University Press, 1998), 169.

8. E.g., Carol Gilligan and David A. J. Richards, *The Deepening Darkness: Patriarchy, Resistance, and Democracy's Future* (Cambridge: Cambridge University Press, 2008), 102–19.

9. Albrecht Koschorke, *The Holy Family and Its Legacy: Religious Imagination from the Gospels to Star Wars*, trans. Thomas Dunlap (New York: Limelight, 1988).

10. Richard Allen Chapman, "Leviathan Writ Small: Thomas Hobbes on the Family," *American Political Science Review* 69, no. 1 (March 1975). Chapman points to Hobbes's chapter 30 and his review and conclusion.

11. Ibid., 77.

12. John Locke, *The Second Treatise of Government*, ed. Thomas Peardon (Indianapolis: Bobbs-Merrill, 1953).

13. E.g., in ibid., section 53, 36–37. Of course, once in the family, Locke argues that the man "as the abler and stronger" should have rule over the family (section 82, p. 46).

14. Ibid., sections 66–69, 37–40.

15. Ibid., section 76.

16. Locke, *The Second Treatise of Government*, section 107.

17. Jean-Jacques Rousseau, *On the Social Contract*, in *The Basic Political Writings*, ed. and trans. Donald A. Cress (Indianapolis: Hackett, 1987), 142.

18. Ibid.

19. Ibid., 227 n. 20.

20. Mostly in opposition in the third. Economy, he argues, originates in the family: but political economy should not be made parallel to domestic economy, since the former depends on the equality of citizens, which does not exist in the natural hierarchies of the family. Jean-Jacques Rousseau, *Discourse on Political Economy*, in *The Basic Political Writings*, ed. and trans. Donald A. Cress, 111–38.

21. Jean-Jacques Rousseau, *Discourse on the Origin of Inequality*, in *The Basic Political Writings*, ed. and trans. Donald A. Cress, 48.

22. Ibid., 62–63.

23. See the 1884 edition of Frederick Engels, *The Origin of the Family, Private Property, and the State*, trans. Lewis Henry Morgan (New York: Pathfinder, 1972).

24. Rousseau, *Discourse on the Origin of Inequality*, 65.

25. John S. Mill, *The Subjection of Women*, ed. Edward Alexander (London: Transaction, 2001).

26. Nadia Urbanati, "J. S. Mill on Androgyny and Marriage," *Political Theory* 19, no. 4 (1991), 626–48.

27. Mill, *The Subjection of Women*, 65–75.

28. Ruth Abbey, "Back to the Future: Marriage as Friendship in the Thought of Mary Wollstonecraft," *Hypatia* 14, no. 3 (1999), 78–95.

29. Mill, *The Subjection of Women*, 79.

30. Ibid., 40.

31. Mary Wollstonecraft serves as the initiator and exemplar of this movement. See Eileen H. Botting, *Family Feuds: Wollstonecraft, Burke, and Rousseau on the Transformation of the Family* (Albany: State University of New York Press), 131–214.

32. Georg Wilhelm Friedrich Hegel, *Hegel's Philosophy of Right*, trans. T. M. Knox (London: Oxford University Press, 1967), 111–12.

33. Ibid., 148.

34. E.g., Jean B. Elshtain, *Public Man, Private Woman: Women in Social and Political Thought* (Princeton: Princeton University Press, 1981), 170–83.

35. Michel Foucault, *Security, Territory, Population: Lectures at the Collège de France, 1977–1978*, ed. Michael Senellart, trans. Graham Burchell (New York: Palgrave Macmillan, 2007); see also the earliest English-language instantiation of these ideas in *The Foucault Effect: Studies in Governmentality*, ed. Graham Burchell, Colin Gordon, and Peter Miller (Chicago: University of Chicago Press, 1991).

36. Foucault, *Security, Territory, Population*, 105.

37. Ibid.

38. Robin Fox, *Kinship and Marriage* (Cambridge: Cambridge University Press, 1983); "The Virgin and the Godfather: Kinship versus the State in Greek Tragedy and After," *Anthropology and Literature*, ed. Paul Benson (Urbana: University of Illinois Press, 1993).

39. For comparison, the Frankish *parentalae* system clearly underlay power and legitimacy in the Merovingian era, and this near the height of church authority. Indeed, it is likely that the ninth-century prohibition of marriage "within the seventh degree" (that is, allowed only to those eighth cousins distant or more) arose from a desire to channel immediate family connections through religious authority rather than kinship claims. See Aline Hornaday, "Early Medieval Kinship Structrures as Social and Political Controls," *Medieval Family Roles: A Book of Essays*, ed. Cathy Jorgensen Itnyre (New York: Garland, 1996), 21–37.

40. Fox, "The Virgin and the Godfather," 109.

41. Anne McClintock points out that *natio* (to be born) forms the root of national-

ism. "Family Feuds: Gender, Nationalism, and the Family," *Feminist Review* 44, no. 3 (1993), 61–80.

42. Rush Rhees, "Some Developments in Wittgenstein's View of Ethics," *Philosophical Review* 74, no. 1 (1965), 21.

43. Bernard Williams, *In the Beginning Was the Deed: Realism and Moralism in Political Argument* (Princeton: Princeton University Press, 2005), 36–37.

44. See chapter 5 of this book for an in-depth example.

45. Linda Zerilli, *Feminism and the Abyss of Freedom* (Chicago: University of Chicago Press, 2005), 65.

46. Ibid., 15–16.

47. I do not exclude political scientists from this hierarchy of care either.

48. Cheryl Hall, *The Trouble with Passion: Political Theory beyond the Reign of Reason* (New York: Routledge, 2005).

49. Gill Valentine, *Public Space and the Culture of Childhood* (London: Ashgate, 2004), 15.

50. See also Corey Robin, *Fear: The History of a Political Idea* (Oxford: Oxford University Press, 2006).

51. Susan M. Okin, "Humanist Liberalism," in *Liberalism and the Moral Life*, ed. Nancy L. Rosenblum (Cambridge: Harvard University Press, 1989), 53.

52. Jacqueline Stevens, *Reproducing the State* (Princeton: Princeton University Press, 1999).

CHAPTER 3: COMMUNITIES AGAINST POLITICS

1. Hegel's entire conceptions of civil society and nationalism depend on this causal chain of becoming truly oneself through overcoming substantive individualism.

2. Arthur M. Schlesinger, Jr., *The Disuniting of America: Reflections on a Multicultural Society* (Knoxville: Whittle Direct, 1991).

3. Ibid., 78.

4. Ibid., 66.

5. Alasdair MacIntyre, "The Privatization of the Good: An Inaugural Lecture," *Review of Politics* 52 (1990), 344–77.

6. The first thorough critique is probably still the best: Michael Sandel, *Liberalism and the Limits of Justice* (Cambridge: Cambridge University Press, 1982).

7. Emile Durkheim is perhaps the most often referenced in this tradition.

8. Amitai Etzioni, *The New Golden Rule: Community and Morality in a Democratic Society* (New York: Basic Books, 1996), 93.

9. See also Amitai Etzioni, *From Empire to Community: A New Approach to International Relations* (New York: Palgrave Macmillan, 2004).

10. James Q. Wilson, *The Moral Sense* (New York: Free Press, 1993).

11. James Q. Wilson, *Thinking about Crime* (New York: Vintage, 1985), 28, 234.

12. Michael Sandel, *Democracy's Discontent: America in Search of a Public Philosophy* (Cambridge, Mass.: Belknap, 1996), 345.

13. Jean B. Elshtain's essay "Catholic Social Thought, the City, and Liberal America," in *Catholicism, Liberalism, and Communitarianism: The Catholic Intellectual Tradition and the Moral Foundations of Democracy*, ed. Kenneth Grasso, Gerard Bradley, and Robert Hunt (London: Rowman and Littlefield, 1995), 97–113, is emblematic of this protective impulse.

14. John Rawls, *A Theory of Justice* (Cambridge: Harvard University Press, 1971), 12.

15. George Kateb, *The Inner Ocean: Individualism and Democratic Culture* (Ithaca: Cornell University Press, 1992), 1–35.

16. Robert Nozick, *Anarchy, State, and Utopia* (New York: Basic Books, 1974).

17. For a clear-eyed but critical exegesis, see James P. Young, *Reconsidering American Liberalism* (Boulder: Westview, 1996), 241.

18. Kateb, *The Inner Ocean*, 174.

19. Ibid.

20. George Kateb, *Patriotism and Other Mistakes* (New Haven: Yale University Press, 1989), 3–20.

21. George Kateb, "Democratic Individuality and the Meaning of Rights," in *Liberalism and the Moral Life*, ed. Nancy Rosenblum (Cambridge: Harvard University Press, 1989), 183–206.

22. Kateb, *The Inner Ocean*, 174.

23. Kateb, *Patriotism and Other Mistakes*, 378.

24. William E. Connolly, *Identity\Difference: Democratic Negotiations of Political Paradox* (Ithaca: Cornell University Press, 1991), passim.

25. Richard E. Flathman, *Reflections of a Would-Be Anarchist: Ideals and Institutions of Liberalism* (Minnesota: University of Minnesota Press, 1998), 23.

26. Each of these arguments, and more, can be found in Andrew Sullivan, ed., *Same-Sex Marriage: Pro and Con* (New York: Vintage, 1997).

27. There is a large body of work arguing that *The Critique of Judgment* is the most efficaciously political work of Kant. Those interested in the history of this argument can consult Hannah Arendt, *Lectures on Kant's Political Philosophy*, ed. Ronald Biener (Chicago: University of Chicago Press, 1982); Ronald Beiner, *Political Judgment* (Chicago: University of Chicago Press, 1983); Dana Villa, *Arendt and Heidegger: The Fate of the Political* (Princeton: Princeton University Press, 1996); and Bonnie Honig, *Political Theory and the Displacement of Politics* (Ithaca: Cornell University Press, 1993).

28. As Stephen K. White has pointed out, this attention to the relevance of aesthetics is a (mostly unacknowledged) inheritance from Burke. See White, *Edmund Burke: Modernity, Politics, and Aesthetics* (Thousand Oaks, Calif.: Sage, 1994).

29. For Kant, freedom means something very different than the ability to act without limitations. It more properly means the ability to judge without limitations, to have intellectual and analytic freedom.

30. See Arendt, *Lectures on Kant's Political Philosophy*, 72.

31. Immanuel Kant, *Critique of Judgment*, trans. Werner S. Pluhar (Indianapolis: Hackett, 1987), §21.

32. See Charles Spinosa and Hubert L. Dreyfus, "Two Kinds of Antiessentialism and Their Consequences," *Critical Inquiry* 22 (1996), 735–63.

33. Ibid., 749.

34. Most famously, see John Rawls's distinction between thin and thick "goods" in *A Theory of Justice* (Cambridge: Harvard University Press, 1971), especially chapter 7. See also his thickening of "thin goods" beyond their original bounds in *Political Liberalism* (New York: Columbia University Press, 1993).

35. Roberto Esposito, *Communitas: The Origin and Destiny of Community*, trans. Timothy Campbell (Stanford: Stanford University Press, 2010), 72.

36. Kant, *Critique of Judgment*, §83.

37. See Immanuel Kant, introduction to *Critique of Practical Reason*, trans. Lewis White Beck (New York: Macmillan, 1985), 3.

38. Kant, *Critique of Judgment*, §91.

39. Esposito describes this as Kant's confusion between two thematics: "between that of a simple intersubjectivity and that of an 'impossible' community." Esposito, *Communitas*, 81.

40. This theory is most commonly associated with Thomas Kuhn, *The Structure of Scientific Revolutions* (Chicago: University of Chicago Press, 1970).

41. This theory descends from political applications of Nietzsche (e.g., the philosophical focus of Canguillem, Foucault, and Connolly).

42. Perhaps the most notable example in the United States over the past few decades has been the disappearance of the debate over adult contraception, which is almost universally seen as a matter of personal choice.

43. Jackie McMillan, "Putting the Cult Back into Community," in *Returning (to) Communities: Theory, Culture and Political Practice of the Communal*, ed. Stefan Herbrechter and Michael Higginsan (Amsterdam: Rodolphi, 2006), 231–43.

44. See Hannah Arendt's discussion of scientists in *Between Past and Future: Eight Exercises in Political Thought* (New York: Penguin, 1968), 226ff.

45. Michael Walzer, *Spheres of Justice* (New York: Basic Books, 1983), 38.

46. See the theorists discussed in the last section of this chapter for exceptions.

47. Samuel Huntington has no interest in overcoming incommensurability; he is more interested in exploiting it. See my critique of him in "Aesthetics as Foreign Policy," in *Challenging Boundaries*, ed. Michael Shapiro and Hayward Alker, Jr. (Minneapolis: University of Minnesota Press, 1996).

48. See Alasdair MacIntyre, *Whose Justice? Which Rationality?* (Notre Dame: University of Notre Dame Press, 1988), esp. 326–403.

49. Charles Taylor, "The Politics of Recognition," in *Multiculturalism*, ed. Amy Guttman (Princeton: Princeton University Press, 1994).

50. Jacques Rancière, *Dis-agreement: Politics and Philosophy*, trans. Julie Rose (Minneapolis: University of Minnesota Press, 1999), 116.

51. Slavoj Žižek, "A Leftist Plea for 'Eurocentrism,'" *Critical Inquiry* 24 (1998), 992.

52. Rancière, *Dis-agreement*, 123.

53. See, for example, Ralf Dahrendorf, *The Modern Social Conflict: An Essay on the Politics of Liberty* (New York: Weidenfeld and Nicholson, 1988).

54. John S. Mill, *On Liberty and Other Writings*, ed. Stefani Collini (Cambridge: Cambridge University Press, 1989).

55. Nicolas Rescher, *Pluralism: Against the Demand for Consensus* (Oxford: Oxford University Press, 1993), 27.

56. Rancière refers to a similar matrix of forces as "the police," which he sees as oppositional to politics.

57. Rescher, *Pluralism*, 3.

58. José Ortega y Gasset, *The Modern Theme*, trans. James Cleugh (New York: Harper and Brothers, 1961), 86–90.

59. Indeed, his attempts to reconstruct community seem to ignore his insights about truth. Cf. José Ortega y Gasset, *Concord and Liberty*, trans. Helene Weyl (New York: W. W. Norton, 1946).

60. Perhaps the best representations of Arendt's commitment to agonistics have been Dana Villa, *Arendt and Heidegger: The Fate of the Political* (Princeton: Princeton University Press, 1996), and Honig, *Political Theory and the Displacement of Politics*.

61. Arendt, *Between Past and Future*, 93.

62. Against this reading, Kirstie McClure argues that for Arendt the social consists of the economic and structural background from which politics can erupt. See Kirstie M. McClure, "The Social Question, Again," *Graduate Faculty Philosophy Journal* 28, no. 1 (2007), 85–113.

63. I make this argument in *William James: Politics in the Pluriverse* (Lanham, Md.: Rowman and Littlefield, 2007).

64. See William E. Connolly, *The Augustinian Imperative: A Reflection on the Politics of Morality* (Thousand Oaks, Calif.: Sage, 1992); and *The Ethos of Pluralization* (Minneapolis: University of Minnesota Press, 1995).

65. Gilles Deleuze and Félix Guattari, *A Thousand Plateaus*, trans. Brian Massumi (Minneapolis: University of Minnesota Press, 1987).

66. Alain Badiou, *Being and Event*, trans. Oliver Feltham (London: Continuum, 2005); Quentin Meillassoux, *Après la finitude: Essai sur la nécessité de la contingence* (Paris: Le Seuil, 2006).

67. William Corlett, *Community without Unity: A Politics of Derridean Extravagence* (Durham: Duke University Press, 1993).

68. Jean-Luc Nancy, *The Inoperative Community*, ed. and trans. Peter Connor (Minneapolis: University of Minnesota Press, 1991), 1–42.

69. Jean-Luc Nancy, *The Experience of Freedom*, trans. Bridget McDonald (Stanford: Stanford University Press, 1993), 75.

70. Alphonso Lingis, *The Community of Those with Nothing in Common* (Bloomington: Indiana University Press, 1994). See esp. chapter 1, "The Other Community."

71. Nancy, *The Inoperative Community*, 43–70.

72. Esposito, *Communitas*, 6–7.

73. Ibid., 138.

74. Ibid., 15.

CHAPTER 4: SILENCE: A POLITICS

1. Deborah Tannen notices how silence is used to negotiate especially stressful situations in her essay "Silence as Conflict Management in Fiction and Drama: Pinter's *Betrayal* and a Short Story, 'Great Wits,'" in *Conflict Talk: Sociolinguistic Investigations of Arguments in Conversations*, ed. Allen D. Grimshaw (Cambridge: Cambridge University Press, 1990), 260–79.

2. Ludwig Wittgenstein, *Tractatus Logico-Philosophicus*, trans. D. F. Pears and B. F. McGuinness (London: Routledge and Kegan Paul, 1961), §7. He later has much to say on these topics, which is one aspect of his philosophy that clearly differentiates the "early" from the "late" Wittgenstein. See my *The Politics of Judgment: Aesthetics, Identity, and Political Theory* (Lanham, Md.: Lexington, 1999), 17–23, 85–89.

3. Cheryl Glenn, *Unspoken: A Rhetoric of Silence* (Carbondale: Southern Illinois University Press, 2004), 15–16.

4. Cingular billboard advertisement, 2001.

5. Cited in George Steiner, *Language and Silence: Essays on Language, Literature, and the Inhuman* (New York: Atheneum, 1976), 32.

6. Cynthia L. Crown and Stanley Feldstein, "Psychological Correlates of Silence

and Sound in Conversational Interaction," in *Perspectives on Silence*, ed. Deborah Tannen and Muriel Saville-Troike (Norwood, N.J.: Ablex, 1985), 31–54.

7. Bessie Dendrinos and Emilia R. Pedro, "Giving Street Directions: The Silent Role of Women," in *Silence: Interdisciplinary Perspectives*, ed. Adam Jaworski (Berlin: Mouton de Gruyer, 1997), 216.

8. S. R. Rochester, "The Significance of Pauses in Spontaneous Speech," *Journal of Psycholinguistic Research* 2, no. 1 (1973), 51–81.

9. See David Crystal, *Language Death* (Cambridge: Cambridge University Press, 2000).

10. Ronald Wardhaugh, *How Conversation Works* (Oxford: Basil Blackwell, 1985), 198–201.

11. Tillie Olsen, *Silences* (New York: Delacorte / Seymour Lawrence, 1978).

12. Ibid., 141.

13. Adrienne Rich, *On Lies, Secrets, and Silence: Selected Prose* (New York: W. W. Norton, 1979), 11.

14. Quoted in Olsen, *Silences*, 174.

15. Rich, *On Lies, Secrets, and Silence*, 13.

16. See Rae Langton, "Speech Acts and Unstoppable Acts," *Philosophy and Public Affairs* 22 (1993), 293–330; Caroline West, "The Free Speech Argument against Pornography," *Canadian Journal of Philosophy* 33, no. 3 (2003), 391–422; and Catharine MacKinnon, *Only Words* (Cambridge: Harvard University Press, 1993).

17. Susan Brownmiller, *Against Our Will: Men, Women, and Rape* (New York: Bantam, 1975).

18. Mary Eagleton, "Ethical Reading: The Problem of Alice Walker's 'Advancing Luna and Ida B. Wells' and J. M. Coetzee's *Disgrace*," *Feminist Theory* 2, no. 2 (2001), 195.

19. See, e.g., Judith Allen, "Evidence and Silence: Feminism and the Limits of History," *Feminist Challenges: Social and Political History*, ed. Carole Pateman and Elizabeth Gross (Boston: Northeastern University Press, 1986), 173–89. Allen's overt use of "silence" means the lack of a self-created historical record by those whose sole historical documentation resides as objects of police surveillance and custody, such as prostitutes in Victorian England.

20. Elisabeth Noelle-Neumann, *The Spiral of Silence: Public Opinion—Our Social Skin* (Chicago: University of Chicago Press, 1984).

21. Peter M. Tiersma, "The Language of Silence," *Rutgers Law Review* 48 (1995), 1–99.

22. Jürgen Habermas, *Between Facts and Norms: Contributions to a Discourse Theory of Law and Democracy*, trans. William Rehg (Cambridge: MIT Press, 1998).

23. See the dissent of Justices Rehnquist, O'Connor, and White, and to a lesser extent that of Justice Stevens, in *Texas v. Johnson*, 491 U.S. 397 (1989).

24. Ron Scollon, "The Machine Stops: Silence in the Metaphor of Malfunction," *Perspectives on Silence*, ed. Deborah Tannen and Muriel Saville-Troike (Norwood, N.J.: Ablex, 1985), 26.

25. Michel Foucault, *The History of Sexuality*, vol. 1, *An Introduction*, trans. Robert Hurley (New York: Vintage, 1980), 101.

26. Thomas L. Dumm, *A Politics of the Ordinary* (New York: New York University Press, 1999), 30.

27. Perry Gilmore, "Silence and Sulking: Emotional Displays in the Classroom," in *Perspectives on Silence*, ed. Deborah Tannen and Muriel Saville-Troike (Norwood, N.J.: Ablex, 1985), 139–62.

28. Ibid., 154.

29. Dumm, *A Politics of the Ordinary*, 30.

30. Haig Bosmajian, *The Freedom Not to Speak* (New York: New York University Press, 1999).

31. Max Picard, *The World of Silence*, trans. Stanley Godman (Chicago: Henry Regnery, 1952), 18. For Picard, the nature of silence is directly related to the ontic in things, and thus he follows Heidegger in decrying the new regimes of noise.

32. *The Piano*, written and directed by Jane Campion, Artisan Entertainment, 1993.

33. Robin P. Clair, *Organizing Silence: A World of Possibilities* (Albany: State University of New York Press, 1998). See especially chapter 7, "When Silence Speaks: A Discussion of Self-contained Opposites."

34. Natalie J. Ciarocco, Kristin L. Sommer, and Roy F. Baumeister, "Ostracism and Ego Depletion: The Strains of Silence," *Personality and Social Psychology Bulletin* 27, no. 9 (2001), 1156–63.

35. See Jack W. Sattel, "Men, Inexpressiveness, and Power," in *Language, Gender, and Society*, ed. Barrie Thorne, Cheris Kramarae, and Nancy Henley (Rowley, Mass.: Newbury House, 1983), 119–24.

36. Wendy Brown, "Freedom's Silences," in *Censorship and Silencing: Practices of Cultural Regulation*, ed. Robert C. Post (Los Angeles: Getty Research Institute for the History of Art and the Humanities, 1998), 316.

37. Oddly, very few other theorists of silence comment upon this rather large role that silence plays in relationships. Susan Sontag, "The Aesthetics of Silence," in *Styles of Radical Will* (New York: Farrar, Straus and Giroux, 1969), 20.

38. Jean F. Lyotard, *The Differend: Phrases in Dispute*, trans. Georges Van Den Abbeele (Minneapolis: University of Minnesota Press, 1988), 3–31.

39. Lisa Block de Behar, *A Rhetoric of Silence and Other Selected Writings* (New York: Mouton de Gruyter, 1995), 7.

40. Ibid.

41. Gail Griffin, *Calling: Essays on Teaching in the Mother Tongue* (New York: Trilogy, 1992), 219.

42. Glenn, *Unspoken*.

43. Friedrich Nietzsche, *Thus Spoke Zarathustra*, trans. R. J. Hollingdale (London: Penguin, 1969), 202–4.

44. Ibid., 153–54. Italics in original.

45. At least eight times, Zarathustra says something along the lines of "Then something said to me voicelessly . . ." as he ascends from part 2 to 3. See ibid., 166–69.

46. See Sonoda Muneto, "The Eloquent Silence of Zarathustra," in *Nietzsche and Asian Thought*, ed. Graham Parkes (Chicago: University of Chicago Press, 1991), 226–43.

47. For further explication of the function of silence in Zen (Chan), see Youru Wang, "Liberating Oneself from the Absolutized Boundary of Language: A Liminiological Approach to the Interplay of Speech and Silence in Chan Buddhism." *Philosophy East and West* 51, no. 1 (2001), 83; and Dale S. Wright, "Rethinking Transcendence: The Role of Language in Experience," *Philosophy East and West* 42, no. 1 (1992), 113–38.

48. Deborah Tannen, "Silence: Anything But," in *Perspectives on Silence*, ed. Deborah Tannen and Muriel Saville-Troike (Norwood, N.J.: Ablex, 1985).

49. Both likely inherited the tradition from the Seekers, though their theological underpinnings cause both to be loath to admit historical influence or precedent. See Stanislaw Zielinski, *Psychology and Silence* (Wallingford, Penn.: Pendle Hill, 1975), and Russell Fraser, *The Language of Adam* (New York: Columbia University Press, 1979), chapter 1.

50. Robert Barclay, *Truth Triumphant*, vol. 2, 353, quoted in Richard Bauman, *Let Your Words Be Few: Symbolism of Speaking and Silence among Seventeenth-Century Quakers* (Cambridge: Cambridge University Press, 1983), 22.

51. Ibid.

52. Thomas Colley, *An Apology for Silent Waiting upon God in Religious Assemblies; With Some Observations on the Nature and Ground of True Faith, and the Application Thereof in the Important Concern of Worship* (Philadelphia: Joseph Crukshank, 1805), 4.

53. Robert Barclay, *An Apology for the True Christian Divinity*, § VI, quoted in Mary Brook, *Reasons for the Necessity of Silent Waiting, in Order to the Solemn Worship of God; to Which are Added Several Quotations from Robert Barclay's Apology* (Philadelphia: Friends Bookstore, 1977), 27.

54. George Keith, *The Benefit, Advantage, and Glory of Silent Meetings, Both as It Was Found at the Beginning, or First Breaking Forth of This Clear Manifestation*

of Truth, and Continued So to Be Found by All the Faithful and Upright in Heart at This Day (London: Andrew Sowle, 1687), 17.

55. See Bauman, *Let Your Words Be Few*, especially 22–31.

56. L. V. Hodgkin, *Silent Worship: The Way of Wonder; Swarthmore Lecture 1919* (London: Swarthmore, 1919), 79.

57. Zielinski, *Psychology and Silence*, 23.

58. John Cage, *Silence* (Middletown: Wesleyan University Press, 1961), 8.

59. See his discussions with Bill Womack and Michael John White in Richard Kostelanetz, *Conversing with Cage* (New York: Limelight, 1988).

60. The pianist Larry J. Solomon is particularly interested in these structural aspects of the piece. See his discussion "The Sounds of Silence: John Cage and 4′33″" at www.azstarnet.com.

61. Sontag, "The Aesthetics of Silence," 10–11.

62. The most extensive investigation which tries to resolve this obscurity is Beryl Lang, whose *Heidegger's Silence* (Ithaca: Cornell University Press, 1996) attempts to foreclose the question by arguing that silence is equivalent to guilt.

63. See Hodgkin's description of a prowar group doing so, "gesticulating violently and shouting lustily" during the First World War in Devonshire, England, in *Silent Worship*, 76.

64. Perhaps the most famous academic essay on silence is Keith H. Basso's description of a Southwestern Native American culture's embrace of silence, often to the extent that Europeans are confused and flustered when confronted with it. See "'To Give Up on Words': Silence in Western Apache Culture," *Southwestern Journal of Anthropology* 26 (1970), 213–30.

CHAPTER 5: I ♥ MY DOG

1. William James, "On a Certain Blindness in Human Beings," *Faith and Morals* (New York: Longmans, Green, 1943), 260. The original essay was published in 1899.

2. Ibid. James also draws a parallel here between the incommensurability of dogs and people and the incommensurability of an "American traveler" and "African savages," the latter of whom, in his telling, do not understand the very basic nature of the written word.

3. Marjorie Garber's book *Dog Love* (New York: Simon and Schuster, 1996) lists a few of these and many other examples of people's love of dogs.

4. The main exception being recent immigrants from countries where dogs are valued differently, either as "filthy animals" or as tasty comestibles (first-generation Iraqi or Vietnamese immigrants, for example, who rarely own dogs as pets). See James A. Serpell, *In the Company of Animals* (New York: Basil Blackwell, 1986), v–vi.

5. Garber, *Dog Love*, 42. Unfortunately, why this is so she never explicitly articulates, other than to say that they bring out extremes of emotion.

6. John Adams to James Warren, October 13, 1775, in *Warren-Adams Letters, Being Chiefly a Correspondence among John Adams, Samuel Adams, and James Warren, 1743–1814*, vol. 1 (Boston: Massachusetts Historical Society, 1917–25), 137; quoted in James Turner, *Reckoning with the Beast: Animals, Pain, and Humanity in the Victorian Mind* (Baltimore: Johns Hopkins University Press, 1980), 9.

7. Harriet Ritvo, *The Animal Estate: The English and Other Creatures in the Victorian Age* (Cambridge: Harvard University Press, 1987), 84–85.

8. Turner, *Reckoning with the Beast*, 74–75.

9. George T. Angell, *Our Dumb Animals*, vol. 1 (1868–69), 37, quoted in ibid., 75.

10. Turner, *Reckoning with the Beast*, 77.

11. Timothy W. Luke, "Beyond Birds: Biopower and Birdwatching in the World of Audubon," *Capitalism Nature Socialism* 11, no. 3 (2000), 7–37.

12. Quoted in Midas Dekkers, *Dearest Pet: On Bestiality*, trans. Paul Vincent (New York: Verso, 1994), 172. This, surprisingly, from the author of *The Foundations of Ethnology: The Principal Ideas and Discoveries in Animal Behavior* (New York: Simon and Schuster, 1982).

13. Andrew Sullivan, "Dog and Man at Harvard," *New York Times Book Review*, November 17, 1996, 11.

14. The hardback version spent over a year on the *New York Times* bestseller list and helped create an avalanche of dog-related books.

15. Michael Oakeshott, "A Philosophy of Politics," in *Religion, Politics, and the Moral Life* (New Haven: Yale University Press, 1993), 122.

16. Ibid., 123.

17. In moral philosophy, this opposition between the practical and theoretical has its own specialized terminology: "the *is-ought* distinction," or the conflict between "value and fact." I will avoid these specialized terminologies, primarily because they tend to delineate matters only at the price of obfuscation.

18. Most overtly, John Rawls, *A Theory of Justice* (Cambridge: Harvard University Press, 1971) and *Political Liberalism* (New York: Columbia University Press, 1993); Richard B. Brandt, *Facts, Values, and Norms* (Cambridge: Cambridge University Press, 1996), esp. 123–63; Robert Nozick overtly lists them in *The Nature of Rationality* (Princeton: Princeton University Press, 1993), 141–50.

19. Rawls, *A Theory of Justice*, 103–4; James Rachels, *Can Ethics Provide Answers? And Other Essays in Moral Philosophy* (Lanham, Md.: Rowman and Littlefield, 1997), ix.

20. Michael Smith, *The Moral Problem* (Oxford: Blackwell, 1994).

21. Mary Midgley, *Heart and Mind: The Varieties of Moral Experience* (Sussex: Harvester, 1981).

22. Bernard Williams, *Ethics and the Limits of Philosophy* (Cambridge: Harvard University Press, 1985), 74.

23. Peter Singer, *Animal Liberation* (New York: Avon, 1990); for a more simplified account, see his "All Animals Are Equal," in *Applied Ethics* (New York: Oxford University Press, 1986), 215–28.

24. See, e.g., Daniel A. Dombrowski, *Babies and Beasts: The Argument from Marginal Cases* (Urbana: University of Illinois Press, 1997).

25. Jürgen Habermas, *The Theory of Communicative Action*, trans. Thomas McCarthy (Boston: Beacon, 1984) and *The Structural Transformation of the Public Sphere*, trans. Thomas Burger and Frederick Lawrence (Cambridge: Harvard University Press, 1989).

26. Quoted in Peter Dews, *Logics of Disintegration: Post-Structuralist Thought and the Claims of Critical Theory* (New York: Verso, 1988), 242.

27. See, e.g., Jürgen Habermas, *Philosophical Discourse of Modernity: Twelve Lectures*, trans. Frederick Lawrence (Cambridge: MIT Press, 1990), or Seyla Benhabib, *Critique, Norm, and Utopia: A Study of the Foundations of Critical Theory* (New York: Columbia University Press, 1986).

28. Actually, there are three, but the "ordinary language" philosophy movement is clearly limited to meaning within human interlocution, and thus is of little relevance here.

29. Dana Villa, *Politics, Philosophy, Terror: Essays on the Thought of Hannah Arendt* (Princeton: Princeton University Press, 1999), 67.

30. Martin Heidegger, *Being and Time*, trans. John Macquarrie and Edward Robinson (San Francisco: Harper, 1962), 237.

31. Jean-Paul Sartre, *Existentialism and Humanism*, trans. Philip Maret (London: Methuen, 1948).

32. "Men," she argues (meaning "humans"), "are conditioned beings because everything they come in contact with turns immediately into a condition of their existence." Hannah Arendt, *The Human Condition* (Chicago: University of Chicago Press, 1958), 9.

33. Exemplary here is Arendt's discussion of love's dependence on the public realm: see ibid., 51–78.

34. Martha Nussbaum, *Love's Knowledge* (New York: Oxford University Press, 1990), 274.

35. Carol Gilligan, *In a Different Voice* (Cambridge: Harvard University Press,

1982); Nel Noddings, *Caring: A Feminist Approach to Ethics and Moral Education* (Berkeley: University of California Press, 1984).

36. Other related political and psychological theories include "object relations theory" and "maternal thinking." See Melanie Klein, *The Selected Melanie Klein* (New York: Free Press, 1987), and Sara Ruddick, *Maternal Thinking: Towards a Politics of Peace* (New York: Ballantine, 1989).

37. Carol Gilligan, "Remapping the Moral Domain: New Images of the Self in Relationship," in *Reconstructing Individualism: Autonomy, Individuality, and the Self in Western Thought*, ed. Thomas C. Heller, Morton Sosna, and David E. Wellberg (Stanford: Stanford University Press, 1986), 240.

38. For an extended discussion of the ethical and political implications of this, see the collection of essays *An Ethic of Care: Feminist and Interdisciplinary Perspectives*, ed. Mary Jeanne Larrabee (New York: Routledge, 1993).

39. Noddings is most explicit in this account.

40. Stan van Hooft, *Caring: An Essay in the Philosophy of Ethics* (Niwot: University Press of Colorado, 1995), 26.

41. Joan Tronto, *Moral Boundaries: A Political Argument for an Ethic of Care* (New York: Routledge, 1993).

42. See, e.g., Lawrence Kohlberg, *Essays on Moral Development* (San Francisco: Harper and Row, 1984).

43. Other than Cuomo and Gruen, another exception is Rita C. Manning, who devotes a chapter to love of animals in *Speaking from the Heart*. Manning's treatment, however, is more a narrative of specific cases of caring (in particular, her decision whether or not to put a horse to pasture), the conclusions of which are simplistic: "those who have had a relationship with animals, with the earth, become, through these relationships, aware of the sacredness of the earth." Manning, *Speaking from the Heart: A Feminist Perspective on Ethics* (Lanham, Md.: Rowman and Littlefield, 1992), 133.

44. Chris J. Cuomo and Lori Gruen, "On Puppies and Pussies: Animals, Intimacy, and Moral Distance," in *Daring to Be Good: Essays in Feminist Eco-Politics*, ed. Bat-Ami Bar On and Ann Ferguson (New York: Routledge, 1998), 129–42.

45. This is not, however, a slip back into a universalism of oppression; Cuomo overtly argues elsewhere that feminist ethics, being contextual and contingent, cannot (and should not) avoid being pluralistic. See her "The Power and the Promise of Ecological Feminism" in *Ecological Feminist Philosophies*, ed. Karen J. Warring (Bloomington: Indiana University Press, 1996), 42–51.

46. Cuomo and Gruen, "On Puppies and Pussies," 140.

47. The above quotation concludes: "the feminist case for vegetarianism becomes even stronger."

48. See Singer, *Animal Liberation*, 22, and Tom Regan, *The Case for Animal Rights* (Berkeley: University of California Press, 2004), 324.

49. Arnold Arluke and Clinton Sanders, *Regarding Animals* (Philadelphia: Temple University Press, 1996).

50. Ibid., 67–71.

51. Though there are certain similarities between the efforts to control their reproduction, the political efforts to create programs to control and minimize the reproductive capacities of "drug addicts" and "welfare recipients" are suspiciously similar to the spaying of genealogically impure or wild dogs and cats.

52. Quoted in Alan Moorehead, *The Fatal Impact: An Account of the Invasion of the South Pacific, 1767–1840* (New York: Harper and Row, 1966), 27.

53. See Glen Elder, Jennifer Wolch, and Jody Emel, "*Le Pratique Sauvage*: Race, Place, and the Human-Animal Divide," in *Animal Geographies: Place, Politics, and Identity in the Nature-Culture Borderlands*, ed. Jennifer Wolch and Jody Emel (New York: Verso, 1998), 72–90, for a sensitive and enlightening treatment of the ways animals are viewed in a culture more prone to sympathize with animals than with foreign cultural practices.

54. E.g., "Question 3," an antiracing proposition passed in Massachusetts in the fall of 2000.

55. For a full range of examples of all these approaches from a variety of popular narratives, see Susan C. McElroy, ed., *Animals as Teachers and Healers: True Stories and Reflections* (New York: Ballantine, 1996).

56. Steven St C. Bostock, *Zoos and Animal Rights: The Ethics of Keeping Animals* (London: Routledge, 1993), 62.

57. Philip Pettit, *Republicanism: A Theory of Freedom and Government* (Oxford: Oxford University Press, 1997), 51–109.

58. Singer, *Animal Liberation*, 255.

59. See McElroy, *Animals as Teachers and Healers*. See also the tales of those whose sexual drive fixes on animals in Midas Dekkers, *Dearest Pet: On Bestiality*, trans. Paul Vincent (New York: Verso, 2000).

60. J. M. Coetzee, *Disgrace* (New York: Viking, 1999). Subsequent citations given parenthetically in the text.

61. For Lurie, this caretaking is not dependent on the recognition of others, even of the dogs themselves. He notes that it matters to no one, not even the dead dogs, how their bodies are treated after death, yet he goes out of his way to solemnize their cremation. Nor does it preclude particularity: he feels a particular attachment to one dog and resists killing it until the final page of the book.

62. Ian Hacking, "Our Fellow Animals," *New York Review of Books*, June 29, 2000, 20.

63. I take this term from Bruno Latour's use of "actant-rhizome ontology." See "On Recalling ANT," in *Actor Network and After*, ed. John Law and John Hassard (Oxford: Blackwell and the Sociological Review, 1999), 15–25.

64. Christopher D. Stone, "Should Trees Have Standing? Toward Legal Rights for Natural Objects," *Southern California Law Review* 45 (1972).

65. The most philosophically formal of these approaches comes from Joel Feinberg, "The Rights of Animal and Unborn Generations," in *Philosophy and Environmental Crisis*, ed. William Blackstone (Athens: University of Georgia Press, 1974). See also Tom Regan's reply and expansion of Feinberg in *All That Dwell Therein: Animal Rights and Environmental Ethics* (Berkeley: University of California Press, 1982), 165–83.

66. Timothy Kaufman-Osbourne, *Creatures of Prometheus: Gender and the Politics of Technology* (Lanham, Md.: Rowman and Littlefield, 1997).

67. Jane Bennett, *The Enchantment of Modern Life: Attachments, Crossings, and Ethics* (Princeton: Princeton University Press, 2001), esp. 17–32.

68. Jim Johnson, "Mixing Humans and Nonhumans Together: The Sociology of a Door-Closer," *Social Problems* 35, no. 3 (June 1988), 298–310.

69. Donna Haraway, "Manifesto for Cyborgs: Science, Technology, and Socialist Feminism in the 1980s," *Socialist Review* 15, no. 2 (1985). It is no coincidence that Haraway's most recent manifesto celebrates the fuzziness of the barrier between pets and humans; see *The Companion Species Manifesto: Dogs, People and Significant Otherness* (Chicago: Prickly Paradigm, 2003).

CHAPTER 6: THE SPACES OF DISABILITY

1. Even the term "disability" is contested. Other conceptualizations such as "handicapped," "crippled," "impaired," or "alternately abled" have their own histories and difficulties, and the field has generally (though not without continued objection) settled on "disabled." While "alternately abled" better—though not precisely—suggests the implications discussed herein, I use the predominant terminology.

2. Erving Goffman, *Stigma: Notes on the Management of Spoiled Identity* (New York: Touchstone, 1986); Simi Linton, *Claiming Disability: Knowledge and Identity* (New York: New York University Press, 1998).

3. The prevalence of deafness in the communities on Martha's Vineyard in the United States, in which most hearing residents were bilingual in sign and sound, serves as a common example. One might also note, as does Lennard J. Davis, that people as famous as Samuel Johnson were partially blind, partially deaf, scarred, depressive, and suffered profound tics (which would today be diag-

nosed as Tourette syndrome), yet few of his writings or others' literary portraits make anything of this. Lennard J. Davis, *Bending Over Backwards: Disability, Dismodernism, and Other Difficult Positions* (New York: New York University Press, 2002), 47–66.

4. E.g., Brandon Gleeson, *Geographies of Disability* (New York: Routledge, 1999).

5. Perhaps the best known of these are Susan Sontag's descriptions of the meanings of cancer and AIDS. Sontag, *Illness as Metaphor and AIDS and Its Metaphors* (New York: Anchor, 1990). See also Rosemarie Thompson, *Extraordinary Bodies: Figuring Physical Disability in American Culture and Literature* (New York: Columbia University Press, 1997).

6. This way of stating the issue can be traced back to Harlan Hahn, "Disability and the Urban Environment: A Perspective on Los Angeles," *Environment and Planning D: Society and Space* 4 (1986), 273–88. A particularly useful recapitulation of the approach is Ray McDermott and Hervé Varenne, "Culture of Disability," *Anthropology and Education Quarterly* 26 (1995), 323–48.

7. This contention, that phenomenology cannot adequately conceptualize this transformation, has proven in discussions one of the most contentious of this book. I assert here that most (though not all) phenomenological understandings of the self-world relation depend upon a concretized or materially manifest engagement, which downplays the possibilities of imaginative conceptual understanding. That is, usually within phenomenology, I must myself experience a profound change in ability (my hammer must break, for example) before my relationships with the world are transformed. Understanding that a hammer might break, or seeing someone else's break, does not generally result in radical change. Thus phenomenological consequence is often reducible to a self-oriented universalism—one that is open to the possibility of radical recentering or transformative consequences, but that ultimately reduces to a new self-centered monadism.

8. Marcia P. Burgdorf and Robert Burgdorf, Jr., "A History of Unequal Treatment: The Qualifications of Handicapped Persons as a 'Suspect Class' under the Equal Protection Clause," *Santa Clara Lawyer* 15 (1975), 855–910, cited in Rosemarie Thompson, *Extraordinary Bodies*, 35.

9. These and further analysis of these dynamics make up the underlying argument of my *The Politics of Judgment: Aesthetics, Identity, and Political Theory* (Lanham, Md.: Lexington Books, 1999).

10. Carol Gilligan, *In a Different Voice* (Cambridge: Harvard University Press, 1982); Nel Noddings, *Caring: A Feminist Approach to Ethics and Moral Education* (Berkeley: University of California Press, 1984); Sara Ruddick, "Maternal

Thinking," *Feminist Studies* 6 (1980), 342–67; Joan Tronto, *Moral Boundaries: A Political Argument for an Ethic of Care* (New York: Routledge, 1993).

11. Ruddick, "Maternal Thinking." It is interesting that even in the midst of her early defense of care, she makes a clear point to identify such "real world" results.

12. Tronto, *Moral Boundaries*, 101–26.

13. Noddings, *Caring*, 33.

14. Hannah Arendt, *Eichmann in Jerusalem: A Report on the Banality of Evil* (London: Penguin, 1964), 49.

15. Maurice Hamington, *Embodied Care: Jane Addams, Maurice Merleau-Ponty, and Feminist Ethics* (Urbana: University of Illinois Press, 2004), 62.

16. Alison M. Jaggar, "Caring as Feminist Practice of Moral Reason," in *Justice and Care: Essential Readings in Feminist Ethics,* ed. Virginia Held (Boulder: Westview, 1995), 179–202.

17. Jane Stables and Fiona Smith, "'Caught in the Cinderella Trap': Narratives of Disabled Parents and Young Carers," in *Mind and Body Spaces: Geographies of Illness, Impairment, and Disability,* ed. Ruth Butler and Hester Parr (New York: Routledge, 1999), 256–68.

18. I investigate the pluralization of things in *Politics in the Pluriverse: William James and the Birth of Pluralism* (Lanham, Md.: Rowman and Littlefield, 2007), chapter 5.

19. Michel de Certeau, *The Practice of Everyday Life,* trans. Steve Rendall (Berkeley: University of California Press, 1984), 61.

20. Ibid.

21. Cf. ibid., 218.

22. Tom McDonough, "Situationist Space," in *Guy Debord and the Situationist International,* ed. Tom McDonough (Cambridge: MIT Press, 2002), 241–65. While this particular quotation (241) merely describes the map, my reading of the map's locational pedagogy relies heavily on McDonough's interpretation.

23. Ibid., 246.

24. Henri Lefebvre, *The Production of Space* (Cambridge: Blackwell, 1991); David Harvey, *The Condition of Postmodernity* (Oxford: Basil Blackwell, 1989); Edward Soja, *Postmodern Geographies: The Reassertion of Space in Contemporary Social Thought* (London: Verso, 1988).

25. Lefebvre, *The Production of Space,* 308.

26. Neil Smith and Cindi Katz, "Grounding Metaphor: Towards a Spatialized Politics," *Place and the Politics of Identity,* ed. Michael Keith and Steve Pile (London: Routledge, 1993), 67–83, esp. 75–76.

27. D. Massey, "Flexible Sexism," *Environment and Planning D: Society and Space* 9 (1991), 31–57; Allan Pred, "Place as Historically Contingent Process: Structuration and the Time-Geography of Becoming Places," *Annals of the Association of American Geographers* 74, no. 2 (1984), 279–97; Steve Pile, *Geographies of Resistance* (New York: Routledge, 1997); Neil Smith, *American Empire: Roosevelt's Geographer and the Prelude to Globalization* (Berkeley: University of California Press, 2003); Heidi Nast, ed., *Places Through the Body* (New York: Routledge, 1998).

28. Jon Goss, "Once-upon-a-Time in the Commodity World: An Unofficial Guide to Mall of America," *Annals of the Association of American Geographers* 89 (1999), 45–76.

29. Ruth Butler and Sophia Bowlby, "Bodies and Spaces: An Exploration of Disabled People's Experiences of Public Space," *Environment and Planning D: Society and Space* 15, no. 4 (1997), 411–33.

30. Eli Clare, *Exile and Pride: Disability, Queerness, and Liberation* (Cambridge: South End, 1999), 2.

31. Tobin Siebers, "Disability in Theory: From Social Constructionism to the New Realism of the Body," *American Literary History* (2001), 737–54.

32. Siebers, "Disability in Theory," 750.

33. I would not except this current chapter from this critique.

34. J. M. Coetzee, *Slow Man* (New York: Viking, 2005).

35. Lennard J. Davis, *Enforcing Normalcy: Disability, Deafness, and the Body* (London: Verso, 1995), 24.

36. Ibid., 26–30.

37. Noddings, *Caring*, 53.

38. Margaret Price, "Writing from Normal: Critical Thinking and Disability in the Composition Classroom," *Disability and the Teaching of Writing: A Critical Sourcebook*, ed. Cynthia Lewiecki-Wilson and Brenda J. Brueggemann (New York: Bedford / St. Martin's, 2008), 56–73.

39. Susan L. Gabel briefly touches on this ability in "'I Wash My Face with Dirty Water': Narratives of Disability and Pedagogy," *Journal of Teacher Education* 52, no. 1 (2001), 31–47.

CHAPTER 7: FAMILIAR LANGUAGES

1. John Searle, *Speech Acts* (Cambridge: Cambridge University Press, 1970); Charles Taylor, "Interpretation and the Sciences of Man," *Review of Metaphysics* 25, no. 1 (1971), 3–51.

2. Address at Baltimore, April 18, 1864.

3. Well, not literally everyone—there exists a considerable body of historical scholarship showing that for many Northerners the issue was partially or primarily material. But as the point of this discussion is Lincoln's terminology, I leave that particular debate to the historians.

4. This particular way of conceptualizing what is at essence a Heideggerian conception of political dwelling is inspired by William E. Connolly, *The Ethos of Pluralization* (Minneapolis: University of Minnesota Press, 1995).

5. W. B. Gallie, "Essentially Contested Concepts," *Meeting of the Aristotelian Society*, 56 (1956), 184–85.

6. Ibid., 190.

7. William E. Connolly, *The Terms of Political Discourse* (Lexington, Mass.: D. C. Heath, 1974), 39; John N. Gray, "On the Contestability of Social and Political Concepts," *Political Theory* 5, no. 3 (August 1977), 342.

8. This is why Quine's work in language is a poor model for theories of political incommensurability.

9. J. L. Austin, "The Meaning of a Word," in *Philosophical Papers* (Oxford: Clarendon, 1979).

10. Genesis 2:19.

11. Throughout this chapter I will be referring to many linguistic theories and grouping them in very general categories. Such groupings will be unusual and, some would argue, untenable, since I include in the same categories philosophers and linguists who considered themselves quite opposed to one another. Examining the details of each subsequent theoretician's critique of the theories that came before is less germane here than is identifying the strategies that they have in common, the relationship between language and meaning that each wants to prove. That is, their similarity in underlying approaches is either to insist on a universalizable intelligibility to words or to recognize their plurality and indeterminacy.

12. This is additionally problematic when the authors are unable to agree on the interpretation that they originally meant; they after all only necessarily agreed on the law's wording.

13. Just about any book of legal theory will mention these problems in passing, though many will claim that these objections are ultimately unfounded.

14. Walter Benjamin, for example, argues that the effects and receptions of words have no bearing on their meaning: "No poem is intended for the reader, no picture to the beholder, no symphony for the listener." Benjamin, *Illuminations*, trans. Harry Zohn (London: Fantana, 1992), 70.

15. Thomas Hobbes, *Leviathan, or the Matter, Forme and Power of a Commonweatlh*

Ecclesiasticall and Civil, ed. Michael Oakeshott (London: Collier-MacMillan, 1962), §4.

16. On the other hand, the thought of such is marvelously entertaining.

17. Alfred J. Ayer, *Language, Truth and Logic* (New York: Dover, 1946).

18. See Rudolf Carnap, *The Logical System of Language* (London: Kegan Paul Trench, 1937), or the essays in A. J. Ayer's collection *Logical Positivism* (New York: Free Press, 1966).

19. Michael J. Shapiro, *Language and Political Understanding: The Politics of Discursive Practices* (New Haven: Yale University Press, 1981), 20. Italics in original.

20. Ferdinand de Saussure, *Course in General Linguistics*, ed. C. Bally and Albert Sechehaye, trans. Roy Harris (La Salle, Ill.: Open Court, 1986), 118. Italics in original.

21. Shapiro, *Language and Political Understanding*, 120.

22. Stanley Fish, "Anti-Professionalism," *New Literary History* 17 (1985), 89–108.

23. Robin Lakoff, *Language and Woman's Place* (New York: Harper and Row, 1975).

24. Lakoff foregrounds these kinds of battles in her later essay "Cries and Whispers: The Shattering of the Silence," in *Gender Articulated: Language and the Socially Constructed Self*, ed. Kira Hall and Mary Buchholtz (New York: Routledge, 1995), 25–50.

25. Deborah Tannen, *You Just Don't Understand: Men and Women in Conversation* (New York: William Morrow, 1990).

26. Catharine MacKinnon, *Only Words* (Cambridge: Harvard University Press, 1993), 17.

27. Ibid., 13. Italics in original.

28. Ibid., 109.

29. This spatial metaphor is sometimes stated baldly: Both Saussure and Ludwig Wittgenstein (in *Philosophical Investigations*, trans. G. E. M. Anscombe [New York: Macmillan, 1958]) describe language as a city in which we live.

30. Ludwig Wittgenstein, *Tractatus Logico-Philosophicus*, trans. D. F. Pears and B. F. McGuinness (London: Routledge and Kegan Paul, 1961), 5.62.

31. This connection is recognized by Charles Taylor in his discussion of "Language and Human Nature," *Human Agency and Language: Philosophical Papers I* (Cambridge: Cambridge University Press, 1985), 244–45.

32. Ibid., 259.

33. J. L. Austin, *How to Do Things with Words* (Cambridge: Harvard University Press, 1962).

34. Ludwig Wittgenstein, *The Blue and Brown Books* (New York: Harper and Row, 1960), 77–83.

35. Wittgenstein goes so far as to argue that two different people in different contexts calling out "slab" are not saying the same thing. See Ring, "'Bring Me a Slab!': Meaning, Speakers, and Practices," in *Wittgenstein's Philosophical Investigations: Text and Context*, ed. Robert L. Arrington and Hans-Johann Glock (London: Routledge, 1991), 12–33, especially 14–19.

36. There are of course notable exceptions: the work of William Connolly, Judith Butler, and Michael Shapiro comes to mind.

37. See the essays collected in Michel Foucault, *Technologies of the Self: A Seminar with Michel Foucault*, ed. Luther H. Martin, Huck Gutman, and Patrick H. Hutton (Amherst: University of Massachusetts Press, 1988).

38. In one interview he overtly states that the transition from phenomenology to structuralism came about when Merleau-Ponty began to address the question of language. See Michel Foucault, "Structuralism and Post-Structuralism," trans. Jeremy Harding, in *Aesthetics, Method, and Epistemology*, ed. James D. Faubion (New York: New Press, 1998), 436.

39. Michael J. Shapiro makes this point in *Language and Political Understanding: The Politics of Discursive Practices* (New Haven: Yale University Press, 1981), 134. But whereas Shapiro interprets this as a form of "neo-positivism" (136), the universalist tendencies of the positivists are in direct opposition to Foucault's project. For Foucault, the speech practices and spoken performances in which we engage are always partial and contestable; the positivist universalism discussed *supra* is intrinsically oppositional to this.

40. Michel Foucault, *The Archeology of Knowledge*, trans. A. M. Sheridan Smith (New York: Pantheon, 1972), 79.

41. Michel Foucault, *The History of Sexuality*, vol. 1, *An Introduction*, trans. Robert Hurley (New York: Vintage, 1980).

42. Ibid., 7.

43. Michel Foucault, *The Government of Self and Others: Lectures at the Collège de France 1982–1983*, trans. Graham Burchell, ed. Frédéric Gros (Chippenham, U.K: Palgrave Macmillan, 2010), 217.

44. Judith Butler, *Bodies That Matter: On the Discursive Limits of "Sex"* (New York: Routledge, 1993). See also her discussion of power in *The Psychic Life of Power: Theories in Subjection* (Stanford: Stanford University Press, 1997), esp. 1–30.

45. David Campbell, *Writing Security: United States Foreign Policy and the Politics of Identity* (Minneapolis: University of Minnesota Press, 1992), 61–79.

46. David Campbell, *National Deconstruction: Violence, Identity, and Justice in Bosnia* (Minneapolis: University of Minnesota Press, 1998).

47. This is Félix Guattari's formulation of his and Gilles Deleuze's project in *Anti-Oedipus*, trans. Robert Hurley, Mark Seem, and Helen R. Lane (Minneapolis:

University of Minnesota Press, 1983). Gilles Deleuze, *Negotiations*, trans. Martin Joughin (New York: Columbia University Press, 1995), 21–22.

48. Gilles Deleuze and Félix Guattari, *A Thousand Plateaus*, trans. Brian Massumi (Minneapolis: University of Minnesota Press, 1987), 79.

49. Ibid.

50. Deleuze and Guattari, *A Thousand Plateaus*, 140. Two other important aspects of a "regime of signs," less important to my purposes, are the *diagrammatic* and the *machinic*; see 147–48.

51. Gilles Deleuze, *Difference and Repetition*, trans. Paul Patton (New York: Columbia University Press, 1994), 204–5.

52. Deleuze and Guattari, *A Thousand Plateaus*, 89.

53. Ibid., 80.

54. Jean-Jacques Lecercle, *The Violence of Language* (New York: Routledge, 1990), 47.

55. Michel Foucault, "Maurice Blanchot: The Thought from Outside," trans. Brian Massumi, *Foucault/Blanchot* (New York: Zone, 1990), 9–13.

56. Deleuze and Guattari, *A Thousand Plateaus*, 113.

57. Ibid., 94.

58. Sanford F. Schram, *Welfare Discipline: Discourse, Governance, and Globalization* (Philadelphia: Temple University Press, 2006).

59. Sanford F. Schram, *Words of Welfare: The Poverty of Social Science and the Social Science of Poverty* (Minneapolis: University of Minnesota Press, 1995).

60. Robert E. Rector and Kirk A. Johnson, *Understanding Poverty in America (Executive Study Backgrounder)* (Washington: Heritage Foundation, 2004).

61. "Research and Markets: America Movil, S.A. de C.V.: Financial and Strategic Analysis Review," press release, *Business Wire*, 24 March 2009.

62. Adam Smith, *The Wealth of Nations*, books 4–5 (London: Penguin Classics, 2000), 465.

63. For example, Jacqueline Stevens and Steven Johnston take this creative view, arguing that the fictions of the national are inherently dangerous and should be contested across a broad range. See Jacqueline Stevens, *States without Nations: Citizenship for Morals* (New York: Columbia University Press, 2009), and Steven Johnston, *The Truth about Patriotism* (Durham: Duke University Press, 2008).

64. That the constitutional elements of this theory come from close readers of Derrida is unsurprising. Derrida's encounters with difference and his suggestion of an ethos of *différance* continue to animate the most interesting political discussions.

65. For a particularly elegant and elegiac account of these dynamics, see Thomas L.

Dumm, *Loneliness as a Way of Life* (Cambridge: Harvard University Press, 2008). For these dynamics as they apply specifically to the relationship between parent and child, see Brian Duff, *The Parent as Citizen: A Democratic Dilemma* (Minneapolis: University of Minnesota Press, 2011).

66. Jean-Luc Nancy, *The Experience of Freedom*, trans. Bridget McDonald (Stanford: Stanford University Press, 1993), 146. Italics in original.

67. Charles Spinosa and Hubert L. Dreyfus, "Two Kinds of Anti-Essentialism and Their Consequences," *Critical Inquiry* 22 (1996), 737.

Abbey, Ruth. "Back to the Future: Marriage as Friendship in the Thought of Mary Wollstonecraft." *Hypatia* 14, no. 3 (1999), 78–95.

Allen, Judith. "Evidence and Silence: Feminism and the Limits of History." *Feminist Challenges: Social and Political History*, ed. Carole Pateman and Elizabeth Gross, 173–89. Boston: Northeastern University Press, 1986.

Arendt, Hannah. *Between Past and Future: Eight Exercises in Political Thought.* New York: Penguin, 1968.

———. *Eichmann in Jerusalem: A Report on the Banality of Evil.* London: Penguin, 1964.

———. *The Human Condition.* Chicago: University of Chicago Press, 1958.

———. *Lectures on Kant's Political Philosophy*, ed. Ronald Biener. Chicago: University of Chicago Press, 1982.

Arluke, Arnold, and Clinton Sanders. *Regarding Animals.* Philadelphia: Temple University Press, 1996.

Augustine. *Confessions*, trans. Henry Chadwick. Oxford: Oxford University Press, 1998.

Austin, J. L. *How to Do Things with Words.* Cambridge: Harvard University Press, 1962.

———. "The Meaning of a Word." *Philosophical Papers.* Oxford: Clarendon, 1979.

Ayer, Alfred J. *Language, Truth and Logic.* New York: Dover, 1946.

Badiou, Alain. *Being and Event*, trans. Oliver Feltham. London: Continuum, 2005.

Barclay, Robert. *Truth Triumphant*, vol. 2 (Philadelphia, 1831). Quoted in Richard Bauman, *Let Your Words Be Few: Symbolism of Speaking and Silence among Seventeenth-Century Quakers.* Cambridge: Cambridge University Press, 1983.

Basso, Keith H. "'To Give Up on Words': Silence in Western Apache Culture." *Southwestern Journal of Anthropology* 26 (1970), 213–30.

Beiner, Ronald. *Political Judgment.* Chicago: University of Chicago Press, 1983.

Benhabib, Seyla. *Critique, Norm, and Utopia: A Study of the Foundations of Critical Theory.* New York: Columbia University Press, 1986.

Benjamin, Walter. *Illuminations,* trans. Harry Zohn. London: Fantana, 1992.

Bennett, Jane. *The Enchantment of Modern Life: Attachments, Crossings, and Ethics.* Princeton: Princeton University Press, 2001.

Block de Behar, Lisa. *A Rhetoric of Silence and Other Selected Writings.* New York: Mouton de Gruyter, 1995.

Bosmajian, Haig. *The Freedom Not to Speak.* New York: New York University Press, 1999.

Bostock, Stephen St C. *Zoos and Animal Rights: The Ethics of Keeping Animals.* London: Routledge, 1993.

Botting, Eileen H. *Family Feuds: Wollstonecraft, Burke, and Rousseau on the Transformation of the Family.* Albany: State University of New York Press, 2006.

Brandt, Richard B. *Facts, Values, and Norms.* Cambridge: Cambridge University Press, 1996.

Brettschneider, Marla. *The Family Flamboyant: Race Politics, Queer Families, Jewish Lives.* Albany: State University of New York Press, 2006.

Brown, Wendy. "Freedom's Silences." *Censorship and Silencing: Practices of Cultural Regulation,* ed. Robert C. Post, 313–27. Los Angeles: Getty Research Institute for the History of Art and the Humanities, 1998.

Burchell, Graham, Colin Gordon, and Peter Miller, eds. *The Foucault Effect: Studies in Governmentality.* Chicago: University of Chicago Press, 1991.

Burgdorf, Marcia P., and Robert Burgdorf, Jr. "A History of Unequal Treatment: The Qualifications of Handicapped Persons as a 'Suspect Class' under the Equal Protection Clause." *Santa Clara Lawyer* 15 (1975), 855–910. Quoted in Rosemarie Thompson, *Extraordinary Bodies: Figuring Physical Disability in American Culture and Literature.* New York: Columbia University Press, 1997.

Butler, Judith. *Bodies That Matter: On the Discursive Limits of "Sex."* New York: Routledge, 1993.

———. *The Psychic Life of Power: Theories in Subjection.* Stanford: Stanford University Press, 1997.

Butler, Ruth, and Sophia Bowlby. "Bodies and Spaces: An Exploration of Disabled People's Experiences of Public Space." *Environment and Planning D: Society and Space* 15, no. 4 (1997), 411–33.

Cage, John. *Silence.* Middletown: Wesleyan University Press, 1961.

Campbell, David. *National Deconstruction: Violence, Identity, and Justice in Bosnia.* Minneapolis: University of Minnesota Press, 1998.

———. *Writing Security: United States Foreign Policy and the Politics of Identity.* Minneapolis: University of Minnesota Press, 1992.

Carnap, Rudolf. *The Logical System of Language.* London: Kegan Paul, Trench, 1937.

Chapman, Richard Allen. "Leviathan Writ Small: Thomas Hobbes on the Family." *American Political Science Review* 69, no. 1 (March 1975), 76–90.

Ciarocco, Natalie J., Kristin L. Sommer, and Roy F. Baumeister. "Ostracism and Ego Depletion: The Strains of Silence." *Personality and Social Psychology Bulletin* 27, no. 9 (2001), 1156–63.

Clair, Robin P. *Organizing Silence: A World of Possibilities.* Albany: State University of New York Press, 1998.

———. *The World of Silence,* trans. Stanley Godman. Chicago: Henry Regnery, 1952.

Clare, Eli. *Exile and Pride: Disability, Queerness, and Liberation.* Cambridge: South End, 1999.

Coetzee, J. M. *Disgrace.* New York: Viking, 1999.

———. *Slow Man.* New York: Viking, 2005.

Colley, Thomas. *An Apology for Silent Waiting upon God in Religious Assemblies; With Some Observations on the Nature and Ground of True Faith, and the Application Thereof in the Important Concern of Worship.* Philadelphia: Joseph Crukshank, 1805.

Connolly, William E. *The Augustinian Imperative: A Reflection on the Politics of Morality.* Thousand Oaks, Calif.: Sage, 1992.

———. *The Ethos of Pluralization.* Minneapolis: University of Minnesota Press, 1995.

———. *Identity\Difference: Democratic Negotiations of Political Paradox.* Ithaca: Cornell University Press, 1991.

Corlett, William. *Community without Unity: A Politics of Derridean Extravagence.* Durham: Duke University Press, 1993.

Crown, Cynthia L., and Stanley Feldstein. "Psychological Correlates of Silence and Sound in Conversational Interaction." *Perspectives on Silence,* ed. Deborah Tannen and Muriel Saville-Troike, 31–54. Norwood, N.J.: Ablex, 1985.

Crystal, David. *Language Death.* Cambridge: Cambridge University Press, 2000.

Cuomo, Chris J. and Lori Gruen. "On Puppies and Pussies: Animals, Intimacy, and Moral Distance." *Daring to Be Good: Essays in Feminist Eco-Politics,* ed. Bat-Ami Bar On and Ann Ferguson, 129–42. New York: Routledge, 1998.

Dahrendorf, Ralf. *The Modern Social Conflict: An Essay on the Politics of Liberty.* New York: Weidenfeld and Nicholson, 1988.

Davis, Lennard J. *Bending Over Backwards: Disability, Dismodernism, and Other Difficult Positions.* New York: New York University Press, 2002.

———. *Enforcing Normalcy: Disability, Deafness, and the Body.* London: Verso, 1995.

Deleuze, Gilles. *Difference and Repetition,* trans. Paul Patton. New York: Columbia University Press, 1994.

Deleuze, Gilles, and Félix Guattari. *Anti-Oedipus: Capitalism and Schizophrenia,* trans. Robert Hurley, Mark Seem, and Helen R. Lane. Minneapolis: University of Minnesota Press, 1983.

———. *A Thousand Plateaus,* trans. Brian Massumi. Minneapolis: University of Minnesota Press, 1987.

Dendrinos, Bessie and Emilia R. Pedro. "Giving Street Directions: The Silent Role of Woman." *Silence: Interdisciplinary Perspectives,* ed. Adam Jaworski, 215–38. Berlin: Mouton de Gruyer, 1997.

Dombrowski, Daniel A. *Babies and Beasts: The Argument from Marginal Cases.* Urbana: University of Illinois Press, 1997.

Duff, Brian. *The Parent as Citizen: A Democratic Dilemma.* Minneapolis: University of Minnesota Press, 2011.

Dumm, Thomas L. *Loneliness as a Way of Life.* Cambridge: Harvard University Press, 2008.

———. *A Politics of the Ordinary.* New York: New York University Press, 1999.

Eagleton, Mary. "Ethical Reading: The Problem of Alice Walker's 'Advancing Luna and Ida B. Wells' and J. M. Coetzee's *Disgrace*." *Feminist Theory* 2, no. 2 (2001), 189–203.

Elder, Glen, Jennifer Wolch, and Jody Emel. "*Le Pratique Sauvage*: Race, Place, and the Human-Animal Divide." *Animal Geographies: Place, Politics, and Identity in the Nature-Culture Borderlands,* ed. Jennifer Wolch and Jody Emel, 72–90. New York: Verso, 1998.

Elshtain, Jean B. "Catholic Social Thought, the City, and Liberal America." *Catholicism, Liberalism, and Communitarianism: The Catholic Intellectual Tradition and the Moral Foundations of Democracy,* ed. Kenneth Grasso, Gerard Bradley, and Robert Hunt, 97–113. London: Rowman and Littlefield, 1995.

———. *Public Man, Private Woman: Women in Social and Political Thought.* Princeton: Princeton University Press, 1981.

Engels, Frederick. *The Origin of the Family, Private Property, and the State.* New York: Pathfinder, 1972.

Esposito, Roberto. *Communitas: The Origin and Destiny of Community*, trans. Timothy Campbell. Stanford: Stanford University Press, 2010.

Etzioni, Amitai. *From Empire to Community: A New Approach to International Relations*. New York: Palgrave Macmillan, 2004.

———. *The New Golden Rule: Community and Morality in a Democratic Society*. New York: Basic Books, 1996.

Ferguson, Kennan. "Unmapping and Remapping the World: Aesthetics as Foreign Policy." *Challenging Boundaries: Global Flows, Territorial Identities*, ed. Michael J. Shapiro and Hayward R. Alker. Minneapolis: University of Minnesota Press, 1996.

———. *William James: Politics in the Pluriverse*. Lanham, Md.: Rowman and Littlefield, 2007.

Fish, Stanley. "Anti-Professionalism." *New Literary History* 17 (1985), 89–108.

Flathman, Richard E. *Reflections of a Would-Be Anarchist: Ideals and Institutions of Liberalism*. Minnesota: University of Minnesota Press, 1998.

Foucault, Michel. *The Archeology of Knowledge*, trans. A. M. Sheridan Smith. New York: Pantheon, 1972.

———. *The History of Sexuality*, vol. 1, *An Introduction*, trans. Robert Hurley. New York: Vintage, 1980.

———. *Security, Territory, Population: Lectures at the Collège de France, 1977–1978*, ed. Michael Senellart, trans. Graham Burchell. New York: Palgrave Macmillan, 2007.

———. *Technologies of the Self: A Seminar with Michel Foucault*, ed. Luther H. Martin, Huck Gutman, and Patrick H. Hutton. Amherst: University of Massachusetts Press, 1988.

Fox, Robin. *Kinship and Marriage*. Cambridge: Cambridge University Press, 1983.

———. "The Virgin and the Godfather: Kinship versus the State in Greek Tragedy and After." *Anthropology and Literature*, ed. Paul Benson, 107–50. Urbana: University of Illinois Press, 1993.

Fraser, Russell. *The Language of Adam*. New York: Columbia University Press, 1979.

Gabel, Susan L. "'I Wash My Face with Dirty Water': Narratives of Disability and Pedagogy." *Journal of Teacher Education* 52, no. 1 (2001), 31–47.

Gallie, W. B. "Essentially Contested Concepts." *Meeting of the Aristotelian Society* 56 (1956), 167–98.

Garber, Marjorie. *Dog Love*. New York: Simon and Schuster, 1996.

Gilligan, Carol. *In a Different Voice*. Cambridge: Harvard University Press, 1982.

———. "Remapping the Moral Domain: New Images of the Self in Relationship."

Reconstructing Individualism: Autonomy, Individuality, and the Self in Western Thought, ed. Thomas C. Heller, Morton Sosna, and David E. Wellberg, 237–52. Stanford: Stanford University Press, 1986.

Gilligan, Carol, and David A. J. Richards. *The Deepening Darkness: Patriarchy, Resistance, and Democracy's Future*. Cambridge: Cambridge University Press, 2008.

Gilmore, Perry. "Silence and Sulking: Emotional Displays in the Classroom." *Perspectives on Silence*, ed. Deborah Tannen and Muriel Saville-Troike, 139–62. Norwood, N.J.: Ablex, 1985.

Gleeson, Brendon. *Geographies of Disability*. New York: Routledge, 1999.

Glenn, Cheryl. *Unspoken: A Rhetoric of Silence*. Carbondale: Southern Illinois University Press, 2004.

Goffman, Erving. *Stigma: Notes on the Management of Spoiled Identity*. New York: Touchstone, 1986.

Gray, John N. "On the Contestability of Social and Political Concepts." *Political Theory* 5, no. 3 (August 1977), 331–48.

Griffin, Gail. *Calling: Essays on Teaching in the Mother Tongue*. New York: Trilogy, 1992.

Habermas, Jürgen. *Between Facts and Norms: Contributions to a Discourse Theory of Law and Democracy*, trans. William Rehg. Cambridge: MIT Press, 1998.

———. *Philosophical Discourse of Modernity: Twelve Lectures*, trans. Frederick Lawrence. Cambridge: MIT Press, 1990.

———. *The Structural Transformation of the Public Sphere*, trans. Thomas Burger and Frederick Lawrence. Cambridge: Harvard University Press, 1989.

———. *The Theory of Communicative Action*, trans. Thomas McCarthy. Boston: Beacon, 1984.

Hahn, Harlan. "Disability and the Urban Environment: A Perspective on Los Angeles." *Environment and Planning D: Society and Space* 4 (1986), 273–88.

Hall, Cheryl. *The Trouble with Passion: Political Theory beyond the Reign of Reason*. New York: Routledge, 2005.

Hamington, Maurice. *Embodied Care: Jane Addams, Maurice Merleau-Ponty, and Feminist Ethics*. Urbana: University of Illinois Press, 2004.

Harris, C. C. *Kinship*. Minneapolis: University of Minnesota Press, 1990.

Heidegger, Martin. *Being and Time*, trans. John Macquarrie and Edward Robinson. San Francisco: Harper, 1962.

Hodgkin, L. V. *Silent Worship: The Way of Wonder; Swarthmore Lecture 1919*. London: Swarthmore, 1919.

Honig, Bonnie. *Political Theory and the Displacement of Politics*. Ithaca: Cornell University Press, 1993.

Hornaday, Aline. "Early Medieval Kinship Structures as Social and Political Controls." *Medieval Family Roles: A Book of Essays*, ed. Cathy J. Itnyre, 21–37. New York: Garland, 1996.

Jaggar, Alison M. "Caring as Feminist Practice of Moral Reason." *Justice and Care: Essential Readings in Feminist Ethics*, ed. Virginia Held, 179–202. Boulder: Westview, 1995.

James, William. "On a Certain Blindness in Human Beings." *Faith and Morals*, 260. New York: Longmans, Green, 1943.

Johnston, Steven. *The Truth about Patriotism*. Durham: Duke University Press, 2008.

Kant, Immanuel. *Critique of Judgment*, trans. Werner S. Pluhar. Indianapolis: Hackett, 1987.

———. *Critique of Practical Reason*, trans. Lewis White Beck. New York: Macmillan, 1985.

———. *Grounding for the Metaphysics of Morals*. Indianapolis: Hackett, 1981.

Kateb, George. "Democratic Individuality and the Meaning of Rights." *Liberalism and the Moral Life*, ed. Nancy Rosenblum, 183–206. Cambridge: Harvard University Press, 1989.

———. *The Inner Ocean: Individualism and Democratic Culture*. Ithaca: Cornell University Press, 1992.

———. *Patriotism and Other Mistakes*. New Haven: Yale University Press, 1989.

Kaufman-Osbourne, Timothy. *Creatures of Prometheus: Gender and the Politics of Technology*. Lanham, Md.: Rowman and Littlefield, 1997.

Keith, George. *The Benefit, Advantage and Glory of Silent Meetings, Both as It Was Found at the Beginning, or First Breaking Forth of This Clear Manifestation of Truth, and Continued So to Be Found by All the Faithful and Upright in Heart at This Day*. London: Andrew Sowle, 1687.

Klein, Melanie. *The Selected Melanie Klein*. New York: Free Press, 1987.

Kohlberg, Lawrence. *Essays on Moral Development*. San Francisco: Harper and Row, 1984.

Koschorke, Albrecht. *The Holy Family and Its Legacy: Religious Imagination from the Gospels to Star Wars*, trans. Thomas Dunlap. New York: Columbia University Press, 2003.

Kostelanetz, Richard. *Conversing with Cage*. New York: Limelight, 1988.

Kuhn, Thomas. *The Structure of Scientific Revolutions*. 2nd ed. Chicago: University of Chicago Press, 1970.

Lakoff, Robin. "Cries and Whispers: The Shattering of the Silence." *Gender Articulated: Language and the Socially Constructed Self*, ed. Kira Hall and Mary Buchholtz, 25–50. New York: Routledge, 1995.

———. *Language and Woman's Place*. New York: Harper and Row, 1975.

Lang, Beryl. *Heidegger's Silence*. Ithaca: Cornell University Press, 1996.

Langton, Rae. "Speech Acts and Unstoppable Acts." *Philosophy and Public Affairs* 22 (1993), 293–330.

Lecercle, Jean-Jacques. *The Violence of Language*. New York: Routledge, 1990.

Lingis, Alphonso. *The Community of Those with Nothing in Common*. Bloomington: Indiana University Press, 1994.

Linton, Simi. *Claiming Disability: Knowledge and Identity*. New York: New York University Press, 1998.

Locke, John. *The Second Treatise of Government*, ed. Thomas Peardon. Indianapolis: Bobbs-Merrill, 1953.

Luke, Timothy W. "Beyond Birds: Biopower and Birdwatching in the World of Audubon." *Capitalism Nature Socialism* 11, no. 3 (2000), 7–37.

Lyotard, Jean F. *The Differend: Phrases in Dispute*, trans. Georges Van Den Abbeele. Minneapolis: University of Minnesota Press, 1988.

MacIntyre, Alasdair. *After Virtue: A Study in Moral Theory*. Notre Dame: University of Notre Dame Press, 1981.

———. "The Privatization of the Good: An Inaugural Lecture." *Review of Politics* 52 (1990), 344–77.

———. *Whose Justice? Which Rationality?* Notre Dame: University of Notre Dame Press, 1988.

MacKinnon, Catharine. *Only Words*. Cambridge: Harvard University Press, 1993.

Manning, Rita C. *Speaking from the Heart: A Feminist Perspective on Ethics*. Lanham, Md.: Rowman and Littlefield, 1992.

McClintock, Anne. "Family Feuds: Gender, Nationalism, and the Family." *Feminist Review* 44, no. 3 (1993), 61–80.

McClure, Kirstie M. "The Social Question, Again." *Graduate Faculty Philosophy Journal* 28, no. 1 (2007), 85–113.

McDermott, Ray, and Hervé Varenne. "Culture of Disability." *Anthropology and Education Quarterly* 26 (1995), 323–48.

McElroy, Susan C., ed. *Animals as Teachers and Healers: True Stories and Reflections*. New York: Ballantine, 1996.

McMillan, Jackie. "Putting the Cult Back into Community." *Returning (to) Communities: Theory, Culture and Political Practice of the Communal*, ed. Stefan Herbrechter and Michael Higginsan, 231–43. Amsterdam: Rodolphi, 2006.

Meillassoux, Quentin. *Après la finitude: Essai sur la nécessité de la contingence*. Paris: Le Seuil, 2006.

Metz, Tamara. *Untying the Knot: Marriage, the State, and the Case for Their Divorce*. Princeton: Princeton University Press, 2010.

Midgley, Mary. *Heart and Mind: The Varieties of Moral Experience*. Sussex: Harvester, 1981.

Mill, John S. *On Liberty and Other Writings*, ed. Stefani Collini. Cambridge: Cambridge University Press, 1989.

———. *The Subjection of Women*, ed. Edward Alexander. London: Transaction, 2001.

Muneto, Sonoda. "The Eloquent Silence of Zarathustra." *Nietzsche and Asian Thought*, ed. Graham Parkes, 226–43. Chicago: University of Chicago Press, 1991.

Nancy, Jean-Luc. *The Experience of Freedom*, trans. Bridget McDonald. Stanford: Stanford University Press, 1993.

———. *The Inoperative Community*. ed. Peter Connor, trans. Peter Connor. Minneapolis: University of Minnesota Press, 1991.

Nathan, Geoffrey S. *The Family in Late Antiquity: The Rise of Christianity and the Endurance of Tradition*. London: Routledge, 2000.

Nietzsche, Friedrich. *Thus Spoke Zarathustra*, trans. R. J. Hollingdale. London: Penguin, 1969.

Noddings, Nel. *Caring: A Feminist Approach to Ethics and Moral Education*. Berkeley: University of California Press, 1984.

Noelle-Neumann, Elisabeth. *The Spiral of Silence: Public Opinion—Our Social Skin*. Chicago: University of Chicago Press, 1984.

Nozick, Robert. *Anarchy, State, and Utopia*. New York: Basic Books, 1974.

———. *The Nature of Rationality*. Princeton: Princeton University Press, 1993.

Nussbaum, Martha. *Love's Knowledge*. New York: Oxford University Press, 1990.

Oakeshott, Michael. "A Philosophy of Politics." *Religion, Politics, and the Moral Life*, 119–37. New Haven: Yale University Press, 1993.

Okin, Susan M. "Humanist Liberalism." *Liberalism and the Moral Life*, ed. Nancy L. Rosenblum, 39–53. Cambridge: Harvard University Press, 1989.

Olsen, Tillie. *Silences*. New York: Delacorte / Seymour Lawrence, 1978.

O'Neill, Onora. *Constructions of Reason: Explorations of Kant's Practical Philosophy*. Cambridge: Cambridge University Press, 1989.

Ortega y Gasset, José. *Concord and Liberty*, trans. Helene Weyl. New York: W. W. Norton, 1946.

———. *The Modern Theme*, trans. James Cleugh. New York: Harper and Brothers, 1961.

The Piano. Directed by Jane Campion. Artisan Entertainment, 1993.

Plato. *The Collected Dialogues*, ed. Edith Hamilton and Huntington Cairns. Princeton: Princeton University Press, 1963.

Price, Margaret. "Writing from Normal: Critical Thinking and Disability in the Composition Classroom." *Disability and the Teaching of Writing: A Critical Sourcebook*, ed. Cynthia Lewiecki-Wilson and Brenda J. Brueggemann, 56–73. New York: Bedford / St. Martin's, 2008.

Rancière, Jacques. *Dis-agreement: Politics and Philosophy*, trans. Julie Rose. Minneapolis: University of Minnesota Press, 1999.

Rawls, John. *Political Liberalism*. New York: Columbia University Press, 1993.

———. *A Theory of Justice*. Cambridge: Harvard University Press, 1971.

Rector, Robert E., and Kirk A. Johnson. *Understanding Poverty in America (Executive Study Backgrounder)*. Washington: Heritage Foundation, 2004.

Rescher, Nicolas. *Pluralism: Against the Demand for Consensus*. Oxford: Oxford University Press, 1993.

"Research and Markets: America Movil, S.A. de C.V.: Financial and Strategic Analysis Review." Press release, *Business Wire*, March 24, 2009.

Rhees, Rush. "Some Developments in Wittgenstein's View of Ethics." *Philosophical Review* 74, no. 1 (1965), 17–26.

Rich, Adrienne. *On Lies, Secrets, and Silence: Selected Prose*. New York: W. W. Norton, 1979.

Ring, Merrill. " 'Bring Me a Slab!': Meaning, Speakers, and Practices." *Wittgenstein's Philosophical Investigations: Text and Context*, ed. Robert L. Arrington and Hans-Johann Glock, 12–33. London: Routledge, 1991.

Ritvo, Harriet. *The Animal Estate: The English and Other Creatures in the Victorian Age*. Cambridge: Harvard University Press, 1987.

Robin, Corey. *Fear: The History of a Political Idea*. Oxford: Oxford University Press, 2006.

Rochester, S. R. "The Significance of Pauses in Spontaneous Speech." *Journal of Psycholinguistic Research* 2, no. 1 (1973), 51–81.

Ruddick, Sara. *Maternal Thinking: Towards a Politics of Peace*. New York: Ballantine, 1989.

Sandel, Michael. *Democracy's Discontent: America in Search of a Public Philosophy*. Cambridge: Belknap, 1996.

Sartre, Jean-Paul. *Existentialism and Humanism*, trans. Philip Maret. London: Methuen, 1948.

Sattel, Jack W. "Men, Inexpressiveness, and Power." *Language, Gender, and Society*, ed. Barrie Thorne, Cheris Kramarae, and Nancy Henley, 119–24. Rowley, Mass.: Newbury House, 1983.

Saussure, Ferdinand de. *Course in General Linguistics*, ed. C. Bally and Albert Sechehaye, trans. Roy Harris. La Salle, Ill.: Open Court, 1986.

Schlesinger, Arthur M., Jr. *The Disuniting of America: Reflections on a Multicultural Society*. Knoxville: Whittle Direct, 1991.

Schram, Sanford F. *Welfare Discipline: Discourse, Governance, and Globalization*. Philadelphia: Temple University Press, 2006.

———. *Words of Welfare: The Poverty of Social Science and the Social Science of Poverty*. Minneapolis: University of Minnesota Press, 1995.

Scollon, Ron. "The Machine Stops: Silence in the Metaphor of Malfunction." *Perspectives on Silence*, ed. Deborah Tannen and Muriel Saville-Troike, 21–30. Norwood, N.J.: Ablex, 1985.

Searle, John. *Speech Acts*. Cambridge: Cambridge University Press, 1970.

Serpell, James A. *In the Company of Animals*. New York: Basil Blackwell, 1986.

Shapiro, Michael J. *Language and Political Understanding: The Politics of Discursive Practices*. New Haven: Yale University Press, 1981.

Singer, Peter. "All Animals Are Equal." *Applied Ethics*, 215–28. New York: Oxford University Press, 1986.

———. *Animal Liberation*. New York: Avon, 1990.

Smith, Adam. *The Wealth of Nations*, books 4–5. London: Penguin Classics, 2000.

Smith, Michael. *The Moral Problem*. Oxford: Blackwell, 1994.

Sontag, Susan. "The Aesthetics of Silence." *Styles of Radical Will*, 1–34. New York: Farrar, Straus and Giroux, 1969.

———. *Illness as Metaphor and AIDS and Its Metaphors*. New York: Anchor, 1990.

Spinosa, Charles, and Hubert L. Dreyfus. "Two Kinds of Anti-Essentialism and Their Consequences." *Critical Inquiry* 22 (1996).

Stables, Jane, and Fiona Smith. "'Caught in the Cinderella Trap': Narratives of Disabled Parents and Young Carers." *Mind and Body Spaces: Geographies of Illness, Impairment, and Disability*, ed. Ruth Butler and Hester Parr, 256–68. New York: Routledge, 1999.

Stevens, Jacqueline. *Reproducing the State*. Princeton: Princeton University Press, 1999.

———. *States without Nations: Citizenship for Morals*. New York: Columbia University Press, 2009.

Sullivan, Andrew, ed. *Same-Sex Marriage: Pro and Con*. New York: Vintage, 1997.

Tannen, Deborah. *Conflict Talk: Sociolinguistic Investigations of Arguments in Conversations*, ed. Allen D. Grimshaw. Cambridge: Cambridge University Press, 1990.

———. "Silence: Anything But." *Perspectives on Silence*, ed. Deborah Tannen and Muriel Saville-Troike. Norwood, N.J.: Ablex, 1985.

———. *You Just Don't Understand: Men and Women in Conversation*. New York: William Morrow, 1990.

Taylor, Charles. "Interpretation and the Sciences of Man." *Review of Metaphysics* 25, no. 1 (1971), 3–51.

———. "Language and Human Nature." *Human Agency and Language: Philosophical Papers*, vol. 1. Cambridge: Cambridge University Press, 1985.

———. "The Politics of Recognition." *Multiculturalism*, ed. Amy Guttman, 25–73. Princeton: Princeton University Press, 1994.

Thompson, Rosemarie. *Extraordinary Bodies: Figuring Physical Disability in American Culture and Literature.* New York: Columbia University Press, 1997.

Tiersma, Peter M. "The Language of Silence." *Rutgers Law Review* 48 (1995), 1–99.

Tronto, Joan. *Moral Boundaries: A Political Argument for an Ethic of Care.* New York: Routledge, 1993.

Urbanati, Nadia. "J. S. Mill on Androgyny and Marriage." *Political Theory* 19, no. 4 (1991), 626–48.

Valentine, Gill. *Public Space and the Culture of Childhood.* London: Ashgate, 2004.

Villa, Dana. *Arendt and Heidegger: The Fate of the Political.* Princeton: Princeton University Press, 1996.

———. *Politics, Philosophy, Terror: Essays on the Thought of Hannah Arendt.* Princeton: Princeton University Press, 1999.

Walzer, Michael. *Spheres of Justice.* New York: Basic Books, 1983.

Wang, Youru. "Liberating Oneself from the Absolutized Boundary of Language: A Liminiological Approach to the Interplay of Speech and Silence in Chan Buddhism." *Philosophy East and West* 51, no. 1 (2001), 83.

Wardhaugh, Ronald. *How Conversation Works.* Oxford: Basil Blackwell, 1985.

Warren, Karen J. "The Power and the Promise of Ecological Feminism." *Ecological Feminist Philosophies*, ed. Karen J. Warren, 42–51. Bloomington: Indiana University Press, 1996.

West, Caroline. "The Free Speech Argument against Pornography." *Canadian Journal of Philosophy* 33, no. 3 (2003), 391–422.

White, Steven K. *Edmund Burke: Modernity, Politics, and Aesthetics.* Thousand Oaks, Calif.: Sage, 1994.

Williams, Bernard. *Ethics and the Limits of Philosophy.* Cambridge: Harvard University Press, 1985.

———. *In the Beginning Was the Deed: Realism and Moralism in Political Argument.* Princeton: Princeton University Press, 2005.

Wilson, James Q. *The Moral Sense.* New York: Free Press, 1993.

———. *Thinking about Crime.* New York: Vintage, 1985.

Wittgenstein, Ludwig. *The Blue and Brown Books.* New York: Harper and Row, 1960.

———. *Philosophical Investigations*, trans. G. E. M. Anscombe. New York: Macmillan, 1958.

———. *Tractatus Logico-Philosophicus*, trans. D. F. Pears and B. F. McGuinness. London: Routledge and Kegan Paul, 1961.

Wright, Dale S. "Rethinking Transcendence: The Role of Language in Experience." *Philosophy East and West* 42, no. 1 (1992), 113–38.

Young, James P. *Reconsidering American Liberalism*. Boulder: Westview, 1996.

Zerilli, Linda. *Feminism and the Abyss of Freedom*. Chicago: University of Chicago Press, 2005.

Zielinski, Stanislaw. *Psychology and Silence*. Wallingford: Pendle Hill, 1975.

Žižek, Slavoj. "A Leftist Plea for 'Eurocentrism.'" *Critical Inquiry* 24 (1998), 998–1009.

Care ethics, 36, 95–96, 113–14, 117,
168 n. 43; theorists of, 115–16
Caregiver, the, 9, 110, 115–17, 122, 124;
conceptualizations of, 120; maternal,
114; theoretical renditions of, 121
Certeau, Michel de, 6–7; *Practice of
Everyday Life*, 118–20
Chapman, Richard Allen, 17
Children, 15, 17–19, 73, 86–87, 92, 116
Citizenship, 29, 43, 102, 151
Civil society, 20–21, 49
Civil War, 141, 146
Clare, Eli, 120–21
Coetzee, J. M., *Disgrace*, 102–5
Commentary, political, 8
Commonality, 8–9, 34, 36, 44, 46, 51, 60,
63–65, 107; silence as constitutive of, 77
Commonwealth, 17
Communication, 68–69, 85; theory, 65
Communitarianism, 6, 36–44, 51, 54–55
Community, 7–10, 23, 27, 31, 33, 35–40, 42,
44–48, 51–52, 54–61, 63, 68, 74, 78, 80,
115, 125, 128, 148, 150–51; antipolitical,
34, 149, 159 n. 39; as created by silence,
76–77, 81; death of, 30; in language,
126, 145; political, 41, 43
Concordia, 15
Connolly, William, 43, 59, 129–30
Consensus, 50
Constantine, 15
Constitutionalism, democratic, 41
Contraception, 159 n. 42
Contract, 130
Cook, Captain James, 99
Corlett, William, 59
Culture wars, 36
Cuomo, Chris, 96, 106
Cyborg, 105

Darwin, Charles, 87
Davis, Lennard, 123
Deafness, 170–71 n. 3

Debord, Guy, *The Naked City*, 118–19
Debt, 145
Definitions: differences in, 131; of family,
3, 146–47
Deleuze, Gilles, 59, 141, 144–46
Demands, 139–40
Derrida, Jacques, 59
Descartian tradition of sensory doubt, 118
Dialectics, 55
Dickens, Charles, 22
Diocletian, 15
Disability, 9, 107, 110, 116, 122–23; defini-
tion of, 170 n. 1; experiences of, 111–13;
interpretations of, 121; role of culture
in, 109; space and, 117, 120; studies, 108,
124
Disgrace, 102–3
Divorce, 15
Dogs, 8, 83, 91–92, 94, 97–98, 102–5;
caring for, 88; as moral models, 86–87;
relationships with humans, 84–86,
97–100
Domestic violence, 135, 149
Domination and relationships, 100–101
Dreyfus, Hubert L., 47
Dumm, Thomas, 6–7, 71

Economy, 155 n. 20
Eichmann, Adolf, 115
Elshtain, Jean Bethke, 39
Embodiment: meanings of, 113, 120–21;
specifics of, 122
Emotion, 96–97; emotional change, 115
Empiricism, 126
Enchanted objects, 105
Engels, Friedrich, 19
Epistemology, 93, 122
Equality, 9, 102
Esoteric knowledge, 6
Esposito, Roberto, 48, 60
Ethics, 24–26, 30–31, 34, 83, 90–94, 97,
101–2, 106, 115, 150; ethical behavior, 116

Individualism, 1, 16–17, 19, 22, 37, 42–43, 115; individuality, 81; in Kateb, 42; liberal, 39–40; rights-based, 40
Intelligence, 93
Intersubjectivity, 94
Iraq war, 42–43

James, William, 59, 85, 165 n. 2
Jaspers, Karl, 94–95
Judgment, 34, 45–51, 53, 92–94, 111, 116, 150–51
Justice, 40; infant, 93; relationship of care to, 116

Kant, Immanuel, 7–8, 44, 47–48, 53; aesthetics as taste, 111; *Critique of Judgment*, 46, 49–50, 52; *Critique of Practical Reason*, 49; influence of, 58–59; Kantian formalism, 47; Kantian formal logics, 114; Kantianism, 51; Kantian reason, 31; "What is Enlightenment," 49
Kateb, George, 40–43
Katz, Cindi, 119
Kaufman-Osbourne, Timothy, 105
Kinship, 22–23
Koschorke, Albrecht, 16
Kuhn, Thomas, 5

Lakoff, Robin, 137, 139
Language, 9–10, 63–64, 66, 85, 93, 125–51; absence of, 76; as constitutive, 134, 140–46; as generative, 144–45; political uses of, 127; as power, 142
Lassie, 86
Latour, Bruno, 105
Law, 56, 69–70, 132–33, 144–45, 174 n. 13; irony and, 133; legal recognition, 104–5
Lecercle, Jean-Jacques, 145
Lefebvre, Henri, 119
Leftism, 36, 54

Legitimacy, 14–15, 106; of human passions, 28
Levinas, Emmanuel, 5
Liberalism, 1, 6, 19, 22–23, 27, 36, 38–39, 41–42, 48, 50, 55, 91, 101–2; constitutional, 40; Kantian, 47, 49; liberals, 37, 40, 43–44, 51, 54
Libertarianism, 91, 143
Liberty, 127–28, 130–31, 148
Lincoln, Abraham, 126–28, 139, 146, 148
Linguistic differences, 129
Linguistics, 9, 128, 140; positivist, 134–35; structuralist, 136–39; theory, 125
Linguistic universalism, 131–39
Locke, John, 18–19, 24, 29–30, 35; *First Treatise of Government*, 17; *Second Treatise of Government*, 17
Logic, 84–85, 91–94, 97–98, 101–2; Kantian, 114
Lorenz, Konrad, 88
Love, 9–10, 25, 97, 101, 105, 151, 168 n. 43; conjugal, 29; of humans for dogs, 85–89, 98–100, 104, 106; paternal, 19
Lyotard, Jean-François, 74

MacIntyre, Alasdair, 37, 53
MacKinnon, Catharine, 138–39, 144–45
Marriage, 15, 18–20, 45–46, 148
Marx, Karl, 19, 48; Marxism, 55–56, 119, 136; post-Marxism, 119–20
Material things, 105
Medea, 25
Meillassoux, Quentin, 59
Metaphor, 133
Methods, 126
Midgley, Mary, 92
Mill, John Stuart, 20, 56; *On Liberty*, 19; *The Subjection of Women*, 19
Molinos, Miguel de, 78
Monarchical power, 17–18, 21
Moore, G. E., 92

Morality: arguments of, 26–27, 38, 43–44, 50–51, 83–84, 90, 92, 128; human, 93; moral distance, 96, 106
More, Thomas, 72
Mothers, 16–18; mothering, 123
Muneto, Sonoda, 76
Music, 79–80
Musical composition, 8

Naming, language, and picture theory, 132
Nancy, Jean-Luc, 59–60, 150
National Book Award, 67
National power, 7, 14, 22, 148
Nazis, 81
Negotiations, 7–8, 10, 24–27, 31, 35, 37, 74, 81
New York, 130
Nietzsche, Friedrich, 76–77, 101
Noddings, Nel, 95, 114, 123
Noelle-Neumann, Elisabeth, 68
Noise, 162 n. 31
Nonhumans, 9, 94, 96, 104; nonhuman animals, 93
Normality, 123
Normativity, 109–10
Nouns, 131
Nozick, Robert, 40–42, 91
Nurturance, 95

Oakeshott, Michael, 91–92; *The Philosophy of Politics*, 90
Oaths, 72
Odyssey, The, 86
Okin, Susan Moller, 29
Olsen, Tillie, 68; *Silences*, 67
Original intent, 132, 135
Ortega y Gasset, José, 58

Parapolitics, 54
Parentalae system, 156 n. 39

Parents, 17–18, 81
Pascal, Blaise, 65
Pastoral power, 21–22
Paterfamilias, 15, 21, 29
Paternal power, 17, 20, 29
Patriarchy, 2, 14, 16, 21, 35, 66–67, 138
Pedagogy, 122, 124
Performance, 77, 79–80
Perlocutionary, the, 144; aspects of language, 140
Pets, 96, 98–100
Phenomenology, 171 n. 7
Philosophy, 64, 91–92, 96, 101–2, 126, 134; philosophical arguments, 26–27
Picard, Max, 72
Picture theory of language, 131–34, 136
Plato, 13, 48, 123, 143
Pluralism, 52, 57–59, 168 n. 45; liberal, 56; linguistic, 167
Pluriverse, 122, 150
Political actors, 8, 84, 90, 105
Political discourse, 23, 144
Political participation, 102
Political philosophy. *See* Political theory
Political power, 17, 20; family as underpinning of, 15, 27
Political science, 8, 54–55, 60, 64, 68; political scientists, 30
Political theory, 6, 13–14, 16, 22, 24, 29–30, 34, 37, 39, 46, 48, 53, 55, 60, 65, 83–84, 89, 92–94, 98, 102, 105–6, 126; liberal, 23; as philosophy, 90; political theorists, 28, 30, 59, 91, 110, 129
Politics, 9, 14, 23, 52, 54, 57, 59–60, 68, 81, 91, 94, 105, 126; electoral, 28; theorizing of, 90
Pornography, 68, 138, 148
Postivism, 134–35, 176 n. 39
Poverty, 147–48
Power, 64–65, 70, 73–74, 81, 89–90, 100; feminist theories of, 105; linguistic

118–19, 175 n. 29; disability and, 117; historicization of, 119–20; meaning of, 121; particularization of, 119–20; pluralization of, 107–8, 110, 122, 124; politics of, 109; social nature of, 113

Speech, 68–69, 81; speech acts, 126, 140

Spinosa, Charles, 47

Stables, Jane, 116

State of nature, 17–18, 23

States, 20–22, 126; democratic, 29; liberal, 43; state power, 7, 14, 22; statism, 36

Statistics, 123

Stevens, Jacqueline, *Reproducing the State*, 29

Stone, Christopher, 104

Structuralism, 136–39, 142

Subjectivity, 101

Sullivan, Andrew, 88–89

Tahitians, 99

Tannen, Deborah, 77, 137

Taylor, Charles, 53, 126, 140

Teachers, 74–75, 81; disabled, 124

Televisions, 147–48

Theology, 14; theologists, 36

Theorists, 43, 90, 93

Thomas, Elizabeth Marshall, *The Hidden Life of Dogs*, 89

Tocqueville, Alexis de, 55

Tolstoy, Leo, 24

Totalitarianism, 58

Transhuman existence, 6

Tronto, Joan, 96, 114

Truth, 56, 64, 94, 135; as produced, 143

Turner, James, 87

Universalism, 9, 50–51, 94, 131–35

U.S. Constitution, 132, 138

Utilitarianism, 91–92

Valentine, Gill, 28

Value pluralism, 6

Values, 38

Veterinary medicine, 94, 97–98, 101

Victorians, 87

Vienna Circle, 134–35

Walzer, Michael, 52

Wardhaugh, Ronald, 66

Where the Red Fern Grows, 86

Williams, Bernard, 24, 92–93

Wilson, James Q., 38–39

Wittgenstein, Ludwig, 24–25, 131, 136, 139, 142; *The Brown Book*, 141; *Tractatus Logico-Philosophicus*, 64

Wives, 15–16, 19

Wollstonecraft, Mary, 19

Women, 8, 15, 19–21, 55–56, 67–68, 72–73, 114; care ethics and, 95, 115; suffrage, 20

Zarathustra, 76–77, 80

Zerilli, Linda, 25

Žižek, Slavoj, 54

Zola, Émile, *Les Rougon-Macquart*, 22

Kennan Ferguson teaches political theory

at the University of Wisconsin, Milwaukee.

He is the author of *William James: Politics in*

the Pluriverse and *The Politics of Judgment.*

Library of Congress Cataloging-in-Publication Data
Ferguson, Kennan, 1968–
All in the family : on community and
incommensurability / Kennan Ferguson.
p. cm.
Includes bibliographical references and index.
ISBN 978-0-8223-5176-4 (cloth : alk. paper)
ISBN 978-0-8223-5190-0 (pbk. : alk. paper)
1. Families—Political aspects.
2. Democracy.   I. Title.
HQ515.F474 2012
306.850973—dc23   2011041899